Homer Croy

Homer Croy

Corn Country Travel Writing
Literary Journalism
Memoir

Edited with an Introduction by
Zachary Michael Jack

Tall Corn Books
North Liberty, Iowa

Homer Croy—Corn Country Travel Writing,
Literary Journalism, Memoir

Copyright © 2010 by Zachary Michael Jack

ISBN 9781888160741

Library of Congress Control Number: 2010921465

Tall Corn Books, a place studies imprint of
  Ice Cube Books, LLC (est. 1993)
  205 North Front Street
  North Liberty, Iowa 52317-9302
  www.icecubepress.com
  steve@icecubepress.com

Manufactured and home spun in the United States of America

The paper used in this publication meets the minimum requirements of
the American National Standard for Information Sciences—Permanence
of Paper for Printed Library Materials, ANSI Z39.48-1992

To the Rugged Individualist of Toad Hollow

Table of Contents

Editor's Preface

Homer Croy was a man of many distinctions, as you'll soon read—a Pulitzer Prize, tagline as the first student of the first school of journalism in America, a reputation as the first person to tour the world shooting motion pictures, and an author of one of just a handful of best-selling anonymous novels in modern American literature, to name a representative few. All these receive long-overdue attention in this first-ever anthology.

Croy hailed from Corn Country, from a far-flung, tall-corn hamlet—Maryville, Missouri—that just happens to have birthed a miraculous number of talented and influential people. Dale Carnegie, author of *How to Win Friends and Influence People*, himself once identified five folks from his hometown, population 5,000, listed in *Who's Who in America*—his chum Homer among them. Toe-to-toe with an anomaly, Carnegie posed the obvious question: "Can any other non-college town outside of the New York suburban area make as good a showing?"

The answer quite simply is no. And yet, strangely, many middle American towns have produced a "human resources" crop nearly as great—my ancestral hometown, West Branch, Iowa, for example, a little burg that birthed Herbert Hoover, sheltered traitor-martyr John Brown, and educated author Walter Thomas Jack, my great-grandfather. The mystery of place, then, of the incalculable vagaries of soul and soil that go into growing a talent as far-reaching and readily forgotten as Croy's is a mystery most poignant, a mystery most timely—as germane to our times as the inexplicability of Bethlehem. More remarkable still is Croy's trenchant appreciation for the gravitational power of his middlewestern home place, and though he tried like the devil to escape it, it kept coming back to him with the force of fate, the certainty of haunt. In sum, that homespun whatever-it-was drew him to greatness, not the other way around.

As a little shaver growing up in eastern Iowa, I happily pledged allegiance each and every day at Henry Wadsworth Longfellow elementary, eyes glued on a limp Stars and Stripes hung in front of the classroom. Under its broad, starry drape, a confederation of fifty wholly different states—the proverbial herd of cats—got corralled. Along with the rest of the class, I stumbled when the oath reached *indivisible*, mumbled through *undergod*, uttered just like that, in one breathless syllable, then got down to the heady business of long division.

Where Croy and I hail from, we really do live our lives by such silly aphorisms as "dance with the one that brung ya." We're America's last surviving Regionalists, considering ourselves first and foremost citizens of a broader Country of Corn, the Corn Belt—an improbable umbrella under which Croy included Illinois, Indiana, Iowa, Missouri, Minnesota, Kansas, Nebraska, Ohio, Wisconsin, and the Dakotas, a list to which I would add Michigan. "These," Croy writes in his exploration of agrarian folkways, *Corn Country*, "are the real article."

To this Republic of Corn I pledge my deepest allegiance. And in these commonwealths, the meekest and therefore the inheritors, I feel most at ease. Here I know what to say in a café, how to talk weather and crops without sounding a fool. Having been raised on an Iowa Heritage Farm, and having lived as an adult across the heart of the Corn Belt—Iowa, Illinois, and Missouri—I natively speak the *lingua franca*—corn, the "most widely grown crop in the United States" as Croy crowed way back in 1943.

For me, Croy and the Midwest he warmly sketched serve as touchstones, part of the literary-familial bread crumb trail by which I find my way forward and back. Connections and confluences abound; my great-grandfather's book of Corn Belt soil lore, *The Furrow and Us*, stands alongside Croy's *Corn Country* in the premier agricultural collection in the United States, Cornell University's Core Historical Literature of Agriculture, a collection selected for historical importance by top scholars in the field.

But the similarities between my great-grandpap, Walter Thomas Jack, and Croy don't end there. Born just two years apart in the late 1800s, these two consummate crusaders for the corn kingdom died within days of one another in May of 1965, leaving behind rich midwest oeuvres and thriving family farms. Both Croy and Jack indulged as their principal historical passion the exploits of outlaws Jesse James and Cole Younger; both Croy and Jack wrote full-length books on the subject. Both men knew Herbert Hoover, Jack having grown up a neighbor to the Hoovers in West Branch, Iowa, and Croy having been a member, along with President Hoover, of New York's prestigious Dutch Treat Club.

For me, Croy's stuff—a well-ahead-of-its-time brew of travel writing, literary journalism, memoir, popular history, miscellany, and humor that these days would fall under the heading "creative nonfiction"—best captures the spirit of the region where I hang my hat and only sometimes grind my axe. Mark Twain, a Croy touchstone, works a similar magic on me. But wily old Sam Clemens is a bit too slippery by my reckoning to be considered a true documentarian of hereabouts, where folks prefer straightforwardness even in their jokes.

Earnest and mischievous, honest Abe and intolerable imp—these, in a nutshell, describe Homer Croy. His was a style drawn from his people, amplified and made all his own, a quintessentially midlands ethos mingling the yarn-spinning ah shucks of the South with the just-the-facts-ma'am reportage of the North. His folksy "midlandism," a style from which he was continually dissuaded beginning with his first book of popular nonfiction, *How Motion Pictures Are Made*, today exemplifies the appeal of Minnesota's Garrison Keillor and Jim Heynen and Nebraska's Ted Kooser and Roger Welsch. But back then, stuck-in-the-mud editors at places like *Harper's* hadn't yet heard the word creative nonfiction, and they called Croy on the carpet for his "lightly and entertainingly written" true tales. In his 1943 memoir *Country Cured*, Croy recalls hearing with incredulity the words of *Harper* bigwigs, who informed him that readers believed the truth "necessarily dull" and preferred an "encyclopedic style" of dry facts. Could Croy please "take out some of the lightness and resubmit"? Thankfully, nonfiction tastes since have fully caught up with the idea of facts properly lit.

Never heard of Homer Croy? Then as now, the Midwest has a way of keeping mum about its literary sons and daughters. Preoccupied with producing and harvesting, industry and agricultural, we characteristically undersell our artists' Grade-A products, mixing the mediocre with the meteoric in much the same way we mingle our corn at the grain elevator. "Pigs is Pigs," we say, embodying the adage made famous by Iowa scribe Ellis Parker Butler. In the process, we play accomplice to the Great Forgetting, the indiscriminate, sacrificial gristmill by which the Breadbasket feeds, literally and figuratively, the rest of a too-often ungrateful or inattentive nation. Pigs is Pigs. It all eats the same to them.

Hence the need for *Homer Croy: Corn Country Travel Writing, Literary Journalism, and Memoir*, the first-ever anthology of his work and the first proper introduction to his life. In our own families we forget our grandparents were once young blades and beauties, shocking in their vibrancies and potentialities, "famous among the barns" as poet Dylan Thomas had it. Similarly, we forget the vivacities and verities of our mostly mothballed regional inheritance. To wit: we forget that Corn Country bumpkin Croy was, for several years anyway, the toast of the literary East, a writer classed with Sherwood Anderson, Sinclair Lewis, and Theodore Dreiser. Still, after scoring a Pulitzer in 1923 with his novel *West of the Water Tower*, Croy, too, gradually became old news among literati on the Coasts, where the Next Big Thing perennially reigns.

Here then is the extraordinary, sadly forgotten work of Corn Country's most faithful, fervent, and funny mid-century chronicler, drawn from a handful of his popular book-length middle American nonfictions. Here live familiar characters, folk legends, forgotten histories, and, most of all, finer appreciations for the land where Corn is king.

Zachary Michael Jack
Jones County, Iowa

Introducing the Inimitable Homer Croy, Chronicler of Corn Country
by Zachary Michael Jack

Homer Croy did it all and laughed all about it. He penned creative nonfiction decades before the first graduate student scratched their head at the oxymoronic term; he worked as a journalist—the first journalist produced from the first university journalism program in the country at the University of Missouri—years before anyone knew what to do with a college-educated reporter; he embraced his native Midwest and its foibles on page, radio, and silver screen two generations before Garrison Keillor's *Prairie Home Companion.*

Among Croy's famous firsts, his *Ripley's Believe It or Not* and *Who's Who* distinction as "the first student of the first school of journalism in the United States," the University of Missouri at Columbia, headlines as it relates to this, the first-ever anthology of his work. Croy is also credited with being the "first person to tour the world shooting motion pictures" by *Contemporary Authors.* Later in his career, not to be outdone by earlier achievements, he wrote the novel *They Had to See Paris*, a story made into the first talking role for Will Rogers in the blockbuster 1929 film by the same name. Add to these distinctions Croy's authoring of one of just a handful of best-selling anonymous novels in modern American literature, 1923's *West of the Water Tower*—a book that sold more than 100,000 copies, won the Pulitzer Prize, and whose film rights were sold to Paramount for the highest price ever paid for an American novel, $25,000. No less than Theodore Dreiser singled Croy out for praise in his seminal *New York Times* piece "Mr. Dreiser Passes Judgment on American Literature," a commentary in which Dreiser puts the then 40-year-old dark horse in the company of icons Stephen Crane and Hamlin Garland. In short, Croy was a phenom, a phenom now largely and unaccountably forgotten at precisely the time when midwestern regional writing, as embodied by Garrison Keillor, Ted Kooser, and Carol Bly, to name just a few, roots anew.

All of this national and international success Croy achieved while proudly assuming the mantle of midwestern writer, a description that leads off his 1965 obituary in the *Missouri Historical Review*. Croy, as the obit points out, wrote more books about Missouri than any other author, a fact that caused author Cameron Shipp to declare him "the tall, towering cornstalk of Missouri letters," the University of Missouri to award him an honorary doctorate, and the State Historical Society to list him in *Historic Missouri* as one of only a half dozen "later Missouri authors" to win national and international acclaim. For his part, Croy made no bones about the source of his inspiration, the 350-acre Nodaway County, Missouri, farm, which he preferred to New York City where he hung his hat, he said, "only to keep something in the icebox." In an era when prominent midwest writers, including Carl Sandburg, Ernest Hemingway, and F. Scott Fitzgerald abandoned their roots to "make it big," Croy perennially returned to his, buying the family place and making twice annual visits to the farm throughout his life. The author would be the first to admit that he made these visits for himself, for the wellness and fullness of his own soul, but the pilgrimages were also an homage, a laying of the laurel at the feet of his people. One of his hosts on such a visit, Maryville, Missouri's E. B. Trullinger, wrote in the hometown newspaper of Croy's 1941 homecoming, "Every journey he takes is a voyage of discovery to him. Like the poet, he partakes of all people as they pass."

A man of letters ... literally

In the only critical biography extant on Homer Croy, a slim, fifty-eight-page volume put out in 1972 by the Committee on The Northwest Missouri State Studies and written by Charles A. O'Dell, the writer describes Croy in his preface as "writer and humorist." While the labels sound to contemporary ears needlessly redundant or oddly mutually exclusive, no description of Croy would be complete without reference to his prodigious talents as raconteur-wit-humorist. In Shipp's send-up essay "About the Author," published in Croy's American humor retrospective *What Grandpa Laughed At*, Shipp relates how his friend's Twain-styled humor infused even his personal correspondence. He recalls receiving letters from all over the world from the globetrotting funnyman, notes penned on a hodgepodge of stationary from the globe's most far-flung places. "I have in my Croy Collection," Shipp writes, "letterheads from a hostelry in Alaska which specializes in reindeer steak, from Lowell Thomas, from the Mount Rushmore Memorial Commission, from Beatrice Fairfax, the White River Boosters League, the Xenia Hotel, and Ambassador Joseph E. Davis." The editors of *Everyweek Magazine* likewise threw up their hands, merrily, at their correspondent's peripatetic ways, noting, "Conducting correspondence with Homer Croy…is like trying to hold a conversation with a grasshopper. He's never in the same place very long…. What's more, you can never tell from his letterheads and envelopes whether he's in Alaska or Australia."

In interviews, Croy claimed the faux letterhead bit developed when, as a young man, he arrived in New York City. Keen to insure his anxious parents all was well in The Big Apple, he convinced a desk clerk at the uppity Hotel Astor to keep him supplied with their stationary and allow him to take the princely hotel's address as his own. While the home folks figured out the ruse in short order, Croy learned it had staying power among his less commonsensical friends in Gotham. Writing for the New York *World-Telegram*, Ed Harris recalls receiving missives written on stationary provided for prisoners at the Missouri State Penitentiary as well as notes signed "Croy, Enemy of Sin and the Hoof and Mouth Disease." In a 1952 interview, Croy explained his favorite slight of correspondent's hand:

> I take a Treasury Department envelope and type across the top of it, Dept. of Fines and Assessments. Everybody feels guilty about his income tax, so I type a person's name and make it fit into the window of the envelope— then very carefully I affix a three-cent stamp in the upper right-hand corner…. When a person gets the envelope he sees the Dept. of Fines and Assessments, and his hand is shaking so bad he can't open the envelope. Never sees the stamp, or notices that I have typed on the envelope.

Jerry Rand likewise writes at length of the humorist's letter-writing technique in his 1952 article "Homer is on the Trail," urging his readers to put themselves in the hilariously unenviable position of being a Croy pen pal:

As one of his acquaintances you receive in the mail an envelope with a return address reading something like this on the outside: Marijuana Distributing Agency, High School Division. Inside, a London tailor's receipted bill and on the reverse side "Met a blonde lady on the street the other day and she asked me for your address. I would not give it to her. She was terribly disappointed. H. C."

Or from Switzerland likewise on the back of a receipted hotel bill, "I am taking a refresher course in yodeling. I am doing rather well except in some of the high trills I shall experience a little difficulty. Next week: apple shooting. The next week after that I take a short spring course in putting holes in Swiss cheese."

Rand goes on to note that the U.S. Postal Service more than once took "an interest" in Croy's marijuana "foibling" and that the pseudonymous letter writer had become something of a marked man among postmasters general. Among the "museum piece" letters Croy shipped out and "returned to sender," Rand cites envelopes carrying such inventions-for-addresses as "Bloody Creek Saloon" and "Rusk's Marriage Bureau, Satisfaction Guaranteed Or Your Money Back."

Like his fellow Missourian Twain, Croy was a man of many guises, one of the original "international men of mystery." And like Twain, who was known to surprise his guests by occasionally appearing in women's clothing, Croy sought genuineness while reveling in disguise. Despite his reputation for plainspoken homeliness, he, like Samuel Clemens, thrived as a prose stylist—especially so in epistles, which afforded him the full tonal range. "Nothing as obvious as 'Monday, Oct. 20' for Homer," Shipp adds, listing the unorthodox datelines in his Croy letter collection as, for example, "Taking Girl to Haymow Day," "Soft Corn Sorting Day," "Calf Weaning Time," "Poison Ivy Time," "Saturday, Just Before Taking Bath," "The Sabbath—Just Before Toddling Off to Sunday School." Croy's sign-offs equally entertained: "Croy, the Rugged Individualist of Toad Hollow," "Croy, the Sir with the Fringe on Top." "Croy, Writer and Roué," "Croy, the Honest Hog Caller," "Croy, Pin-up Man of the Harems," "Croy, the Man Who Hates Sin and Form 1040," "Croy, the Man Who Wants to Live to be 90 and Be Shot by a Jealous Husband," "Croy, a Fine Man in a Fine

Body (No Laughter, Please)," "Croy, a Good Force in a Naughty World," "Croy, General Custer's Last Surviving Scout," "Big-hearted, Tousle-headed Croy," "Croy, Terror of All Evildoers."

Omnipresent in such myriad, mock calling cards is Croy's midwestern self-deprecation and folksiness, a simultaneous acknowledgement that middle America was both easy to fool and prepared to laugh at. Croy's persona, again like Twain's, blended emphatic earnestness with cultivated tomfoolery, the two perfectly calibrated both to disarm and to persuade. "Homer's the kind who'll catch you off guard," Harris opines, "About the time you say to yourself, *here's a rube*, Old Homer's got you right where the hair is short."

Croy's foolin' went beyond fabricated epistles to a kind of textual play seen only lately in post-modern meta-fictions and nonfictions. But unlike contemporary meta-writing, so self-referential and academic, Croy's brand of "messin'" was organic—arising from sympathies shared with his everyman reader. A case in point: book indices. When Croy was told he needed one for *Corn Country*, he eventually relented, but with a wink to the reader about the inanity of it. Former *New York Times* personnel director, author, and Croy confidante Harry King Tootle recalls that following the *Corn Country* index entry for "Canton," Croy offered this nudge, "not the one in China, but the one in South Dakota." The listing for his daughter, "Carol Croy," he subverted as "daughter of; hard to get up in the morning." For Iowans, he sneaked in this satiric gem "Iowa, only one person out of two and a half in the state raises corn; rate higher for those who drink it." One reviewer, Tootle observes, was so amused by the genius of the unorthodox index, he reviewed it instead of the book. In making light of truth-telling's flimsy claims to objectivity, Croy underscores the biases and blind spots inherent in traditional media. On research trips, he routinely staged gags and mock photos intended both to whip up publicity and bring the high-falutin' down to size—as when he posed for a faux mug shot with the Pima County, Arizona, sheriff Ed Echols. The pic, showing a frowning, aghast Croy wearing a prison number around his neck, turned up splashed across newsprint.

Like Twain, and, more recently, comic writers Roy Blount Jr., Calvin Trillin, and David Sedaris, Croy gravitated toward folkways and families—intimate regionalisms with a universalistic twist. As such, he never ran short of material. At the time of his death in 1965, Croy had produced an incredible fourteen novels, fifteen nonfiction books, at least two autobiographies, eight movie scripts, an unknown number of radio plays (still occasionally coming to light, such as Croy's authoring of the radio program *Showboat*.) and possibly television scripts, plus an incalculable number of magazine articles, short stories and, of course, jokes.

A "Towering Cornstalk of Missouri Letters" is born

Homer Croy was born on March 11, 1883, a date he did his best to withhold from would-be biographers, piquing their interest with hints at "the year the Brooklyn Bridge was built," or "the year Mark Twain's *Life on the Mississippi* appeared." As in many Corn Belt farm households, only a few books decorated the shelves of the Croy farm six miles north of Maryville in far northwest Missouri. One of the few periodicals to reach the Croys was *Wallaces' Farmer*, edited by "Uncle Henry" Wallace in nearby Iowa. In one of two memoirs excerpted in this collection, *Country Cured*, Croy recalls taking *Wallaces' Farmer* to bed with him, letting his mind wander to inventions he might concoct to make the pages of the famed farm glossy. As he tells it, his ruminations resulted in a prototype for a section of rubber hose used to wean calves. *Wallaces' Farmer* published his contraption while Croy was between twelve to fourteen years old according to O'Dell's calculations, and young Homer was "off and running, chasing the will-o'-the-wisp of literary fortune for nearly seventy years of continuous writing." While still a teen working on the farm, Croy published many additional for-pay pieces—humor, short story, and miscellany—in *Wayside Tales, Texas Siftings*, and ultimately, in Eastern outlets such as *Grit* and *Puck*. From the beginning, in keeping with his farm upbringing, he was a working writer, selling his first article to the humor magazine *Puck* while still in grade school.

Encouraged by his teen successes, Croy worked summers at nearby newspapers the St. Joseph *News-Press* and *Gazette* between 1902 and 1904, enrolling in the University of Missouri in 1904, where he worked his way through school partly on checks received for published work run in the *Gazette, News-Press*, and Kansas City *Star*. In an article entitled "Harry King Tootle Gives Inside Dope on Homer Croy," Northwest Missouri's Author,

Tootle relays a story told him by Harold Hall, who recalled "while the other young reporters were playing poker in the back room Homer Croy would be pecking out an article on his typewriter." Fond of portraying his rise to prominence as accidental, these and other reminiscences of Croy's salad days as a journalist intimate his ambition and work ethic. O'Dell quotes a newspaper clipping from the *Star* from February 9, 1906, testifying to the Kansas City newspaper's pride in its rising star. The piece cites "a recent announcement of the features of *Judge* during 1906" in which "Homer Croy of the University of Missouri is given as one of the prominent humorists." The article goes on to praise Croy's "leading article of the week" as it appeared in that January's issue of *Puck*.

Even as his work garnered notice in the "Big City" Kansas and Missouri newspapers, Croy found time to contribute on campus, where he worked for the University of Missouri newspaper, *The Independent*, and for the university humor magazine he helped created, the *Oven*. These and other journalistic dabblings led him to the university's fledging journalism program. While the iconic School of Journalism would not be officially established until 1908, Croy's trailblazing laid foundations. As early as 1906 the journalism "program" was operational in practice, unfolding as an unprecedented co-curricular practicum whereby nine University of Missouri students were offered room and board in St. Louis to put out an occasional issue of the St. Louis *Post-Dispatch*. The *Dispatch* published the student-produced number under the banner St. Louis *Post-Dispatch Junior* and listed Croy as its editor in chief.

Habitually spread thin and all the more so after his apprenticeship in St. Louis, Croy barely kept up with his studies back in Columbia. Before long, his burning of the candle at both ends caught up with him, and he failed his major subject, English, an asterisk which follows him to this day as a "sidelight" in *Contemporary Authors*. Though his failure to graduate would keep him humble throughout a life as a jet-setting, best-selling author, and though he would always regard his academic foolishness with good humor, at the time, his inability to obtain a degree dogged him. Withholding the particulars from even his future wife, Croy waited almost 50 years, on the occasion of an honorary doctorate offered him by the University of Missouri in 1956, to come completely clean. "In my senior year I took an advanced course in Shakespeare," he told Ed Wallace in the article "Firstest Journalism Major to Get College Diploma 49 Years Late." "On the final examination I passed everything else, but there was a question in Shakespeare to explain the line 'tickle o' sere.' I missed it."

In *Country Cured*, he recalls, "I walked down the campus, meeting students I knew. Each time a pang of bitterness went through me…soon they would know." At about the same time, his farming father, Amos, still mourning the loss of his wife, Homer's mother, Susan, wrote he would be visiting Homer for the first time at the university. After showing his father the university's experimental farm, Croy broke the bad news to his pa, who'd left the plow in the field to come see him. To his credit, the no-nonsense, hard-to-please Amos Croy said, "Homer, I don't care what these professors say, I still think you're smart." Croy, expecting the worst, recollects, "In all my life I don't think I ever received such a lift, such a soaring of hope and inspiration and renewed determination." He parlayed his father's confidence into a job after "graduation" at the St. Louis *Post-Dispatch*, and, after a short stint there, into the audacity requisite to test his mettle in New York City.

Homer Croy heads east

Charles O'Dell lists Croy's position at the *Post-Dispatch* as police reporter, though the 1912–1913 edition of *Who's Who* mentions him as "Sunday Writer." Croy himself offered conflicting accounts of leaving the *Post-Dispatch*, from being "let out" because he "fumbled a story," as he writes in his second memoir, *Wonderful Neighbor*, to the rosier version of *Country Cured*, wherein he recalls selling so much of his writing that he resigned to try greener pastures out East.

This eastward migration, Croy's first serious parting from his native Corn Country, would be repeated throughout the writer's lifetime, as his heart called him back to his family's midwest farm and his career pulled him to literary centers New York and Paris. Typical of his born-on-the-farm generation, wanderlust and nostalgia waged war inside Homer Croy, wanderlust winning out more often than not but never achieving a decisive victory. Before heading East to make his literary fortunes in 1908 and after his botched matriculation at the university, Croy cooked up countless, aborted journalism travel schemes, half-baked quests ranging from a trip announced in the St. Louis *Republic* in 1906 ("Homer Croy and William C. Matthews…will work their way around the world….from Columbia, Missouri in June, without money") to a university-funded expedition to Jamestown, Virginia, in 1907. From there, according to O'Dell, Croy refused to return to Missouri with the university group, attempting, instead, to earn passage from Newport News, Virginia, to Havana, Cuba, by working as a coal shoveler and dishwasher with just sixty-five cents to his name.

Croy's early, failed trips amounted to practice, to ascertaining the route and the escape velocity required to overcome the gravitational pull of his native Midwest. When he did leave his newspaper job in St. Louis around 1908, he went first to Boston, where he met up with two University of Missouri alums—Frank Burch and Roscoe F. Potts—to form *The Baseball Magazine*. Deferring to his experience, Burch and Potts appointed Croy editor of the sports periodical, an irony Croy notes in his essay "Bathing in a Borrowed Suit" from *Our American Humorists*, wherein he admits to never having the "slightest interest" in baseball. Even so, he put on his game face, editing issues of the serial until 1909, when he left Boston for a reconnaissance trip to The Big Apple.

In New York City, Croy's midwestern connections once again proved guardian angel, as a friend from the Show-me State tipped him off to a job with the Butterick Publications as an assistant to the legendary writer Theodore Dreiser. Whether by twist of fate or by cruel "literary joke" as O'Dell cites Dreiser biographer W. A. Swanberg called it, Dreiser, the author of *Sister Carrie*, had become "the high arbiter of dainty stories for dainty women, the iconoclast turned hymn singer." In any case, Dreiser admired midwesterners and had several already on staff from Missouri.

Croy, audacious in his luck, prospered under Dreiser's tempestuous but instructive mentorship. While *Contemporary Authors* lists Croy's position as "assistant" to Dreiser and *Who's Who* listed him variously as "assistant" and "associate" editor for the women's magazine Dreiser oversaw, *Delineator*, it's clear that Croy was a key consultant in Dreiser's "cabinet." According to biographer Robert Elias, Dreiser believed that women's magazines ought to be serious, yet light, and it was for this leavening, comedic touch for which Dreiser turned increasingly to the young Missourian. Croy contributed, along with Franklin P. Adams and a young H. L. Mencken, to the magazine's comedic "Man's Page" and later to Dreiser's "little magazines" such as the monthly *Bohemian*, which included skits and short fiction from the likes of O. Henry and Croy. Dreiser's growing appreciation for his employee's fictional and dramatic abilities was evident not only in practice but in word. Swanberg references a *New York Times* interview of 1923 in which Dreiser, snubbing Sherwood Anderson and Sinclair Lewis, mentions the still green Croy as a writer in the company of Stephen Crane and Hamlin Garland

In fact, by 1923, the year of his best-selling, Pulitzer Prize-winning novel, *West of the Water Tower*, Homer Croy had established himself as a writer on a meteoric path. Leaving the steady salary of Butterick Publications behind in 1910, he returned to his bread and butter, free-lance writing, turning out material for *Harper's Weekly* and the New York *Evening Telegram* in 1910 before starting up his own, short-lived but successful advice magazine for working writers, *The Magazine Maker*, in 1911. By 1914, Croy had sold *The Magazine Maker* at a profit and had once again returned to freelancing, this time with more regularity. A blurb from the January 24, 1914 *The Universal Weekly* lists the thirty-year-old Croy's remarkable resume: a serial humor column in *Judge*, a weekly humor installment for *Leslie's Weekly*, and a once-a-week dash of wit for *Colliers*. Croy's biography as run in *The Universal Weekly*, an organ of Universal Pictures, served the additional purpose of advance promoting an across-the-globe trip Croy was to make with backing from *Leslie's Weekly* and Universal Pictures, for whom he was to film his circumnavigation. The voyage, a kind of belated playing out of the author's thwarted post-university globetrotting aspirations, was subsidized by *Leslie's Weekly* in return for an exclusive series of humor dispatches titled "Laughing Around the World with Homer Croy" and by numerous other ad companies who let Croy dip into their corporate coffers in return for product placement en route. Explaining the unique arrangement, Croy writes in *Country Cured* that he was obligated to "smoke a certain kind of pipe tobacco, use a certain kind of toothpaste, and chew just one kind of gum." When the ad companies somehow bought the scheme, Croy next "singled out the Universal Film Company as being susceptible," and, as he puts it, "tripped gaily in" to appeal directly to the head of Universal, "Uncle Carl" Laemmle. When Laemmle initially rebuffed him, Croy ambushed the movie mogul, jumping in Laemmle's moving car as Uncle Carl drove off to the bank. Whether in deference to Croy's self-promotional genius or to his shear desperation, Laemmle acquiesced to all of Croy's demands, assigning him a cameraman, as requested, and naming him "director" of what would become a forerunner of reality television. Ultimately, the trip, begun in Honolulu, made it as far as Bombay, where Croy's camera was confiscated and where the author was marooned for several weeks before his friend, love interest, and future wife, Mae Belle Savall, wired him the cash necessary to return to the States. A year later, the two were married in a ceremony that qualified for another worldwide first according to the groom—"the first couple in the world to be put on a [Universal] newsreel."

During the year of "Laughing Around the World With Homer Croy," Croy also published his first, Midwest-set novel, *When to Lock the Stable*. Bobbs-Merrill published the book in conjunction with an advertising campaign intended to capitalize on the author's growing fame as a Corn Belt humorist. The press produced and distributed a brochure with a biographical sketch introducing Croy to his readers and accompanied by caricatures of the author drawn by another Missouri connection, Croy's University of Missouri artist friend, Monte Crews, who also illustrated the novel. The brochure, reports O'Dell, trumpeted Croy's off-the-cuff, hot-off-the-presses speed as a writer, boasting that the author had written the text in just forty-two days. Analyzing the novel's literary merit, O'Dell criticizes the writing for its "thinness" and its "stereotypes." He also notes its similarities to Mark Twain, as suggested by the protagonist's name, "Clement" (akin to Samuel Clemens) and plot, which features Clem's running away from a repressive family (akin to Huck Finn). Closer analysis, however, suggests *When to Lock the Stable* is perhaps less purposefully derivative of Twain than it is simply autobiographical. Not coincidentally, the setting of *When to Lock the Stable* is the midwestern town of Curryville, also tellingly named to echo Croy's hometown of Maryville. Clem, declaring, "someday, somehow, I'm going to be a hero," is the spitting image of a young Homer Croy as he appears in his memoirs, *Country Cured* and *Wonderful Neighbor*. The names of the novel's lesser characters, too, suggest the story's autobiographical source; Clem's friend, Rencie is similarly named to the real-life Renzo who served as Amos Croy's hired man; Clem's love interest, named Miss Mary Mendenhall is phonetically similar to the name of the young woman Croy was courting as he completed the novel, Miss Mae Belle Savall.

Croy's debut novel, meditative in places, foreshadows the essayist's voice the writer brings to full flower in his later midwestern nonfiction, as when the narrator muses, "The quickest way to the heart of a man west of the Mississippi River is to say a good word for his town. The people may quarrel among themselves, but when a stranger comes within their gates they are shoulder to shoulder, swearing their own city is the rose-bed of the national flower garden." Perhaps because *When to Lock the Stable* remained too close to Croy's experience, resisted further fictional flights of fancy, its sales disappointed.

For his next work, *How Motion Pictures Are Made*, Croy returned to nonfiction, producing a classic still considered foundational in the study of American cinema. Hailed by the December 22, 1918 *New York Times* as "one of the first and most immediately accessible descriptions of the progressive invention and growth of motion pictures," the book, a history and how-to film primer in one, offers a close, demystifying read of how early pictures were made. In the book's closing chapters, the author offers personal prognostications for the nascent industry. Croy declares that the weekly magazines so important to Middle America would gradually be superceded by the motion picture, "which arouses an enthusiasm unapproached by even the best daily papers." Especially noteworthy in *How Motion Pictures Are Made* is the author's enthusiasm for the emerging medium, a keenness he showed in directing his own trip around the world. A journalist by trade, Croy praises the very media he claims will one day supplant the daily paper, a media where "finer shades of feeling and temperament are now conveyed to the screen in sincerity equal to the best in the older form of art." Following up on his film monograph, Croy also wrote the entry on "cinema" for the twelfth edition of the *Encyclopedia Britannica* and accepted a position as director of "Overseas Weekly," a post which charged him with providing "film entertainment" for the American Expeditionary Forces in Paris. In his biographical sketch of Croy in *Contemporary Authors*, Creath Thorne offers still more specifics about Croy's nine-month wartime service in Paris, which entailed working with the YMCA as a "liaison man with the Signal Corps."

How Motion Pictures Are Made established Croy's long association with Harper Brothers, now Harper Collins, which published his book-length work exclusively from 1918 to 1945 with the exception of Croy's other early work of nonfiction *88 Ways to Make Money by Writing*, published in 1923 by midwestern press J. K. Reeve. In 1918, the year of *How Motion Pictures Are Made*, Harper Brothers also published the first of its many Croy novels, *Boone Stop*, another semi-autobiographical novel the author once called his "best book" but which did not sell well, perhaps because of its wartime release. *Boone Stop* was followed two years later by what Croy called his "worst book," *Turkey Bowman*, a melodramatic coming-of-age story set in the era of Indian raids in the West. Like *Turkey Bowman*, *Boone Stop* is the story of an insecure middle American male. In the book, hero Cleveland Seed wrestles with his father's, Pa's, religious fanaticism while trying to form his own beliefs. While O'Dell attributes the historical source of Pa's apocalyptic precepts to the American prophet William Miller's prediction of the end of the world on October 22, 1844, Croy's nonfiction reveals more recent alleged "end times"—the drought and grasshopper plagues of Croy's childhood in Missouri. In any event, citing *Boone Stop* and *Turkey Bowman* in particular, O'Dell locates the strength of Croy's early novels in the author's "treatment...of the insecure young man, the fellow who is certain all the other boys know how to act around girls while being equally certain he can't do anything right." Croy's characters' awkwardness around the fairer sex likewise strongly suggests an autobiographical source, as two Croy essays excerpted herein from *Wonderful Neighbor*—"Our Hat-tipping Problem" and "I Lose My Manhood"—make abundantly, uproariously clear. Accurate as O'Dell's comments may be, they overlook the deeper wellspring of Croy's protagonists' opposite-sex awkwardness: the wider, rural Midwest he returns to again and again in his nonfiction and its habit of treating "girls and womenfolks" as, to use Croy's words, "suddenly and mysteriously...fascinating."

To his midwestern upbringing, Croy also owed his first breakthrough success, the best-selling 1923 novel *West of the Water Tower*. In *Country Cured*, Croy describes walking along a street near his adopted home of Forest Hills, New York, in the early 1920s, "barely making a living," when, "for no reason at all," he thinks of a childhood incident where he had witnessed a Missouri neighbor boy flee to a barn. The boy, Croy later learned, had been shamed because he had "got into trouble with a girl." He remembers: "As I rode along, the frightened expression on the boy's face rode with me. Goodness knows, I had had all the yearnings the boy had had, and I told myself that it was only by the grace of God I wasn't running to the barn." Within a month of the memory's resurfacing, he had begun a novel about the shunned boy. "It was my own town," Croy recollects in *County Cured*, "my own people, and I knew that boy and girl. It [the novel] took me ten months."

The gestation period—twice Croy's usual—proved auspicious for its literary virtue. "Very shortly," O'Dell writes, savoring the irony implicit in the historical moment, "Homer Croy found himself a best-selling but anonymous writer, with nearly ecstatic reviews from the critics." The reviews to which O'Dell refers rolled in from the biggest newspapers. Writing for the New York *Tribune* on April 22, 1923, writer Leon Wilson said the book was the best in its genre since E. W. Howe's *The Story of a Country Town* in 1917. Allan Nevins in the March 5, 1923 *Literary Review* applauded, "As...a study of a community it has highly unusual merit." H. L. Mencken, who Croy had come to know via his work for Dreiser's humor publications, praised the book's "striking portraits." The acclaim took Croy completely by surprise; he had, he writes, almost become "ashamed" of the novel and Harper's decision to publish it anonymously on the grounds that its controversial subject matter conflicted with the author's reputation as a humorist.

But Harper's marketing decision soon paid ironic dividends. "My heart," Croy recalls in *Country Cured*, "which had been down around my knees, shot up like a balloon at a country fair. Guesses poured in as to who had written it. I felt pretty good about that, for I was right up there in the front pews. Booth Tarkington, Sherwood Anderson, Harry Leon Wilson, Sinclair Lewis, Theodore Dreiser." Croy managed the circumstantial irony attending his anonymity with characteristic good humor, writing, "Never in all my life had anything so exhilarating happened to me, me, the author of a bestseller! Assisted, of course, by Anonymous."

Once again, Croy's interest in and aptitude for film intervened, as he necessarily sacrificed his anonymity for an offer from Jesse Lasky at Paramount Pictures, who negotiated for the film rights to the book. Even after the author signed on the dotted line for $25,000—the largest sum ever paid for an American novel at the time—Croy's secret remained intact until a chance meeting at a party when Croy's friend, Don Marquis, spilled the beans to Percy Hammond, a columnist for the New York *Herald Tribune*. Croy assumed Hammond, a professional journalist, would keep his secret, though a tell-all but complimentary column a few days later proved otherwise. Directed by Harper Brothers to deny the Hammond story because the book's anonymity had boosted its sales—numbered at more than 100,000 in Croy's obituary in the *Missouri Historical Review*— the author penned an evasive note to the reviewer. It was too late, however; the cat was fully out of the bag. "Every critic in the country knew, then, who had written it," Croy recalls in *Country Cured*, "and the mystery was over. But it'd been thrilling while it lasted."

Once more, Croy had drawn explicitly on his midwestern ethos and upbringing to tell a universal story that was, except for the protagonist, Guy's, fathering of an illegitimate child, significantly autobiographical. The action in *West of the Water Tower* takes places in the midwestern burg of Junction City, a setting widely regarded by critics ever since as a thinly veiled representation of Croy's hometown of Maryville, Missouri. Characterized by O'Dell as "a picture of a young man wanting the best of both the world of the town and the world of his father, and getting neither," Guy Plummer represents Croy's youthful ambitions and fears. Sin and Puritanism, preoccupations throughout the author's childhood, dog Guy, who prays after having premarital sex with his lover, Bee, a respectable, hometown girl, in the backroom of the Owl Drugstore where Guy works. As Guy and Bee, alone in the pharmacy, warm up to their romantic inclinations, Bee criticizes a pin-up girl Guy's friend, Cod, had given him to hang on the wall—a picture Guy shamefully and surreptitiously attributes to the fellow who had worked at the store before him. This scene is literally reminiscent of the adolescent exploits Croy recounts in his memoir *Country Cured*, wherein the author, newly graduated from high school, moves to St. Joseph, Missouri, for the summer to work as a newspaper reporter. Before Croy leaves, his mother cautions him against "bad girls," but, once having established himself in St. Joe's, he finds himself looking for any pretext to witness the goings-on inside a St. Joseph bordello. Posing as an artist, Croy goes upstairs with a girl not to make love, but to sketch her in the nude. In real life, then, Croy drew exactly the kind of suggestive picture

Bee denounces prior to her illicit lovemaking with Guy. After leaving the house of prostitution with his drawing, Croy suffers a shame similar to the kind Guy feels after making love to Bee. Croy writes, "I could hardly believe I had done such a cheap thing. A fit of self-scorn laid hold of me. I was low and unworthy. Then, suddenly, I though of what Billy Sunday had said, and terror laid hold of me. I would be punished, just as he had said lustful men would be." In *West of the Water Tower*, Guy's punishment is doled out by the people of Junction City, who "gathered in front of the drugstore, whispered, and then stared at the curiosity which had suddenly come among them. Entering, they bought lozenges while they looked at the strange animal."

O'Dell cites an interview Croy gave on June 23, 1923 to his old employer, the St. Joseph *News-Press*, in which Croy labels Guy Plummer a "thief" and "seducer" while claiming that he, the author, took "an aloof point of view of the goodnesses and pettiness of small-town life." And yet, for all his attempts to distance himself from his controversial novel before an audience of home-state readers, Croy admits to trying to "lift off the top of his [Guy's] skull and let the reader peer down into his inner workings." Here again, Croy stakes out middle ground—a borderland between anything-goes artistic integrity and conservative Regionalism. O'Dell cites a passage from W. Tasker's study *The Adolescent in the American Novel 1920–1960* as evidence of a similar middle road taken by Floyd Dell in *Mooncalf* and Dreiser in *An American Tragedy*. Mentioning *West of the Water Tower* alongside the work of Dreiser and Dell, Tasker claims such novels "represent a transition between the unquestioning condemnation of premarital intercourse and pregnancy found in the novels of the genteel tradition, and the almost casual treatment of these problems in later novels." Here again, the influence of the Midwest in general and Missouri in particular as literal and figurative midland between the conservatism of the South and the liberalism of the Coasts, dictates Croy's artistic outlook, at once enabling the then—risqué story he tells and insuring its baseline palatability.

The financial success of *West of the Water Tower* enabled Croy to pay down the mortgage on his expensive home in Forest Hills, Long Island, and to continue to pay the mortgage on the Croy farm back in Maryville, land he had promised his father before his father's death that he would hold on to at all costs. Croy and his more cosmopolitan wife

Mae Belle also made multiple trips with their children to Paris, a city which Croy writes in *Country Cured* he had to see for himself. On that first trip overseas, Croy wrote to Walter Lippmann to ask for a personal meeting and was allowed to buy the celebrated journalist and political commentator a drink. Later, while staying in the Grand Hotel in Saint Maxime along the French Rivera, Croy entertained Dale Carnegie, who would later dedicate his seminal book *How to Win Friends and Influence People* to him. "How sweet it was," Croy opines, "to consort with the famous, elbow to elbow, no looking up and no looking down." And yet for all his sudden fame, the author found Paris "disappointing" and the French "aloof and artificial" by comparison with the midwestern folks he had grown up with. As he toured the French countryside, he couldn't help but find the nation's agriculture primitive by comparison with midwestern farming, recalling: "Often I thought how I would like to take one of them [French farmers] to my farm and show him the long, straight, stoneless rows, three horses abreast swinging down a black loam field, a whole hill covered with steer." When Croy and family returned to Paris in the spring, Croy's son, Homer Jr., took ill with an unknown malady and passed away in what Croy describes as "that lonely Paris hotel." Americans turned out in sympathy for Croy, Mae Belle, and their young daughter, Carol, a phenomenon Croy later wrote "made America seem very close." Recalling how the coffin, covered with an American flag, made its way down the Parisian streets, he recounts in *Country Cured* how "the Frenchmen lifted their hats," adding, "It all helped and yet, at such at time, nothing helps, for when the big crises come we enter them alone. But some way or other we do stand them, we do go on living, we laugh again."

One of the things that brought joy to the Croys during the difficult twenty-two months they spent in France was their daughter, Carol, their sole surviving child, who Croy describes as a "fine little girl who thought the *Punch and Judy* show on the Champs Elysees was the finest earth had to offer." Acknowledging the joy he felt taking her there, the proud father concludes, "And soon we move from one stepping stone to another on a path that we don't understand, that we have never chosen, and ends we know not where." Another positive legacy of their time in France turned out to be Croy's first major success after *West of the Water Tower*, a novel he titled *They Had to See Paris* (1926), a based-on-real-life story of an unhappy

American businessman Croy had known in Gay Paree, and reflecting Croy's own disappointment with the French. The story, lightly comedic, follows the fictional Pike Peters, a garage owner from Oklahoma who suddenly becomes wealthy—not unlike Croy—and moves to Paris at the behest of his socially-climbing wife, only to find the city incomprehensible and its citizens inhospitable. The novel, writes Thorne, was "well-received on its appearance...because it reflected the misgivings many Americans felt at the time toward the European experience." The novel was released as a film by the same name in 1929 and famously starred Will Rogers in his first talking role. Thorne calls the movie a "major success" for Fox and the "first real success" Rogers enjoyed on the silver screen. More importantly, the Croy-Rogers collaboration created a lasting friendship unique among screenwriter and film star, and one which Rogers trumpeted. Describing his Thanksgiving in a *New York Times* dispatch entitled "Will Rogers Reports on his Turkey Day," a pleased Rogers wrote, "Homer Croy, author of *They Had to See Paris*, as hungry as an author can be, was here."

Croy, whose novels were turned into Rogers films with greater frequency than any other writer's, devotes an entire chapter of *Country Cured* to his friendship with Rogers. Much later in 1953, he would author a book-length appreciation, *Our Will Rogers*. In his memoir, Croy recalls the first time he and Rogers "really felt drawn to one another"—a discussion on humor in which they agreed that humor consisted of truth, only exaggerated. The two men shared much—a background writing commentaries for newspapers, an appreciation for the people and folkways of the Great Plains, an aversion to pretense, a gift for colloquialism, and, above all, celebrity, though Rogers's was of a different order. Both men had gone to school in Missouri; both lacked college degrees, playing up their ignorance when it suited them. Meeting Rogers must have been, for Croy, like meeting a version of himself. This doppelganger effect fostered in him an intense fascination for what made his pal tick. "I realized," Croy writes in *Country Cured*, "that the qualities were what the public saw, but I also realized that there must be qualities that were not so discernable." Rogers's secret, as Croy distills it, amounts to "showmanship," an evolution by which Rogers "built himself up until he became, both on and off the stage, the Will Rogers the public knew." By contrast, Croy refused to play the "Hollywood game" in which salaried writers milked projects at the encouragement of greedy agents, and where writers and the treatments they wrote were heroes one day and goats the next. "One of the things that makes you think twice," Croy laments, "is to see a studio decide to do a 'different' kind of story.... The idea, as deep in a studio as a design in a rug, is to play safe. Never experiment. Don't monkey with the box office."

Croy's abiding, midwestern sense of fair dealing served him poorly in Hollywood, where his treatments and adaptations, ranging from a commissioned adaptation of the Broadway play *Lazybones* to a scenario for a sequel to the popular *They Had to See Paris* entitled *Down to Earth*, poorly matched the vision of studio executives. In several instances, including *Down to Earth*, Croy was compelled to cede control of his project to studio writers brought in to give the script box-office "punch." In Will Rogers's *Down to Earth*, for example, Edwin J. Burke is listed as the sole writer despite the fact that the scenario and the original screenplay belonged to Croy. Even Croy's foundational role in the box-office hit *They Had to See Paris* was minimized in the film's credits, which acknowledged Croy as creator of the novel on which the story is based, but listed Sonya Levien as the writer of the for-film "story."

These slights, coupled with Croy's feeling that he had badly undersold his rightful interest in *They Had to See Paris*, caused the author to feel a growing disconnect between his rising reputation as a writer for page and screen and his dwindling bank account. In *Country Cured*, he remembers returning, depressed, to his home in Long Island, what he called the "Little House with the Big Mortgage." Croy muses, "My name was in the papers. I had sold the first talking picture for Will Rogers at what everybody assumed to be a whacking price; and I let them think so, uncomfortable as I sometimes felt." The bank, too, wanted to know why Croy, the famous scribbler, couldn't pay his mortgage if he had sold a film starring Rogers. "I told them [the bank]," Croy explains, "I had got only a crumb or two from Mr. Fox's table; they said they knew how to handle people like me." Still, despite his grim financial standing, he kept up appearances in literary circles in New York City, persisting in the generosity he had been taught as a child and which had earned him countless friends. When *They Had to See Paris* came out, Croy recalls visiting his favorite club to buy rounds for all his admirers with "money that should have been going to...the grocer." Wryly characterizing the irony of his financial straights, he writes, "It is sweet, indeed to nibble the fruit of success—the first I had had since *West of the Water Tower*. But there was no fruit in the bank."

Money had not been the sole factor tempting Homer Croy to Hollywood; instead, it had been a sense that he had something genuine Hollywood lacked. He writes that he decided to go to Hollywood to see if it missed, as he suspected, the "homey-touch" that was his greatest strength. His early experiences in Hollywood, roughly corresponding with the Dustbowl years, confirmed the illusion of a promised land. In each studio he called on, Croy asked for what he felt his free-lance film work was worth and what his two mortgages required—$500 a week. Mostly, Hollywood declined his services, except for admirers in women's and civic clubs aching to have him speak. "Sometimes the pay is your lunch," Croy recalls with a note of bitterness, "sometimes it is a banquet dinner, sometimes they take you home in a swagger car. The rest is heartfelt appreciation."

Increasingly between jobs, Croy wrestled questions of identify, refusing to sell the family farm back in Missouri on the grounds that his feel for the farm remained "deep and abiding" as it was "wrapped with tender and useful memories." At the same time, he had increasingly to confront his reputation as a New Yorker by attrition, a point driven home in the popular press by friends like Jerry Rand, who needled, "Homer for a time posed as a 'farmer straight from the Missouri soil.' Periodically he would disappear from his city haunts after explaining that harvesting time had arrived and he was needed on his acres." Thereafter Rand landed the punch line, "As time went on, skeptics noted that the calluses were confined to the right hand. Except for its size, the left might have been a society bud's." For a January 9, 1944 story for the Kansas City *Star*, reporter E. B. Garnett visited the Missouri legend who had made his long-ago migration to New York City with "an open countenance and round cheeks so sunburned they resembled nice Jonathan apples." To his surprise, the reporter found a dual citizen, a product of ambivalence, on the other side of the automatically locking door of Croy's flat. "And behind his vaunted rusticism and frank credulity," Garnett wrote, "you find a very professional, urbane novelist keeping the orthodox morning office hours of a writer in a big, cooperatively owned [New York] apartment."

Twice-mortgaged, oft-caricatured as a "subway farmer," and ever-questioning the tragic loss of Homer Jr., Croy turned philosophic, pausing for serious, dark-night-of-the-soul reflection for the first time since *West of the Water Tower* had made him an overnight sensation. By this time, having lost a second son, Creighton, to an accident in Texas, personal grief had made Croy fully circumspect. He writes that he could not find meaning in any of it—the Hollywood or New York literary scene, the popular novels—but only in, for example, the sweetness of his daughter Carol, who was then developing into a talented girl writer, and in the solace of the farm and his midwestern past, days of "simple faith," he wrote, when "I put my hand on the pommel of my saddle and promised God I would never 'have anything to do with girls.' God was right up there, then; now I don't know where he is."

Further indignities followed. The gas was cut off at the Croy house in Long Island; the roof leaked. Finally, the bank took the house and the Croys moved into a small cooperative apartment on West 183rd Street in New York. Though, during these troubled days, Croy was elected a member of the famous Dutch Treat Club, a group of elite writers, editors, publishers, and artists, he reported feeling "uncomfortable" and "ill at ease" in the company of men "much more prosperous." Even the stories of O' Henry that he once loved now seemed "merely glamorous claptrap contrived for a trick ending." During this period of "readjustment," Croy recalls in *Country Cured*, "I had an example of the influence of the farm. This influence came into my life every day, and into my thinking, and into my attitude toward the world.... Who can ever get away from his early influence?"

Homer Croy's true tales from Corn Country

Increasingly, Croy's mind returned to his birthright, to the small towns and mid-sized farms of the Middle West. While as a young man he had craved the sentimental, feel-good stories of O'Henry, as a middle-aged soul he wanted truth, as deep and real and folksy as he could get it. He didn't want verities garbed even in the benign showmanship of Mark Twain or Will Rogers, but in the direct, simple way he recalled from his youth. "I began to try, as I never had before," Croy reflects, "to understand my life and my place in it.... I began to appreciate the things that gave me moments of exaltation, a lift, a flash of something spiritual." At his lowest, he made lists of what he called "homey satisfactions"—the spiritual bread crumb trail that would lead him back home. These personal inventories included such items as "the whistle of a train at night," "the welcome of a dog," "the smell of coffee cooking early morning," "a walk all by myself on a country road." Such sensations became talismans and totems, sheltering him as he entered uncharted territory in the last stage of an incredibly productive writing career: a documenter of the true tales of his native Corn Country and the men and women who called it home. Though advancing years and mounting debts forced him to sell the Missouri home place in 1957, he understood well the artistic gift it had been to him. In a 1957 interview given the newspaper where he got his start, the St. Joseph *News-Press*, Croy's tone turned wryly circumspect. "A peculiar thing though is that I made more writing about the farm than I ever made operating it. I guess I took in the worst paying professions in the world—farming and writing."

After penning two mid-1940s volumes of popular memoir, *Country Cured* and *Wonderful Neighbor*, Croy continued to connect his personal past with the zeitgeist of post-World War II Middle America. In 1948 he returned to his bread and butter, humor. With the discriminating ear of a man who had heard countless jokes in his nearly seventy years, he selected, compiled, and edited a retrospective anthology of American humor, *What Grandpa Laughed At*. Applying the hypothesis that "the history of this country could be told by its jokes," the book celebrates the good humor bubbling up from the nation's Heartland especially, and specifically from beloved regional wits Will Rogers, Williams Jennings Bryan, and Mark Twain. A year after *What Grandpa Laughed At*, Croy turned his writerly attentions to the history-making deeds and misdeeds of the real-life heroes and villains of his middle section in titles such as *Jesse James Was My Neighbor* (1949), *He Hanged Them High* (1952), *Our Will Rogers* (1953), and *The Trial of Mrs. Abraham Lincoln* (1962), among others.

In his biographical sketch published in *Dictionary of Literary Biography*, Thorne calls Croy's later-life nonfiction "among the most lasting of his books," even considering the popular success of his early novels. The *New York Times*'s Harry King Tootle approved of his friend's return to popular nonfiction, writing, "He [Croy] is as much a story as anything he has ever written.... The saga of the country boy from Nodaway County is as entertaining as any of his brainchildren.... His personality is always popping out of anything he writes, from anecdote to novel." Tootle's assessment was born out in the marketplace, where Croy's middlewestern memoirs performed well, selling well over 100,000 copies, a tally that included an order placed by the Armed Services for 97,000 of *Country Cured*. Readers around the country benefited from the release of Croy's nonfiction in affordable, pocket-sized editions that, while they netted the author less than a penny in royalties per unit, nonetheless made his a household name.

The embrace of his midwestern nonfiction by his home people delighted Croy, who passed away in 1965. The true tales of his native Corn Country interested him most, and he traveled widely and well to find them. Ignoring conventional wisdom that the really interesting stories happened in the nation's most romantic places—places like New England and California—Croy made whistle stops in Arizona, Oklahoma, Missouri, and Kansas. Commenting on Croy's research trip to Oklahoma in search of material about Judge Parker, writer Jerry Rand writes, "He [Croy] found eastern Oklahoma as rich in history as scrub oaks. Where other biographers had appraised only the forest, Homer took the individual trees to wind up with the book called *He Hanged Them High*." Rand's article "Homer is on the Trail" captures the incongruity of the incomparable and by-then famous Croy beating the streets of Oklahoma City for "clues for his book." Rand renders the scene thusly:

> Last spring he dropped off a train in Oklahoma City, tracking down clues. Thereafter, he cloppity-clopped (his own uncopyrighted term) along Broadway, Main Street, and Grand Avenue, pedestrians stopped dead in their tracks to study this largish person clad in a checkerboard suit, nothing in the way of headgear to cover a pate, completely devoid of foliage. And spread out over a manly chest like a bonfire on a prairie, a necktie of such brilliant red that pedestrians shielded their eyes.

More remarkable still, according to Rand, is that the unmistakable Croy visage proved as "identified and identifiable whether in Oklahoma, Siam, Singapore or Cairo, in Egypt or Illinois." Unlike fellow midwesterner Ernest Hemingway, whose popularity likewise spanned genres, Croy's sirens did not call him away from the United States, but inexorably and ebulliently back to the center of it. And he never stopped learning. After he returned home in 1941 to eat fried mush and commune, his host E. B. Trullinger took solace, writing in the January 16 edition of the home newspaper, "Even in this part of the world, overlooked by poets, painters, and fiction writers, Croy had varied and amusing experiences enough to fill a new novel."

In *Country Cured*, Croy describes the existential revelation that caused him to turn back to his native landscape and the stories of its people. He writes, "As I began to better understand life, I felt that instead of standing alone, I was part of a vast kinship with all other human beings, and that as I suffered, so they suffered; and as I yearned, so they yearned; and that as I felt defeat, so they must experience it, too." This, then, may be the finest expression of Croy's abiding service to the salt-of-the-earth, of his "gift for friendship" as Harry King Tootle put it. His warm regard for his fellows, for friends near and far, was fully reciprocated, as evidenced by a column published by Croy friend and fellow writer Don Marquis in the New York *Tribune* in 1923, the year of Croy's great early success with *West of the Water Tower*. Marquis' words serve as well-earned grace notes, echoing as they do, throughout Croy's long and generous life:

> I never saw a man whose success…was hailed with more genuine rejoicing on the part of his fellow workers; each member of the whole writing gang feels tickled as if something good happened to himself. And this is a tribute to the man's fine, loyal, game personality. For his is a nature that has permitted him to meet his own personal misfortunes and disappointments with endurance and gallantry and gentleness.

Homer Croy's death at the age of 82 in late May of 1965 merited an unusually lengthy, eighteen-paragraph write-up in *The New York Times*. His claims to fame—from his hardscrabble youth in rural Missouri, to his trip around the world sponsored by Universal, to the phenomenal success of *West of the Water Tower*, and finally to his Hollywood heyday with Will Rogers and the popular western and midwestern nonfictions that followed—made for impressive copy. But even twenty column inches in the nation's most prestigious newspaper failed to capture his enduring influence. As a writer, he rejected the doom and gloom realism of Sherwood

Anderson and Hamlin Garland, earning praise from critics for "serious realistic work which has something of the spirit of [Thomas] Hardy and Dreiser…but…more hopeful." As a popular literary humorist whose universal appeal sprung, paradoxically, from a particular plot of ground in Corn Country, he earns a spot in the line-up of great American literary humorists from Mark Twain to David Sedaris. As an early documentarian and champion of film, he stands as a forgotten pioneer who, uniquely, embraced the camera as an extension of the pen, not a threat to it. And as a beloved personality and prankster in both New York City and Hollywood, Croy prefigures such legendary literary luminaries and socialites as George Plimpton and Truman Capote.

All this *joie de vivre* arrived bound in a singularly folksy, drop-dead funny package. Indeed, few figures in the twentieth century can boast a best-selling novel, hit films and radio shows, and stage play successes (His novel *Family Honeymoon* was turned into a play.). Still fewer have kept company with their era's best-loved humorists, novelists, dramatists, journalists, and screenwriters without sacrificing their spot at the kitchen table with the folks back home. Precious few have had the ear of Presidents, industrialists, celebrities, writers, and artists alike.

"The great Croy," Cameron Shipp concludes in the magazine *True*, "has so many astonishing, lovable and downright scandalous distinctions that setting them down all in one paragraph would be distracting. But as millions of readers know, Croy is the tall, towering cornstalk of Missouri letters, the author of *Corn Country, Country Cured, They Had to See Paris, and West of the Water Tower*, among a spate of exceptionally fine books, all bestsellers, and also of innumerable motion pictures, short stories, radio sketches and magazine articles." In its way, Croy's life proved as meteoric as F. Scott Fitzgerald's, as restless as Hemingway's, and as sweetly sad as Faulkner's. Somehow he managed to laugh through it all, refusing to sell himself or anyone else out. He introduced a subversive dash of Corn Country loam to the airy drawing rooms and high-brow cliques of New York, L. A., and Paris. For him, Corn Country yielded a crop of miracles. Of his own particular plot of Earth, of Eden, Homer Croy once said:

> Almost every square yard of it brings back memories. Not
> far away, buried on a farm, are my father and mother. A
> "pioneer cemetery" we call it. A cornfield comes up on

two sides; a pasture is on the other, and there are water maples branching over the graves. Some way or another, it always looks beautiful.

Part I
Travel Writing and Literary Journalism

Homer Croy's 1947 classic *Corn Country* (Duell, Sloan & Pearce, 1947) stands as one of the first and best treatments of Corn Belt history and culture—more so with the advent of academic programs in Regional Studies, Midwest Studies, and Place Studies. Recently selected by top scholars in the field for inclusion in Cornell University's prestigious Core Historical Literature of Agriculture and, at the time of its publication, selected by Erskine Caldwell for the American Folkways series featuring such writers as Wallace Stegner and Louis Bromfield, *Corn Country* comes with a pedigree.

In spite of its inclusion as part of the relatively high-brow American Folkways, *Corn Country* makes for vintage Croy—occasionally lyrical, often factual, and always sentimental. In *American Novelists of Today*, the University of Florida's Harry Warfel detours from a page-long study of Croy's fiction to make special mention of *Corn Country*, wherein the author "spins humorous yarns in the midst of excellent reporting on the social life and manners of the Middle West." Part travel writing, part journalism, part history, and part folklore/ethnography, the book's mixed genre anticipates the work of contemporary midwestern writers such as Carol Bly, Michael Martone, Michael Feldman, Jim Heynen, and former U.S. Poet Laureate Ted Kooser. Croy, a mature writer by 1947, recognizes his book's departure from the tonal conventions of scholarly nonfiction, and respectfully asks his readers' indulgence, writing in the first chapter: "The Corn Belt is my country. I grew up there, my heart is still there; so if I become a little too enthusiastic in this book…please make allowances. Maybe, during the course of this book, I can win you to an appreciation of the corn section. I would like that. It has no equal."

The final readings in this grouping of Croy's most lasting midwestern travel writing and literary journalism broaden the author's writerly reach to the very edge of the Great Plains and Border State hill country. In an excerpt from "Small-town Writing" the Missourian debunks the myth that the deck is stacked against the midwestern writer sequestered away from the city. In "Perambulating Preacher of the Ozarks" he profiles the Christ-like Guy Howard, a native Iowan who ministers to Missouri's hill folk on foot and for free. "Introduction" appears here from the author's 1949 biography of his childhood hero/antihero, Jesse James. The result of over 5000 miles traveled for interviews with friends and family members of the infamous outlaw, *Jesse James Was My Neighbor* (Duell, Sloan, & Pearce, 1949) well suits the journalistic mood and method of Croy's *Corn Country*.

These Are the Corn States

First, before I set down the names of the corn-producing states, I must point out that corn is the most widely grown crop in the United States; every state in the Union grows it.

There is more corn grown than wheat; indeed, the corn crop, measured in bushels, is about three times as large as the wheat crop. More corn is grown than cotton and hay lumped together. In fact, the Department of Agriculture tells me, one-tenth of all our farm land is given over to corn. The Department also tells me that the corn crop of this country is worth twelve times as much as the orange crop. I hope that gives Florida and California something to think about.

Sometimes corn is the biggest crop in states that are not known at all for corn! For instance, Colorado is known for its sugar beets; yet, year after year, Colorado makes more money, in terms of value although not of cash, from corn than it does from sugar beets.

Louisiana is famous for its sugar cane, but good old corn is its fourth biggest crop. (Here they are in the order they come under the wire: cotton, sugar cane, rice, corn.)

North Dakota is the biggest flaxseed-producing state in the Union. But corn makes it tick.

Florida is, of course, the orange state. I'd like to say it really raises more corn than oranges; I can't, however, quite do that. But corn is bigger than its tangerine crop! Take that, Florida.

You'll be surprised to know which state produces the least corn. Its not Rhode Island, nor is it Delaware—it's Nevada. In fact, Rhode Island produces about five times as much corn as Nevada. (You see how interesting corn statistics are!)

The Department of Agriculture lists twelve Corn Belt states and they are, indeed, corn producers: Ohio, Indiana, Illinois, Michigan, Wisconsin, Minnesota, Iowa, Missouri, North Dakota, South Dakota, Nebraska, and Kansas. In addition, outside of the recognized Corn Belt, are two pretty good corn states: Kentucky and Tennessee.

For years the National Corn Husking Contests was the official organization of the farm journals of the corn-producing states. (We've got a chapter on that; but don't turn to it now.) Each year the championship was settled. The official list, when the last contest was held, was the same as the states above, except for two changes: North Dakota had dropped out and, for some strange reason, Pennsylvania had come along, fancying itself as a corn state. The rules were loose; any state that had had county elimination contests could send two shuckers—this added to the contest, the officials said; made more people turn out. But the number of states was still twelve.

Two of these states were only semi-corn states, not the real thing: North Dakota, Michigan. They dabbled in corn, but corn wasn't the principal crop. And now, little by little, I get down to the list of the great corn producers:

Indiana
Illinois
Iowa
Missouri
Minnesota
Kansas
Nebraska
Ohio
Wisconsin
South Dakota.

These are the real article. Ten in all. Its interesting to note that the first three begin with the letter I. Two begin with M. The next five states spell KNOWS.

Corn is not grown all over these states; indeed, in some, only a small section raises corn. But that section raises enough corn to make the state rank as a producer. As an example, only a dab of Minnesota raises corn, but it's excellent corn. And so with Wisconsin; only a small section grows it, but does the job exceedingly well. The same is true of South Dakota.

These states pare down still more. Only eastern Nebraska produces corn in a big way; the same is true of Kansas. And only northern Illinois and northern Missouri come across handsomely. In fact, Iowa is the only state in the Union that is all corn. And even this is not true... . You have to watch your step when you make flat statements about corn. For Iowa produces many other crops for instance, wheat, clover, hay, soybeans, and goodness knows what. So even a real corn queen has other dresses in the closet.

When I say Iowa is the real thing, it sounds as if everybody in the state were out in the fields working like mad. This is hardly true, for Iowa has a population of two and one-half million, but only one million are engaged in farming. The rest are selling life insurance. At least, it seems that way when you see how many people in Des Moines are mixed up in it.

Why should the corn belt be exactly where it is? The answer is simple: the glaciers. They came plowing down from the north, scraping off the rich black soil and, finally, obligingly they melted. The black soil they left is the Corn Belt. But the glaciers didn't do it quite all, for there are the wind-driven and silt-loam soils; they're pretty good at this corn business, too.

Corn soil isn't a single and unchanging matter. I saw a soil map at Iowa State College, Ames, which opened my eyes. It is as big as a wall and is laid off in many colors, with endless swirls and swaths, so that when you look at it you have the feeling of seeing a dream on paper. Its purpose is to show how the soil of Iowa changes—sometimes within five miles. In other words, one stretch of soil will produce excellent corn; the swirl next to it will hand up a second-rate article.

The whole thing is again complicated by the fact that it changes from season to season; one kind of corn soil will produce during a wet season; another is better for a dry year. If you try to understand it, it will drive you nuts.

Geographically the Corn Belt is in the middle of the United States, of this black loam country. It stretches from western Ohio to the eastern part of Kansas; north and south, from the lower part of Minnesota to the middle of Missouri. In shape it is like a giant meat platter—quite a bit longer than it is wide, with rounded corners. Plop a meat plate down in the middle of the map of the United States and draw a line around it and you'll not be far wrong. Meat platter seems to be a good comparison, for, in one sense, it is exactly that; it does produce a tremendous quantity of meat. And a tremendous quantity of bacon. Other states and other sections produce steaks (Texas, for instance), but not much in the way of bacon. Sometimes, so amazing is this rich midriff of America, it seems to me it produces just about everything. The Corn Belt is my country. I grew up there, my heart is still there; so if I become a little too enthusiastic in this book you have purchased (I hope), please make allowances. Maybe, during the course of this book, I can win you to an appreciation of the corn section. I would like that. It has no equal.

ANECDOTE

At the end of each chapter, I am going to put in some odds and ends about corn and the corn-producing section. Here's a starter:

If you put Iowa's corn crop for one year into freight cars, the train would reach from New York to Fresno, California. Nobody, however, seriously contemplates doing this.

Corn is used in the production of penicillin. Also in the production of face powder, but much more for the latter. It just shows.

The Barbed-wire Fence

My father always said he had farmed ten years before he ever heard of a barbed-wire fence. He used to angle (as he called it) across the prairie to town; no fences; least, not enough to bother. When he arrived, there was not a single rod of fence on our farm; and there wasn't a tree or a stone. How, then, was he going to take care of his livestock? At first he tethered; that is, he put a rope on an animal's foot.

The first was the Osage mock orange—the meanest, most trouble-making fence ever spread on the face of this earth. It had thorns as long as clothespins; nothing seemed to give is so much pleasure as to jab one into a barefoot boy. I tell you, it had the Devil in it. For a distance, it would be hog-tight and bull-proof; then, like a bald spot on a scalp, there would be an open space. A farmer who depended entirely on his hedge was, half the time, chasing his stock. (I shudder to think of the harsh words that must have been uttered by farmers trying to find their escaped cattle.) There was little timber, so it was almost impossible to bolster the holes. The thing that was most often tried was a combination of hedge and smooth wire. A farmer wove the two in and out like an Indian making a basket. But this was like throwing a challenge to the farm animals.

In no time at all the cows would be in the corn, or the horses would be romping the range. My father and my uncles used to make a trip to the 102 River to cut poles which would be nailed to upright posts, thus making a crude sort of fence; but the trip was long, so mostly only the horses and cow-lots were enclosed.

Then—almost in the twinkling of an eye, so quickly did it come— there arrived something that changed the prairie. And this was the barbed-wire fence. It was invented in DeKalb, Illinois, by Joseph F. Glidden; in the early days it was called the Glidden Fence. Glidden was a farmer, with the troubles of all farmers. One morning he found that his cattle had pushed through his smooth wire fence and gone off on missions of their own. As he saw the pulled-out staples dangling helplessly on the wire, an idea entered his head. Maybe if he fastened these staples to the wire, they would slow up the cattle. He began to experiment with the different types of barbs and ways of securing them to the wire. It is said that he used an old coffee mill to twist the coiled barbs. Anyway, at last he had a fence with barbs strung along it like clothespins on a line.

Now comes the wrangle; no two historians seem to agree. In this same town another man turned up with a barbed-wire fence—Jacob Haish. A bit of an oddity here: that, in the whole United States, the two inventors should be in the same town. Immediately the men were at each other's throats. I went to DeKalb with the idea of trying to understand the situation; the more I looked into it, the more befuddled I became. I, now, don't know anything about it at all. The two men began suing each other; this resulted, I was told, in the longest drawn-out litigation in patent infringement jurisprudence on record. Anyway, they both made money; in fact, everybody connected with the manufacture of this much-needed fence appears to have made money. Today, in DeKalb, there is a Glidden Hospital and not very far away there is a Haish Memorial Library. The two appear about ready to spring at each other.

People would have nothing to do with the fence; said it was cruel and that the stock would saw themselves to pieces. Some of them did. But it had so many advantages that its shortcomings were overlooked. The ranchers took it on, first; then, little by little, the farmers. The effect on the prairie lands was amazing. It changed the open range to farms. The cattlemen hired thugs to beat up farmers who were stringing wire. A war began between the cattlemen and the farmers that lasted for years.

A farmer could fence a pasture and have more acreage for his stock; then he began to raise cattle; then hogs to run after them. A cycle was started that is still going on—CHC, as its called; corn, hogs, cattle. And to this could well be added another C—clover.

This new fence was threaded into the bald spots in the hedges; but this was only the beginning. Whole fields were fenced with it. No farmer now got up in the morning, wondering where his cows were.

So successful was the barbed-wire fence that the Osage hedge had to go. It was found that on each side the Osage hedge drained half a rod of corn land; the corn was pale and yellow and sickly. And now the farmers started to chop out and to try to kill this hedge. I came along at this unfortunate period. In order to kill it, hedge has to be grubbed in August and its roots salted. The hottest work in the world is grubbing hedge roots along a cornfield in August. The sun boils down, and a kind of shimmering heat lays over the hedge rows as if a million oven doors had suddenly been flung open. You have your jug in the shade, but the water is warm; ants are sucking at the moist corncob stoppers. There is a chirping of the insect world which rises and falls with a hypnotic cadence. A train goes roaring by with rich people sitting on plush seats. I tell you, it's heartbreaking.

At last hardly a farm had a hedge fence; sometimes, in the sloughs, a few clumps might be left for steer shade. And there the fattening cattle would stand, half asleep, the whites of their eyes glazed, their sides going in and out like a blacksmith's bellows; now and then they swing their heads to scare off a fly; as they swing their heads, a fine ribbon of clover saliva goes sailing through the air. Clomp! goes a foot as a steer shakes off a deer fly. A steer moves over to get in the shade; the muscles of his ankles make little crackling sounds—That was about all it was good for, this once prized and tremendously sought-after fence.

Then came the all-weather, dependable farm fence consisting of woven wire at the bottom and three lines of barbed wire at the top, a fence that was shoat-proof and bull-strong. What a tumbleweed, Russian thistle, and ticklegrass catcher it was! I've seen the mess piled as high as the fence itself; sometimes a Devil-filled boy would come along, strike a match, and set it on fire…which would bring his father on the run. It was not a good idea to do this…. The only time the fence met defeat was in the spring when the old sows rooted under it; this was solved by placing rings in their noses, or a line of barbed wire at the bottom. Farmers learned how to put dead men at the bottom of corner posts, and how to brace the posts with a crosspiece and twisted smooth wire so that the corner posts would stand a two-way strain.

Many schemes and devices were employed to make woven-wire fences. Once my father hired a man who had a great loomlike machine that wove a wire fence on the spot, all operated by handpower. In no time I made the horrifying discovery I was to be the handpower. The machine crossed and recrossed the wires like a monstrous steel spider at her spinning. I tell you it was hell. In fact, it made me sick. I didn't recover until the fence was finished.

I was twenty-six years old before I ever saw a stone fence; it seemed to me the crudest, most wasteful thing I had ever seen in my life. Weeds and grass and vines surrounded it; nothing could be planted for six feet. Stones had fallen out and became misplaced; it showed disrepair. I suppose a stone wall, with chipmunks flipping around over it, is picturesque. But still it's a waste of good land. I'll take a nice, well-kept-up barbed-wire fence.

The corn country is ever changing. Machinery has made it possible for stock to be fed in barns by grains fetched from the field; yes, silos. Stock doesn't have to shift for itself as in the days when I was a young sprout. No one ever hears of a steer burrowing into a strawstack till it caves in and smothers him to death. Sometimes, around a cornfield today, there is not a furlong of fencing. It makes me blink.

Electric fencing is coming in—single strand, or sometimes double, hooked up with a circuit. A rambunctious steer comes along, touches a live wire, and sets off down the pasture with his tail sticking out like a buggy-tongue. But its not completely successful, for farmers have been electrocuted; and animals, too. Some day, I suppose, this will be solved. Anyway, on the Croy Farm there is a two-strand wire fence exactly where I used to just about die grubbing hedge. It makes me feel I was born too soon.

When I was a boy we liked fence-building time; it wasn't lonesome work like plowing, hedge-cutting, or cocklebur-chopping. The neighbors came in and we all worked together and enjoyed it. In the fall, after the summer rush, Pa would go to town in the wagon and bring out two or three spools of barbed wire and then I would know that exciting fence-building time was here.

The morning we were to build, two or three of the neighbors would come down the road, carrying their spades and long-handled wire-seizing pliers. I could hardly wait.

Pa and I (mostly Pa) would hitch up our team and have our tools ready by the time the neighbors arrived. Lots of jokes and weather talk and neighborhood news and who had the epizootic. Then we would all hop on the wagon and go rattling out to where the fence was to be built. There, lying on the ground in a long row, would be the posts. That was ominous. Somebody would have to dig the holes.

Stretching the wire was fun and nailing the staples was fun. Everybody liked that.

Pa would go along laying down his measuring pole, then picking it up again and putting it down again so as to get exactly right the distance between posts. He didn't have use for anybody who didn't do a good job setting posts. Pa was a good farmer. But he made people work.

Then we would all have to begin digging holes. Hard work, but not as bad as hedge-cutting, because we could talk and have a good time. Sock the spade down, put your foot on it, and push. Wiggle the spade, then throw the dirt out. We had a long, split-handled, round dirt-lifter; we would jab it into the loose dirt in the bottom of the post hole, then bring the split handles together (watch out for fingers). This would squeeze the dirt, like a giant nutcracker. Then we would pull it up, open the handles, and the dirt would fall out. It was more fun than digging with a plain spade. But it was still work. Nobody in his right mind could be blind to that. On the other hand, it was nice to be together, visiting and talking and asking conundrums.

Now and then the men would get off by themselves and start to tell a funny story about a preacher, a widow, and a parrot; I would begin to edge up. Then Pa would make me go away so I couldn't listen. Then, in a minute, I would hear the men roaring with laughter. I tell you it was trying.

At last there would be a row of post holes and into the holes would go the posts. Then Pa would sight along them to see if the posts made a straight line. He didn't have any use for people who didn't have even posts. Of course, it meant work, but today—with the neighbors in and with everybody talking and visiting—it was fun. Finally we would tamp the dirt in.

Homer, do you want to run off the wire? Pa would say and I'd want to. It was lots of fun. Two of us would put a broom handle through the hole in the barbed-wire spool and start down the row of posts. As we walked, the spool unwound and left the wire along the line of posts. But somebody, as the spool whirled over, had to hold the wire down to keep it from leaping off. If the wire suddenly jumped, it would cut your hands to pieces.

Now and then we would sit down and rest. Everybody liked that.

We would fasten one end of the wire to the corner post, then go twenty or thirty posts away and put on the wire-stretchers. By pumping the handle back and forth we could make the wire as tight as a fiddle string; as it got tight it would make a singing noise. An inexperienced person was not a good wire-tightener, because if you got the wire too tight it would snap and rip hell out of somebody. Stretching wire was the most fun of anything. I always volunteered for this.

When the wire was exactly right, the men would go along driving in the staples. I would put my ear down to the wire and it would make a singing noise; then there would be a pecking. That was the men driving the staples. Sometimes a staple would twist and turn and wouldn't go into the jack oak; and there it would hang on the wire, all twisted and contorted out of shape, like a cripple.

Finally the whole row of new fence would be finished; then we would sight along it to see how straight it was and would stand there admiring it.

"Well, we turned in a purty good job," Pa would say.

"It's as straight as Daniel Boone's gun-barrel," Newt Kennedy would say. "You helped me right good, Amos."

Then they would laugh, because that was on the joking side.

We would clean off the spades, put the long, split-handled dirt-squeezer into the wagon—and the empty spools, because they could be used for milk stools. Then we'd hop in and start back home, everybody tired. Not many jokes now. No funny stories.

"Now you folks come in and eat some supper," Pa would say. If a man didn't ask the people to supper, he was mean. After a while nobody would neighbor with him.

It was manners to protest and make excuses and say you didn't have time, but finally give in. Then we would wash up and my mother would bring out the Vaseline for the cut hands.

Then we would go in and sit down at the table with two coal oil lamps going; one lamp was enough when we didn't have company. Pa would lean forward and say grace. Then we would all pitch in. But we wouldn't laugh and talk and joke as we'd been doing while building fence. Eating in the house with the women-folks made us self-conscious. But it didn't do anything to our appetites. We could eat on fence-building day, no matter how many women were around.

After a while we'd again be out on the porch; as soon as we got there we could talk easier and laugh more. But it didn't last long. Pretty soon the neighbors would pick up their tools and start down the road toward home, walking slow now. The day's fun would be over.

"Homer," Pa would say, "it's time to chore. Get the milk buckets." I would, slow-like.

ANECDOTE

The Ringling Brothers Circus originated in McGregor, Iowa. There were seven brothers who started giving performances in their back yard. Then they went on the road. Alf Ringling was the juggler and acrobat; one of his feats was to balance a plow on his chin. It made the farmers popeyed. Later the brothers joined up with P. T. Barnum and the combination became the P. T. Barnum and Ringling Brothers Circus. Tell Junior the next time you have to stop work to take him.

The Incredible Grasshoppers

I never saw a grasshopper year, but it was very real to me. I caught a little of the effect it had on the pioneers, for my father always spoke of Grasshopper Year with a kind of hushed awe. Sometimes my parents, or our neighbors, would say, "It was before the Grasshoppers," or "It was after the Grasshoppers." And so terrible was it that everybody knew the year meant.

"They would even eat corncobs," my father would say as if he still couldn't quite believe it.

Nothing under the sun would eat dried corncobs; they were fit only for fuel. But the Grasshoppers ate them.

There were really three grasshopper years (1874, '75, and '76), but the first was immeasurably the worst and was the one everybody meant when Grasshopper Year was mentioned.

It was a favorite topic of the old settlers. Always the conversation got back to Grasshopper Year; they would talk about where they were and what they did to combat the grasshoppers as veterans will talk about a battle they were in; a kind of note-comparing.

My Aunt Viola had just been married and had moved on a prairie claim. She had brought from the East, as a wedding present, a pair (as she always called them) of lace curtains. The grasshoppers ate them. She always spoke of this with a catch in her voice, so tragic was the event.

Uncle Jim Croy (my favorite uncle who had shot buffaloes and who almost said he had once scalped an Indian but never *quite* said it) was at work in the field with his team when he glanced up and, to the northwest, saw a cloud. His first thought was that a storm was coming and that he should unhitch; then, as he looked more closely, he saw it wasn't a storm cloud at all, but something sailing through the sky. As it drew closer he heard a roaring; as the insects came slanting in on their wings it took only a moment to realize they were grasshoppers, but never had he seen them on such a vast, bewildering scale. He unhitched and started to the house; on the way they got up his trouser-legs, "almost drivin' me crazy," he would say.

The stories of what they did were endless. One was that they loved onions. The pioneers told how the damned grasshoppers would start down an onion stalk and devour it till there was only a hole in the ground. Some of the settlers said they could smell onions on their breath, as the grasshoppers went by in a cloud. We always laughed a little at this, yet we believed it; I still think there was truth in it.

One woman had a treasured cabbage patch. When she saw the grasshoppers devouring the cabbages, she ran to the field, got some hay, scattered it along the edge of the patch and set the hay on fire, hoping the smoke would drive them away. It did, but for only a short time; so she got more hay and spread it over the cabbages themselves, hoping the grasshoppers would eat the hay instead; they did, but they ate the cabbages first.

Another story our people told was what happened to the chickens and turkeys. When the grasshoppers first began failing, the chickens and turkeys chased them with huge delight. But more and more came; the chickens and turkeys gorged until their crops were distended; then the chickens and turkeys would stand around, blinking at the astonishing good luck that had come to them. But chicken and turkey nature still held forth. When a hen would see a grasshopper light, her instinct would make her waddle toward it and she would go through a half-hearted peck; then, at the last possible moment, she would suddenly realize she couldn't eat another and would turn sadly away. So much did the chickens and turkeys gorge themselves that our people always said they had a peculiar taste. Some even said that the pork had a grasshopper flavor. And indeed this might be true. They said the fish in the streams tasted. This, also, might be true.

When I was making notes for this chapter, I thought I remembered a grasshopper story. It was to this effect: the pioneers raised castor plants— the very plants from which castor oil was made. But the pioneers raised them because they were pretty, grew fast, and could stand drought. When the grasshoppers came they would have naught to do with the castor plant. I asked an aunt if I had remembered correctly and she said I had…. I guess it was something no boy was likely to forget.

Also I thought I remembered that guineas would not gorge till their flesh was tainted; they were the wildest, closest-to-nature fowl a pioneer had. But this aunt said that, to the best of her recollection, their flesh also had a peculiar taste.

Incredible stories were told, as I have mentioned. One was recounted by my father. He said the grasshoppers ate one of his pitchfork handles till the wood was roughened. Uncle Jim might stretch things a bit, but my father always stuck pretty close to the truth.

This is as far as my personal experience goes, but I wanted to get all out of this chapter I could, so I looked up some information and talked to the state historians in our section and turned up some unusual facts. I think the most astonishing is that grasshoppers once stopped a Union Pacific train near Kearney, Nebraska. The evening had turned cool; grasshoppers were along the railroad and crawled up on the steel rails to get the heat. The tracks became so oily and greasy that the wheels slipped. The sand in the box was used, but still the train would not go. So brush was cut and the train crew was set to raking and scraping the grasshoppers off the rails. At last the train was able to creep away.

Not only were families eaten out, but also towns; in a few every family moved away. One family started east in a covered wagon; on the canvas was painted, "The Grasshoppers Got Us." Communities sent representatives east to raise money; barrels of clothing and food were shipped to the sufferers. Sometimes these barrels and boxes were taken to the church, opened and the clothes passed out. In Plumb Creek, Nebraska, word was sent that a shipment of food and clothes was to arrive on a certain day; four hundred families were waiting when the train pulled in and there, on the depot platform, the boxes and barrels were opened.

So desperate was the situation that the United States Government passed a law appropriating money for relief. A United States Army officer was sent to see that relief was properly administered; he brought with him a supply of army shoes and uniforms. So, now and then, a farmer would be seen plodding about his work dressed as a Union soldier. Well, they were thankful to have anything.

Settlers arriving in a lonely valley in Kansas had seen playful little grasshoppers leaping picturesquely around a waterfall, so they named the place Grasshopper Falls. It grew into a town and all was well. Then came Grasshopper Year and millions of pests. The people were so disgusted that they rushed off a committee to the legislature and had the name of the town changed to Valley Falls. And that's what it is today.

People doted on horse racing. One day at Fort Scott, Kansas, just as the races were getting started, the grasshoppers came in on a wind. The track became so deeply covered that the horses began to slip; the owners said it was too dangerous to continue, so the races were called off and a set of the maddest people who ever assembled in the state of Kansas went home cursing.

A town in South Dakota was started and took the impressive name of Kampeska City; a plat was drawn up and bonds were offered for sale in the East. But, alas, the town was launched Grasshopper Year. The locust hordes swooped down upon it and ate up everything; one by one the families moved away; finally, not a single soul remained in Kampeska City; it belonged to the grasshoppers.

Sioux Falls is the biggest city in South Dakota. In the early days it got off to a good start and boomed along until it had a population of 600. Then the grasshoppers struck. The people began to move away, beaten by the scourge. A few, however, stayed; and the town survived. But it took two years to get its population back to 600.

Indeed the situation became so desperate that the Governor of Missouri issued a proclamation setting aside a day of prayer and fasting against grasshoppers—June 3, 1875.

Inventors got to work and turned out grasshopper exterminators. Here and there an exterminator machine would go lumbering across the field at its deadly work; at least, at what the inventors said was deadly work. One machine was pulled by a team of horses; a long tin trough was so arranged that when the young grasshoppers flew up they would fall into it; it was filled with coal oil which settled their hash. Every now and then the farmer emptied the hoppers on the ground and set fire to the oil. But the thing didn't work; before the man got back to the end of the row, there would be just as many insects in the row as he had exterminated. Some farmers in Nebraska got the idea that concussion was the answer; so they bought quantities of black powder, placed it in the ground over the fields, and set it off. The theory was that the concussion would kill the eggs. It didn't; one farmer, later, said ruefully, "It just seemed to give 'em ambition."

In fact, nothing worked; nothing under the sun.

Towns offered what was called "grasshopper bounties." That is, if a farmer's boy brought in a bushel of dead grasshoppers he would be paid fifty cents. The dead grasshoppers were piled on the street and set on fire. The stench was dreadful. The towns had to give up the idea, for a bushel of grasshoppers was no more important than a drop of water in a rainstorm.

I think the following is as striking as any I have come across (thanks to Will G. Robinson, Pierre, South Dakota). Jefferson, in South Dakota, was a small pioneer town which seemed to be particularly in the path of the ravenous insects. Finally, all human means having failed, the priest announced a day of prayer. Protestants and Catholic alike turned out; the priest took the principal role and led a procession of townspeople through the streets and out into the country. So poor and poverty-ridden were the people by this time that many of them were barefooted. The procession, headed by the priest, marched in one direction, then turned in another until the route they traveled was in the form of a giant cross. At the end of each arm a simple cross was erected; the procession had been so planned that in the middle of the cross would be the cemetery; here a large cross was erected. Then services were held, men, women, and children joining, in prayer. At dusk the people went home. The next day the plague began to wane; finally the grasshoppers were no more. The cross still stands in the cemetery at Jefferson.

Damnable, destructive, and detestable as the grasshoppers were, now and then they served a good purpose, surprising as this seems. Kansas had been experimenting with drought-resisting alfalfa, led by Dr. Edgerton R. Switzer, of Salina. He had two acres of second bottom land which he had planted to alfalfa. He had paid thirty dollars a bushel for the seed in San Francisco, an exceedingly high price. The precious seed sprouted, the field bloomed, and the doctors heart became young and gay. Then suddenly, in August, came a cloud of grasshoppers which fell upon the alfalfa and ate it to the ground. He gave up the idea that alfalfa could be grown in the state and turned to other things. But in September it rained and magic happened on the second bottom. To the doctor's astonishment that alfalfa sprang up and grew again. He said, "If this alfalfa can survive both drought and grasshoppers, it's exactly what we want." He returned to his experiments and, from this crucial test, pioneered alfalfa in Kansas; it is now one of the great sources of income in the state.

(I asked Mrs. A. M. Campbell, curator of the Saline County Historical Museum, in Salina, if there was a monument, or marker, to the doctor and she said there wasn't. Well, I've seen plaques to less deserving.)

An astonishing situation grew out of the plague. During Grasshopper Year there was an election in Nebraska and a great many chosen to the State Legislature were grasshopper sufferers. They passed a law which required all able-bodied citizens to fight grasshoppers; that is, when the road supervisor sent out word that the grasshoppers had hatched, every male over the age of sixteen was to turn into a grasshopper fighter and had to fight up to ten days. They fought with fire and flails and by plowing, trying to get rid of the young hoppers and of unhatched eggs. If a man didn't turn out, he was subject to fine and imprisonment. But most of them turned out.

So serious were the state legislators that, in 1877, they passed what became known as the Grasshopper Constitution. A vital part of this was that the state should not borrow money. The legislators had found (which, alas, is all too true) that people borrow money when interest rates are high; then they improve and spend more money than they ordinarily would. Along comes a pinch and Trouble is upon them. So the legislators passed the law that Nebraska should not borrow money. And it never has from that day to this; it has always had a pay-as-you-go policy. It went through the depression without borrowing a dollar; and today the state has no debt (one of the few in the Union, I believe); there is no state income tax and no sales tax—thanks to the Grasshoppers.

What of today? Are there grasshoppers? The answer is yes, but they don't strike terror to the hearts of farmers as they once did. One reason there are few scourges today is that the breeding grounds have been broken up; that is, plowed; the great ex-buffalo ranges no longer exist. And then farmers have a way of fighting back; they put out poison bran, usually through the Farm Extension Service. When a plague seems imminent, the farmer goes to the county agent who helps him get the poison meal. There are now government spreaders which scatter the meal over the ground like fertilizer. The county agents don't wait for the grasshoppers to arrive; they have egg counts. That is, samples of the soil are spaded up and the eggs actually counted. It can then be judged how severe the plague may be. And so even before the grasshoppers arrive, fighters are at them.

The very latest, as I peck this off, is the grasshopper-fighting plane. Dust is squirted, like smoke from a sky-writing plane. This has been tried only in a few sections; but the report is favorable and it would seem that in the future airplanes will go up and attack from the sky. It would have made Pa blink. Anyway, the plague that once broke the hearts of the pioneers is no longer a serious menace. There are grasshoppers and they hop, but I haven't heard in years of a farmer telling how they nibbled his pitchfork handle.

FAVORITE CORN-BELT ANECDOTE

A county agent walked out over the ill-cared-for land of a lackadaisical farmer who was noted for his Peter Tumble-down ways. The county agent suggested better methods for the man to use, but each time the shiftless farmer shook his head. Finally he said, "I guess what-all you say is likely correct, but, hell!, I ain't farmin' now half as good as I know how."

How Some of Our Towns Got Their Names

This section, which was to become the Corn Belt, was developing fast; towns were springing up. The way they were named is astonishing especially the casual, offhand way they came by their names. A good example of the latter is Bloomfield, Iowa. It was pulled out of a hat. Three names were put in: Jefferson, Davis, and Bloomfield. Bloomfield came out. The town now has about twenty-five thousand people—all very proud of, the name.

Another example: a group of people, arriving in Iowa, decided to found a town. One day as they were trying to get a heavy piece of machinery across a creek, this piece of machinery (a cylinder) fell into the water and was lost. This gave the people an idea and they named the town Cylinder.

Usually about half a dozen early settlers had to do with the naming of a town. Sometimes they didn't agree. But they had a way of settling this, as they had of most problems a practical way, indeed. This time they decided to play a game of poker; the man who won was to have the town named in his honor. They pitched in and E. Harrison Cawker won. Just plain Cawker, Kansas, wasn't enough, so they gave it a really fitting name—Cawker City. Many of the towns were named *City*—made a good impression on the Easterners who were considering coming west and investing, they said. Omaha was first named Omaha City; as soon as it became a city it dropped the City.

Sabetha, Kansas, so far as I know, is the only town named for an ox. A religious zealot, on his way to the gold rush in California, had reached the eastern plains of Kansas where his favorite ox took sick and died. He wanted to honor the faithful animal; the day of the week was the Sabbath, so he changed the word a little and called the camp Sabetha. In time the camp became a town where it still flourishes. The town is proud of its name.

The University of Missouri (a fine institution) has a separate School of Mines. The town where the School of Mines is located sprang up almost overnight, for it was a railroad town. When time came to choose a name, the citizens couldn't agree. One of the men was from North Carolina and argued long and loud for it to be called in honor of his hometown of Raleigh. He described the glories of Raleigh so vividly and so feelingly that a vote was taken and Raleigh won. The head of the committee wrote it down and sent it to the Post Office Department in Washington and in due length of time word came back that the name was now official. The head of the committee had written the name just as the North Carolina man had pronounced it and there it was on the official documents—Rolla. The North Carolina man was so disgusted he moved away.

Another town in Missouri was being platted. One of the men helping was John Kirkpatrick; the others said that for the fine work he'd done they'd name the town for him Kirkpatrick. He said, "This place will never amount to anything; I don't want it named for me." So they had to cast around for another name and finally chose Odessa. It's going strong.

Women were scarce; anything in skirts looked good, so towns were named in their honor. Sometimes it was the first woman into a town, sometimes it was the wife of one of the settlers, sometimes it was merely a girl who happened to pass through. Beatrice, Nebraska, was named for a girl who never saw the place but twice.

I'll choose my own county as an example of the way names were arrived at. The county seat was named for the first woman there. Her name was Mary, and *ville* was added. (No s, please.) She lived to be an elderly woman; I once saw her, but never got to speak to her.

Near where I was born is a town...I can give you an idea as to its size when I tell you that the post office is open every day of the year. Yes, Christmas, too. It is the highest point on the Wabash Railroad between St. Louis and Omaha. When town-naming time came, the richest man in the community was named Wilcox; he had two hundred acres of land. He said he wanted the town named in his honor; no one could speak up against two hundred acres, so Wilcox it was and is.

Another town is Orrsburg. A man named Fred Orr started a store and named the town after himself. No one had any objections, for that was the way things were done.

A few miles away from Orrsburg is Parnell (home of Ben Jones, trainer of the famous racehorse Whirlaway). A man in the settlement was an ardent admirer of the Irish Parnell; he talked Parnell so much that one of the other men, in a sort of desperation, said, "Let's call the town Parnell and give him all the damned Parnell he wants." And thus they honored the great patriot.

In the same county is Graham; yes, after the first settler. Pickering was named after a railroad official; and so was Hopkins. However, there was an exception to this early-settler, railroad-official name-choosing way. And this is Quitman which was named after a southern general in the Civil War. How he wandered into the picture no one seems to know. (It's interesting to note that Senator Forrest C. Donnell was born here. Present population 150. When Forrest was born, 180. You'd better come back, Forrest.)

Near the Croy Farm was a schoolhouse (the Davis School); a blacksmith shop came, then a grocery. But still there was no name; we just said, I'm goin over to the corner. One day a farmer, in talking to another farmer, said, Well, I guess I'll drive to Pumpkin Center. Soon the whole neighborhood was calling it that. It wasn't long before the name was on the map and *Punkin Center* (our pronunciation) was a flourishing village. And there it is today, as up and coming a place as you'd want to see.

I have dealt with my own county at some length as it is typical of the section. Early settlers, women, railroad officials, whimsy, chance—that's the way it went.

Even tongue-slips entered in. The important thing was to get a name so the town could have a post office and so town-lots could be sold; then it could *develop* as the settlers put it.

A town in northeastern Iowa was to be christened; a platform was built and the people came for the great occasion. It was to be named Harmon in honor of a pioneer. The mayor mounted the platform and spoke at length on what a flourishing city this was soon to be. But—*alas!*—that morning he had been reading a novel by Sir Walter Scott and its spell was still upon him, for his tongue slipped and he said, "And now I pronounce the name of this town to be Waverly." Consternation was upon the faces of the people; the committee got together as soon as it could, but decided it was too late to do anything. Thus Harmon became Waverly. It shows what novel-reading will do to a person.

A friend of mine (Uel W. Lamkin, the educator) told me how the town where he was born got its name. The town is California, Missouri. When time came to select a name, the committee couldn't agree, as so often happened. While they were wrangling, a man known as California Wilson came up, listened, then said, "I'll tell you what I'll do! If you'll name the town for me I'll give you a demijohn of whiskey." The committee said that was the best idea they'd heard and gratefully named the town California. In no time at all the whiskey was gone, but the name had been nailed down.

Not far away was a settlement fast growing into a town but no name had been arrived at. One day the county commissioners came to look the place over and to choose a name. In the settlement was a couple who ran a tavern—Mr. and Mrs. Jesse Kirk. Mrs. Kirk was the cook and, in honor of such distinguished visitors, she spread herself and gave them a wild turkey dinner. The commissioners ate and ate; finally they pushed back, stuffed and gorged and at peace with the world. Then one of them said, "I think, as a tribute to this wonderful meal, we should name the town Kirksville. And it was and is an exceedingly fine town, famed as the home of the Kirksville College of Osteopathy."

Chance. This entered, too; in fact, countless towns came by their names exactly this way. In this same state was a thriving town by the name of Tanglefoot; the reason was simple. It was made there. But as the town grew, the people became sensitive about the name. At last a meeting of the board was called; the Bible was to decide. The chief commissioner was blindfolded and the Bible opened at random. The commissioner put his finger down on a page. The sentence read: "Then Agrippa said unto Festus, I would also hear the man himself. His finger was nearest the word Festus and so Festus became the town's name. Tanglefoot was still sold.

Jokes were relished, for the early settlers were a roistering, fun-loving crew. Sometimes a joke carried the day. In South Dakota a town had sprung up alongside a railroad track, as so often happened. The officers of the town met in the railroad office to decide on a name. But they couldn't agree. Finally one of the men glanced at the Marvin safe and said, "Why not call it Marvin? That's a good, safe name." The men laughed and the town of Marvin, South Dakota, was born.

Not far away was another railroad siding; a man put up a refreshment shack. Two or three other buildings straggled in. Meantime the train crews stopped there for a particularly good kind of coffee that the man in the cook shack prepared. The railroad men began to call the place Java in honor of the coffee. And Java it is today. I tasted some of its coffee, but it didn't make me want to name a town.

Another example of chance. In 1906 the Milwaukee Railroad started to build a bridge across the Missouri River in South Dakota; a telegraph operator was stationed there to wire back daily work reports. The location had no name, so he began signing the words *Missouri Bridge*. This he shortened to Mo. Bridge. Pretty soon it was known up and down the line. The town took it up, dropped the period, and thus Mobridge, South Dakota, came into the geography of names.

I went to see the faces of four of our presidents carved on a mountain in the Black Hills and while there learned how the mountain came by its name. In the late 1870s a lawyer from New York came to the Black Hills, then a gold camp. The New York lawyer's name was Charles E. Rushmore. Hiring a horse and buggy, he started to drive through the hills and promptly became lost. He continued on for a while, growing more and more confused. Seeing a group of miners, he went up to them, one of whom recognized him. After a few moments of sociability, the lawyer pointed to a great granite peak and said, What's the name of that mountain?

"It's called Mount Rushmore," said the wag.

The lawyer went back to New York and, so far as anyone knows, never saw the mountain again. And thus, by mere chance, the mountain where the breathtaking faces are carved was named. (Note: I've tried to find what happened to Lawyer Rushmore, but haven't succeeded. If any reader knows, I wish he'd write me. I'll send him an autographed copy.)

Yes, queer names and queer reasons. One of the towns in South Dakota is Canton; the people believed the town was diametrically opposite Canton, China. Becoming curious myself to know if they'd hit it on the nose, I wrote to the Department of the Interior, Geological Survey, Washington, D. C. I'll have to report they didn't. Canton, China, is opposite a point in the Atlantic Ocean, south and a little east of Bermuda. Fortunately, the people of Canton, South Dakota, didn't know this and went happily ahead.

In Nebraska is a fine, flourishing town named for a strong man. This was the kind of man the early settlers admired. His name was Antoine Barada and he was so strong he could snap a canoe paddle in two with his hands. Once he was captured by the Indians, but escaped. When time came for the naming of a town, it was named in his honor and there it is today—Barada, Nebraska. His descendants live in the vicinity. They are not very strong.

John I. Blair, of Blairstown, New Jersey, came into this section and grew so rich and powerful that he named towns right and left. (More of him in a few moments.) He had a son-in-law back in New York; this son-in-law was Charles Scribner, founder of the publishing house of Charles Scribners Sons. So he named a town for him—Scribner, Nebraska. But there's no publishing—its all hogs and pure-bred cattle.

One day Judge John Eckman and his daughter from Ohio arrived in a small town in Iowa that was in the process of being named. The judge told them if they would name the town after his daughter he would buy a lot. The town planners said Yes. That's the way Exira, Iowa, came into existence. Its pronounced Ex-ire-a. Lots of *ire*.

Danville, Iowa, needed a church and, after a time, a man named Rudd was found who said he would contribute a thousand dollars to a church if they would name the town for him. The city fathers said this could be arranged; the change was sent to Washington. When the pinch came he didn't pay the money, but the name has been established and it's still there; no one knows what became of Rudd. The worst is hoped.

Nealtown, Iowa, needed a doctor. The city fathers looked around, but couldn't tempt one. Finally they heard of Dr. Crawford who lived in another county. They had a meeting and told him if he could pull up and come to them they would change the name of the town to Crawfordsville. He pulled—and thus Crawfordsville, Iowa, came into being.

A town needed a church; for a church, people said, attracted settlers. Madison Letts said he would subscribe a hundred dollars. The townspeople were so grateful they named the town after him; and there it is today—Letts, Iowa; two churches now.

An Iowa settlement was having trouble deciding on a name; it got so that no one liked any name suggested. Finally one of the residents came across with an inspiration. Why not stop haggling and take the first letters of the names of the six prettiest girls in town? This was done and thus Le Mars, Iowa, was born. Another oddity: the town has a college named Western Union. Many pretty girls attend.

Another town in Iowa tried it, but without using the names of pretty girls. They chose the first letters of the surnames of the eight most prominent citizens. The result: Primghar. Try to pronounce it. The pretty-girl way seems better.

A name even more difficult to pronounce was Kjaldahl. The town had been named for a preacher, the Reverend Mr. Kjaldahl. When the city fathers found no one could pronounce it, they changed it to Sheldahl. The Reverend Mr. Kjaldahl took it calmly.

Here is the story of Emma. She was what was known, in the rough-and-rugged days of South Dakota, as a popular prostitute. Her admirers didn't have the authority to name a town after her, but they named three mines in her honor, One is near Galena, a second is near Lead; the latter was sold to the Homestake (owned by William Randolph Hearst) and has been incorporated into its holdings. The mines and the settlements around them are now vastly conservative; they wouldn't dream today of perpetuating the name of a low woman.

A town in eastern Iowa was being built; but no name had been arrived at. One day, as the committee was deliberating, they saw the steel rails for the new railroad piled beside the track; the rails were imported from England and each rail had stamped on it the name Low Moor. They grabbed it.

Another town in Iowa was in the course of construction, but still had no name. One of the laborers, doing the rough work, was a Spaniard who kept talking about his home city of Madrid, Spain, and how wonderful Madrid was. The inevitable happened.

At Kingman, Kansas, was a fabulous stagecoach driver by the name of D. R. Green; he drove so fast that he came to be known as "Cannonball" Green. People came from miles around to see his coach whirl by in a cloud of dust, with Canonnball sitting on top, lines in his hands, urging the horses to even greater speed. He boasted that, with the help of his men, he could change teams faster than a passenger could walk around the coach; then off in a cloud of glory (and dust). Time came to name a new town and it was named for Cannonball Green. But there was no post office; two miles away was a town named Jaynesville. One night the patriotic citizens of Greensburg quietly yoked up oxen to a sturdy wagon, drove to Jaynesville, and loaded the post office onto the wagon. By morning Greensburg had a post office. Soon a post-office inspector arrived. He looked the situation over—and said he would report that he thought the change was a good one. Nothing further was heard about it; the town continued to boom and the post office to do a fine business. Part of the old stagecoach route is now followed by United States 54; it is still called the Cannonball Highway. In Greensburg is a firm that ships live jackrabbits to all parts of the United States. Even the jackrabbits seem especially speedy.

Towns were named so fast that spelling was sometimes neglected. A town in Iowa was named for Johann Gutenberg, the German inventor of movable type. There was an error in the plat and the town became Guttenberg. It still is.

Stephen Watts Kearny was a famous general in our war with Mexico, and a developer of the West. A town in Nebraska decided to name itself in his honor. But an error crept into the records and the name came out Kearney; a law was passed declaring this to be the correct spelling. Nothing can be done about it.

A town in Iowa had many Tennessee people; when time came they wanted to name it in honor of Governor Senter of Tennessee and sent a letter petitioning the state legislature to name it Senterville. The legislature thought the people had made a mistake in spelling and changed it to Centerville. The Senterville enthusiasts were indignant, but it was too late; it's still Centerville.

Harrisburg, South Dakota, is an exception to the quick and casual naming. It started off as Harrisburg and this it was for years; they thought they could do better, so called it Salina. This didn't look so good, after all, so they changed it to Springdale. They got tired of this and finally went back to Harrisburg. That's permanent, they reckon.

And now I come to the town-namingest person who ever swept across the corn lands—John I. Blair (already mentioned). He was from Blairstown, New Jersey, which was named for one of his family, and came to the Middle West where he left a trail of towns behind him as a Daniel Boone might leave a trail of blazed trees. He was the richest man who ever had anything to do with the business affairs of Iowa and was chief promoter and builder of the Chicago & Northwestern, and a couple of other roads. In fact, when time came for him to go to his heavenly reward he was director in seventeen railroads.... I hope this was considered an asset. His railroads were flowing across the country like water over the kitchen linoleum, and new towns had to have names. He took care of that. He had a friend, Oakes Ames, so he named a town for him; and there it is today—Ames, Iowa, home of the Iowa State Agricultural College. With a fine family feeling he named a town for his daughter Alta and was very proud of his good deed. But a family is a complicated affair with many currents and cross-currents sweeping through it; so it was even in rich Mr. Blair's; for Alta's sister Aurelia became jealous. Father Blair took care of this, as only a railroad builder could, by naming a town for her Aurelia, Iowa. It is now the home of a large Cement Blocks Works. He had a dog he was exceedingly fond of; the dog followed him around. One day the dog was killed by a construction train. Mr. Blair was so upset that he named the town for the dog; and there it is today—Cob, Iowa.

It seems, in the course of his railroad building, that Mr. Blair suddenly realized he didn't have a town named for himself; it must have been a distressing moment. He promptly took care of this by naming a post office in Pottawattamie County—Blair. (Later it curled up and died; so he named a new place Blairstown.) He was now in his stride, so he named a village, in Hamilton County—Blairsburg. He flowed over into Nebraska and named, curiously enough, Blair, Nebraska, for himself. Now comes a twist. A town in Cherokee County, Iowa, wanted to get the new railroad he was flinging across the state; so the people got together and named the place in honor of Mr. Blair—Blair City, they called it. But it didn't work; he shunted the railroad past the town.

So two daughters, a dog, and himself all had towns named after them. No town, however, was named after Mrs. Blair; she seems to have been the family martyr.

Becoming fascinated by this town-naming gentleman, I looked up his later history and found that he died in Blairstown, New Jersey, and was buried in Blairstown Cemetery, no doubt just the way he wanted it. Maybe a little part of his heaven is Blair Heights.

This, exaggerated as it is, illustrates how casually names were given to towns. The railroads were going through and so were wagon roads; even old hay camps were turning into towns; they had to be named. Especially did the railroads name towns. They'd name 'em for presidents and vice-presidents and construction superintendents and foremen, even for locomotive engineers. It got so you were nobody in railroad circles if you didn't have a town named after you.

In the early days, when a blizzard came upon them, the pioneers put up an extra stove. This was a hayburner; it had two cylinders. Hay was twisted by a machine and stuffed into the cylinders where a spring pushed it forward into the fire. The people loved their hay stoves and affectionately called them "hay-ties." A town was looking for a name and finally chose Haytie. It was sent to Washington but the wise people there thought the South Dakota residents wanted to name it for Haiti in the West Indies, but had spelled it wrong. So back came the official papers with a compromise—Hayti. But no hay-burning stoves now; only Grandpa remembers them.

One day a man from back east turned up in Kansas and announced that Kansas needed developing. This indeed struck a responsive chord. Then the man said he would do that himself. His name was Rose and it soon became evident he had extraordinary conversational powers. He went across the Missouri River to the capitalists in St. Joseph, Missouri, and said that the spot just opposite in Kansas would make a splendid location for an enterprising town. The capitalists were interested; in fact, a group of them remained up all night so as to be at the bank the next morning when it opened in order to give their money to the hypnotic man. Immediately construction started and almost as promptly the man named the town after himself—Roseport.

Things went along boomingly.

Then, one day, another man showed up and told the citizens something that made their eyes pop. He said this rose would smell just as sweet under another name. In fact, he said the man's name wasn't Rose at all, but Ingraham. And that he was an ex-convict, with a record of brazen swindling transactions in the East.

At first Rose tried to deny it, but sold out as speedily as he could and left town between suns. The town promoters were dumbfounded, but only briefly; they got together and said they wouldn't let the town die. Nor did they. They named the town after their leader—John B. Elwood. And there stands Elwood, Kansas, today—the only town I have been able to discover that was at first named after an ex-convict. The town is intensely upright and law-abiding.

Dexter, Iowa, was named for a horse. Kingsdown, Kansas, was decided by drawing a card from a deck, a King. Big Whiskey Creek and Little Whiskey Creek, Iowa, were named for whiskey that was buried there. (None—alas!—buried there now.) Indianola, Iowa, was named from a newspaper clipping. Tribune, Kansas, was named for Horace Greeley's paper. Chadron, Nebraska, was named for a squaw man. Olathe, Kansas, was named by the first settlers for what they thought was the Indian word for beautiful … the word turned out to mean something else. Florence, Kansas, was named for a girl, who later became the wife of Senator Arthur Capper of Kansas. Stanley, Kansas, was named for Henry M. Stanley, the reporter who found David Livingstone in the wilds of Africa. Akron, Iowa, was thus named because the people thought it would soon be the size of Akron, Ohio. (Present population: 1,400.)

What Cheer, Iowa, was so named because, to the early settlers, it seemed exactly that. (It's the birthplace of Hal O'Flaherty, famous newspaperman.)

Once it was believed that Topeka was the Indian word for Potato, but this has been proved wrong. They made it up out of whole cloth.

Atchinson, Kansas, was named for a Missourian. Oh boy!

I don't want this chapter to drag out too long, so I'll give a few names without stopping to tell how they were chosen. They're all from my own state (but with all that it hasn't got as many odd ones as Iowa has) and all have post offices:

Braggadocio
Bachelor
Devil's Elbow
Boss
Peculiar
Seventy-six
St. Patrick
Ink
Chloride
Romance
Speed
Cureall
Neck
Tiff
Blue-eye
Ponder
Cyclone

Sank

Hurricane

In the animal and insect line it proudly has: Rat, Swan, Buffalo, Roach, Turtle, and Gobler. Also it has a Zebra, but alas, no Mule.

And these are towns but do not have post offices: Nonsuch, Pansy, Seed Tick, Sinkin. Sinkin and Sank, as might be expected, are fairly close together.

A place, in the state, that makes one read the name twice is Tit Saw Bottoms. It's pronounced Teet. I thought you would like to know.

Yes, that's the way the corn section came by its town names. Women were the greatest influence, the early settlers were next, then the railroads, then came the names specifying localities or geographical formations (such as rivers), and then came chance and whimsy names. But I treasure them. I'm glad we've got 'em. It gives the section character.

The First Homestead

Three and one-half miles northwest of Beatrice, Nebraska (pronounce it Be-at-rice, please), is a farm that, to me, is very touching. You have to have your wits about you; otherwise you will shoot by it. Indeed, that farm marks the most important act for the welfare of the common people ever passed in the history of the United States. It should have a monument as high as a singing tower.

The story begins a good many years ago and has to do with the expanding of this country. We had taken in the Louisiana Purchase; we had more land than we knew what to do with.

Here's an item for my thoughtful readers. The whole land thing had been a troublemaker from the word go; it showed the great difference between Alexander Hamilton and Thomas Jefferson. The former thought new land should be sold to large corporations and to big business, and that then the money should be used to meet the governments expenses. Thomas Jefferson said it should be given, as nearly free of charge as possible, to the small man. Right there was a fork in the road of thinking in America; thank goodness, we took the Jefferson turn.

The problem, now, was to get the people on the land and producing. Should it be sold? The House of Representatives and the Senate powwowed about it and got nowhere at all. Daniel Webster made a speech on the subject that lasted two hours and thirty-five minutes, or about two hours longer than the average listener's interest. Then another man got up and orated for an hour and twenty minutes; he was never quite able to explain why he was so brief.

The thing was kicked around for years; finally a bill was passed to give the land free to the people—a revolutionary step, indeed; never before had the people of the United States been able to get even a sandlot without paying for it. Abraham Lincoln signed the bill and, on the stroke of midnight, December 31, 1862, the land was opened to "filing."

But there were sandburs under the surface: one was that you had to be at least twenty-one years of age; however, if you were not you could depend on Time to get in there and pitch. Another was that you had—practically—to be a Union soldier, for the Civil War was going full blast; indeed it was really engineered to help the Boys in Blue, though the words were framed more politely. They said, If you have never borne arms against the United States Government, or given aid or comfort to its enemies… That knocked the socks off the "Gone With the Wind" people. They burned worse than Atlanta, but it was the law and nothing could be done about it. Another burr was that you had to fork over fourteen dollars in order to file. But, on the other hand, that entitled you to a quarter section, an exceedingly cheap price.

At this time a member of the secret service of the Northern army had been sent into Nebraska to do some scouting for the Union cause, but what he could turn up in his own territory I don't know. His name: Daniel Freeman. He appears to have had an easy time of it, for, when the climax came, he was cutting a rug at a New Year's party at Brownville, Nebraska. He had been keeping an eye on the Free Homestead thing; in fact, he had found a piece of land on Cub Creek that was just what he wanted. Not only this but he had built a log cabin and had staked out what was called squatters rights; this did not mean he owned the land but that he could raise hell with anyone who tried to put him off.

Just like a stage play, on the night of the ball orders came through for him to report to St. Louis; he wished now he had been an ordinary doughboy instead of being with the department of Psychological Warfare of the day.

He had been planning to wait till the land office opened on January second and then file. He couldn't file January first, for that was a holiday. Daniel Freeman was up against it; there was his farm and there was St. Louis. The hell of it was that St. Louis had the rank.

His mind, however, was chewing over the idea.

He went to the agent in charge of the government land office who also was whacking away at a rug and told him that he would like to file before he left. The agent was sympathetic but said it couldn't be done because of the holiday.

"Couldn't you open up for just five minutes?" asked Freeman.

"It wouldn't be fair to the others," said the agent and waved his hand over the GIs gracefully hopping around the floor.

"Put it to a vote," said Freeman. He hadn't had psychological-warfare training for nothing.

The land agent thought this over, then said, "'Taint regular."

However, the land agent quieted the orchestra, then told the men what the problem was, and asked if it would be all right for Dan Freeman to be the first one to have a go at the filing. The men gave a lusty whoop and said it certainly would be all right, then went back to their genteel hopping.

The agent and Dan Freeman hurried as fast as they could to the government land office, in Brownville, arriving at five minutes after midnight. (On the stage it would be one minute after.) Then Dan Freeman signed—

Entry Number I
Proof of Residence Number I
Recorded in Book Number I
On Page Number I

and thus became the first homesteader in the history of the United States. It turned out to be extremely important, for it opened up a new era. In fact, one million people, since that day, have had land given to them free of charge by our Government. The average man got 120 acres.

Daniel Freeman got on a steamboat and went to St. Louis and back to his secret-service business. He had a brother who was engaged to a girl in Iowa, but his brother fell in the war. When the war was over, Daniel Freeman went to Iowa to console the girl and, just like a story, it happened.

He put her in a buckboard and they started west and at last arrived at Beatrice. The prairie grass had grown up close, but the cabin was safe and secure. He opened the door and the two went in—one room, that was all. But it was home, just as any place is if the heart is right.

And then Dan Freeman did what so many of the returning soldiers did—worked in his blue uniform. At last it disappeared and was no more.

Things went along nicely on the First Homestead until one day in '76 when suddenly the sky was darkened and there was a distant faraway roaring, those omens that the settlers came to know so well. The grasshoppers took his crop and that year was an exceedingly hard one. But he kept his faith and his hope, just as the early settler learned to do. His farm was excellent corn land and, bit by bit, he became prosperous. The one-room cabin grew into a "framehouse" and, after a time, this became a brick house, this latter extremely unusual for the prairies. Fire, however, swept through it, gutting it so badly that the bricks were torn down and another house built. So now, on the First Homestead, no original building stands.

There, on that homestead, Freeman lived until death took him in 1908. But not until the hardy old gentleman was eighty-two. His widow lived twenty-four years longer, but she was much younger.

I did indeed shoot by and was beyond Cub Creek before I knew it; I returned and there, swinging on a wooden post, was a rustic sign: Entering Homestead National Monument.

I got out and walked around the old homestead and it made a sentimentalist of me. I was thinking of my father who came to the prairies and was almost a homesteader himself and I thought of all the homesteaders I had known and of their stories which had always so thrilled me. And now I was upon the very first!

The old gentleman and his lady are buried, side by side, on the very spot where the cabin stood. I thought, as I stood beside the granite shaft, of the decision that night at the dance and how this very shaft came to be and of what a strange affair is chance. The old farm itself is being allowed to go back to prairie grass, but all around it, like a frame around a picture, is corn.

I walked down the road to the nearest neighbor, and there I thought a dog was going to have my leg. I found that Harold Graff lived here; also I found that he was not much impressed by Daniel Freeman. I asked him if he had known him, but he hadn't; however, his father had known the old man. "He never done much work," said Mr. Graff. I must tell you I was shocked, for I had thought of the old gentleman as working his head off. "He was always tradin' around, damnedest trader in the township. He wasn't much of a farmer. Lots of men here could farm rings around him. People here always thought he got money from back home. He was sheriff for a while, even ran a bakery. Also he was a doctor, a sort of jack-of-all-trades. If he hadn't got the first homestead he would have been just like anybody else."

I got away as fast as I could. I couldn't stand it.

I went to see Mrs. Webb Carre, daughter of the old homesteader, who lives near the Lutheran Church, in Beatrice. She was lying on a sofa with a spread over her shoulders; her son was taking care of her.

"The control of the thing has passed out of our hands," she said. "All sorts of people are now mixed up in it. They never tell us anything. They're commercializing it."

"There were six of us children. I was the oldest. Both my parents were highly educated for their day. My mother graduated from Abingdon College, Abingdon, Illinois. My father went to the Electic School of Medicine in Ohio. My father added to his original homestead until he had, at one time, eight hundred and forty acres of land. He was an exceptionally good farmer and a great asset to the community."

I left, feeling better now.

The opening of this homestead was a powerful factor in changing the whole Middle West, for homesteaders came in vast numbers, eager to get free land. That was the call everywhere; and a thrilling call it was—Free Land! The words went across the Atlantic and thousands upon thousands of land-hungry Europeans came to the Middle West and entered up land. The statement has been made that from the day of the allowing of the Freeman homestead and up to the year 1920, twenty-five million immigrants came into the great Middle West section.

The Middle West was no longer a ranch country; farms now, small tracts. Then came the barbed-wire fence and, with its coming, fields could be enclosed and corn was practical. It was the "money" crop; for that matter it still is. In a sense the granting of the Freeman homestead marked the end of one era and the beginning of another.

Before I left, I drove back past the old homestead and again saw the farm and again the feeling laid hold of me. It is a significant and touching place. I don't see how anyone can see it and fail to be moved.

NATURE NOTE ABOUT THE BIRD THAT WEARS SHOES

Kansas's most famous emblem is the Jayhawk, a bird that never existed on land or sea. The cartoon of this fabulous creature was created by a junior at the University of Kansas in 1912—Henry Maloy. I thought it would be interesting to find what happened to him, and here it is:

He was born in Eureka, Kansas, and still lives there. He is a printer on The Eureka Messenger. He is a bachelor and lives in a house he himself built. He was not paid for that first drawing and does not know what happened to it.

The Rainmakers

To us, in the Corn Belt, it seems as if every known hazard in the world attacks corn: drought, hail, wind, cutworm, the European corn borer. It passes from crisis to crisis, like a growing child; and always the trouble that has our corn in its grip at the moment seems the worst.

Corn must do its growing, ripening, and maturing in 120 days—very precious and dramatic days, indeed. A thousand things can go wrong; at least it seems like a thousand. Some seasons, when wet or drought have had their way, there is hardly any corn at all. There may be some "bottom corn," or "hill corn," or it may be "spotted,"—depending on the season and the hazards. But corn is really a healthy child; it may look peaked and have dark circles under its eyes and twitch at night, but usually it comes through in pretty good style.

One of the hazards is drought. This was much more true in my early days than it is now, for drought-resisting corn has been developed. (I'll tell about hybrid in another part of the book.) There is nothing that quite takes the heart out of a farmer so much as to see his corn "burn up." There it is, row upon row, and acre upon acre, and it lies there in its grayish bed, like a sick child, growing more and more pale, and there is nothing in the world he can do for it. A farmer looks out across his corn field; a wave of flickering, eye-stinging heat goes up. He can gaze into it only a minute, for it makes his eyes water and his heart heavy, for this is the corn-killing drought-heat that all corn raisers dread. He gets up early of a morning and studies the sky and knows there is no hope today; that burning, withering, suffocating, devilish south wind. The corn that had been blackish-green a few days before is now a sickly grayish-white; the leaves curl up, the silk withers and becomes so brittle it falls at a touch. When everything is at its worst, grasshoppers come; they go through the field like Sherman to the sea. The farmer walks out across his field a lonely, sad figure. When he comes in his wife asks, "How is it?"

"We may get some nubbins."

Then she goes back into the house; that ceaseless, unending, heartbreaking drudgery of running a farm home. Especially in the early days. Conditions are better now; much better, indeed. (More of this later too.)

Maybe I can bring out how exceedingly important this was by recounting something that happened when I was just a boy.

One day my father said, "Get ready and we'll go to town and see the rainmaker."

No work! Maybe a candy mouse. Maybe some *lickorish* (as we called it). There were always wonderful things to be had in town.

It was not long before we were in the hack and jogging along the dusty road; there, on each side of us, was the suffering, gasping, dying corn.

It did not seem queer to be going to see the rainmaker; at this time a great many people indeed believed in rainmakers. Of course, some scoffed; they were usually the kind who stood outside a church at a revival and told funny stories. At least, that's the way we thought of them. The papers were filled with accounts of the wonders rainmakers accomplished and lists of precipitation. I did not know at first this was just plain rain; it was disappointing that such a fine and impressive word could mean anything so simple as rain, for I was beginning to love words. As we drove along I would study the advertising ads and think how I would change the words, or choose others.

It was like county fair; teams were jogging along; great clouds of dust arose. The women-folks sat with veils over their mouths to keep from sucking it down. But we boys sat proudly with our faces bared, taking the dust as it came. Sometimes a team would try to pass. I would want Pa to race. But he never would; too conservative. Then I would wish I had a father like Newt Kennedy, who would race anything on the road.

And there suddenly it was—the water tower—the first herald of town. How high it stood above the trees, filled with tons and tons of water! What would happen if the tower fell? I almost wished it would. What excitement!

The vitrified brick pavement sent up waves of heat. "It's hotter here than in the country," my father said. He always said that and believed it, too. The rest of us would murmur, "It don't seem as hot to us."

No flags across the street, no bunting, no platforms in the courthouse yard for speakers, no toy balloons, no squawkers which would shoot out and tickle a girl. But otherwise it did seem like a street fair. Boys on every street corner selling lemonade. Parasols which could be rented for weak ladies.

69

Everybody studied the sky. At the post office a daily weather bulletin was posted in a little gray-metal frame. The bulletin was filled with strange, weird lines called "isotherms." Only Professor Hawkins could understand them. Pa would put on his spectacles and shake his head. "It don't look good." What we wanted to know was if there was any possibility of rain. The rainmaker might creep around and see for himself and thus know how long to hang on.

The Corn Belt had many rainmakers; everybody knew their names and believed in them or didn't, just as people believe in certain racehorses or don't. Some called them "fakes," and some believed in them as implicitly as they did in their preachers. Nearly every street corner had an argument going. Some rainmakers made a flat charge of five hundred dollars, let the rain fall where it might; some charged half-a-cent an acre; some charged by the number of acres of cultivated land. Some charged by the number of miles from the place where they made the rain attempt. But there was one good thing; all rainmakers worked on the basis of "No rain, no pay." The distressed farmer—seeing his crops perishing before his eyes—wanted the rainmaker to try. If the rain came, there would be enough corn to pay him. If there was no rain, he wouldn't have to pay him.

Soon the whole town—yes!, the whole county—was on its way to the depot, people on foot, the farmers walking in the street, city people mincing along the sidewalk. And me running ahead to explore, then coming back to tell Pa and Ma and Phebe. Then darting away again, like a dog off a leash. No candy mouse. Hoarhound candy, surely the finest, the most wonderful a boy ever put in his mouth. The lickorish was good, too; could spit tobacco juice, then.

As we drew near the depot, the crowd became thicker; thousands upon thousands, it seemed to me. The railroad had set the rainmakers car on a siding and there it was the mysterious, the wonderful boxcar that was going to save the crops. I was a little skeptical, but I wanted deeply and earnestly to believe. A rope had been stretched so the crowd would not get too near the car, for it was a secret how the man made it rain. Little by little I worked my way near and at last caught a glimpse of the wizard, for that was exactly how I thought of him, and so, for that matter, did most of the people. I was disappointed, for I expected to see an exceedingly tall man, with long hair and maybe a cape. Instead he was of medium height, and had stooped shoulders.

In a moment the disappointment was over. I believed in him; yes, that little stooped man could perform miracles.

The railroad had converted a whole boxcar to his use; windows had been cut. One end was for sleeping and eating, my peeking revealed, and the other was for the chemicals and gases that were going to save our corn. And in the roof, over this end, was a hole. The little stooped man climbed the iron ladder to the roof of the car where he studied the clouds—we held our breath.

Down again he went and our hearts, too—what if the clouds were not right? But he sent out word the clouds were right. Now there was a great stirring inside the mysterious car and in a few minutes a grayish gas began coming out the stovepipe hole in the roof. In no time the gas hit our noses—the most evil-smelling stuff we had ever encountered. But if it took that to make it rain, why, all well and good; we could stand it. The theory, as most of us knew by this time, was that this gas went up and drops of moisture coagulated around the particles and down came the rain. It seemed simple and logical to us. And, for that matter, it seemed simple and logical to county officials, and to state ones, too.

Up went the gas and up went our eyes and up went our hopes. How long would it take? Stories had come back from other towns and other states; sometimes it took only two or three hours, but sometimes it took two or three days.

People visited; neighborhood news was exchanged, corn news. Always corn news. From all parts of the county it was the same—the corn was "burning up," yellow sickly stalks, cutworms taking them—the devils that flourish best in corn-killing weather. People joked a little, but not much; the situation was too desperate for fun. But a man did come among us with a keg of umbrellas. That did make us laugh a little, but even with all this some people bought, mostly city people who were delicate and couldn't stand to get wet, not farmers who had to take the weather as it came. It made us smile, as we saw the city people picking through the umbrellas, for it always seemed to us the city people were queer and did unaccountable things. They could look down on us because we were poor and because we didn't have good clothes, but—thank God!—we didn't buy umbrellas when there wasn't a cloud in the sky.

A long wait. Children played, men fed their horses out of the back ends of hacks, the city people went home to dinner, the gas continued to go up, still smelling like hell but—so we said—worth it.

Suddenly there was great excitement; someone shouted, "There's a cloud!" And sure enough there was one about as big as a horse-blanket. And now a great many jokes, for we knew this was the start. It was going to rain. We gazed upon the rainmaker as if he were a god. This wonderful, this splendid man was going to save us.

As suddenly as it had appeared, the horse-blanket disappeared. A silence, for this was a calamity, not something to joke about.

The afternoon wore on; people came and went; the evil-smelling gas continued to rise. But not a cloud. And down our hearts went. Smart-alecks said, "I told you so. He can't make it rain. He's a fake." But the believers stuck by him. I did. My faith never wavered.

But chores are chores and cows must be milked, so when evening drew upon us, Pa and Ma and Phebe and I went to the hack; there, in the back, were the stripped corncobs where the horses had had their dinner. Pa threw the cobs out and brushed the grains onto the ground. Soon we were jogging home. I turned and there, standing out over everything, like a friendly sentinel, was the water tower. Finally it bobbed out of sight.

When we came to the Croy Farm, Pa's eyes read everything, as they always did, to see if all were right—if the gates were closed, if a horse might be on the barbed wire, if the windmill had raised water for the cattle, the thousand and one things those eyes of his could see. "We're late tonight. Homer, I guess you'll have to milk an extra cow." I groaned to myself. Work. Always work. When I got big I'd go to the city and lead a soft life. But I'd have more sense than to buy an umbrella when there wasn't a cloud in the sky.

We put the lanterns away, after the chores were done, and sat on the porch and looked out across the dying corn and our hearts were heavy. Pa spoke of taxes. There would be trouble, this year, paying them. Movers would be going by people who had lost their farms; tramps would be begging for food. If you didn't give it to them, they'd open your gates and let the cattle out; they might even set fire to a haystack.

Pa studied the sky. He was the weather prophet of the family. "Well, I dunno." He came back and sat down in the rocking chair. "I...just dunno," he repeated. But it looks a little more on the favorable side."

Bedtime came. The heat filled the rooms like smoke in the smokehouse. And it was almost as suffocating. Corn-killing weather. We'd be lucky to get nubbins.

Pa took another look. "I'm gettin' to be more hopeful."

The windmill went into gear. "Do you hear that!" said Pa.

Suddenly there was a sput on the porch steps—then another and another. The dog came in and curled up.

Our spirits leaped and so did the spirits of the farm. Soft, heart-filling moos came from the cows, the mules began to kick up their heels, the sows grunted contentedly—sweet, lovely music.

We went to bed, the rain spattering on the roof; the rain barrel began to roar.

When we got up the next morning, a thrilling sight greeted our eyes. Water was everywhere, the hens were huddled under the shed, clucking softly; the dog had darted in and out, and there on the porch were his footprints. But that was all right; everything in all the world was all right. The drought was broken. And we knew why it had been broken. City people might scoff, but we knew. And were we thankful to God for the fine, wonderful man who had come among us!

So much for boyhood memories. How vivid they are! I go out on that porch (all modernized now) and look across the cornfields and think of the old days. I get real moony. How important rainmakers were! But now no one ever mentions them. When I told my daughter, Carol, I was writing this chapter and mentioned rainmakers, she thought it was a "gag." And so it goes.

Wanting, for the purposes of this book, to enlarge my memories, I went among old-timers, poked through newspaper files, and wrote the state historians and gained some surprising bits of information. One had to do with "Melbourne, the Rainmaker." He was said to have come from Australia, but this is not certain. He was one of the earliest and most spectacular, a kind of barnyard Barnum. He came into our section when people already half believed in rainmaking, for that was the tradition of the prairies. When the Indians had wanted rain they had set fire to the plains; rain follows battles.

He usually went to the fair grounds (the Barnum touch) where he erected a building with four windows, one opening to each point of the compass. Into this were wheeled tanks and coils and electrical batteries, all covered with tarpaulin and battened down so no spy could peek. The utmost secrecy prevailed. Melbourne would not even answer questions; ropes were stretched around the building; no one but his own men could enter. In the roof of the building was a flue; from this the mysterious gases were allowed to escape.

He made a flat charge of five hundred dollars; this guaranteed rain to fall for fifty to one hundred miles in all directions. He had three days to produce results and it nearly always rained. Then he would collect his money and move on to another suffering locality. His fame spread; he was the most talked-of-man in the Corn Belt. But Melbourne—alas!—was human. He liked to go to horse races, something no self-respecting person would do. He did too, letting the corn wither and perish. Curses were heaped on him, but Melbourne didn't care; he wanted to see which horse came in first. He lived high, demanding ten dollars a day extra for hotel expenses. The committee groaned, but what could it do?

Sometimes he won and sometimes he didn't. Sometimes it would rain fifty or one hundred miles away; then he would explain the wind had drifted the gases. But mostly he won. Once it rained so hard that a committee waited on him and demanded that he shut off the rain. He calmly sat at the hotel (the race tracks being muddy) and told them he would do nothing about it. And he didn't.

But it wasn't all easy. He had critics and detractors. Some said he was a fake; others believed in him earnestly and deeply and sincerely.

At last luck ran against him; a series of cool and windy nights set in and, try as he would, he could not produce rain. His detractors increased. But the people of Goodland, Kansas, where he had established headquarters, believed in him; they'd seen results. A call came from Nebraska. So he sold to a group of citizens in Goodland the right to use his gases and his secret formula for rainmaking, and got on the train and left for that parched and suffering flatland.

So implicitly did the people of Goodland believe that not one but three rainmaking companies were organized. Their names were: The Inter-State Artificial Rain Company; The Swisher Rain Company of Goodland; and The Artificial Rain Company.

Goodland was the rainmaking headquarters of the Corn Belt. Business boomed. They ranged far and wide and money flowed back to the banks.

Meantime, working quietly and unspectacularly for the Rock Island Railroad was a train dispatcher named C. B. Jewell. He had been experimenting, but he lacked means. A friendly official of the road heard of his work, called on him, and volunteered to take it up with the road. The officers were interested; if they helped the farmers produce, then the road would get more hauling. So impressed were the officers that they told Jewell he could give up dispatching and go out and make it rain. He trained two other crews; the railroad converted boxcars into rainmaking laboratories and these went up and down the line, stopping wherever it seemed advisable. Jewell was now, suddenly, as popular as Melbourne had once been; in addition, he wasn't interested in horse races. That was hopeful. So important—so sought after—was he that he went to South Dakota where he had one triumph after another. Everything he touched turned to rain. He had a telegram from a man in Britton, South Dakota, saying he lived near a river and the waters had become so high that his calves were in danger of drowning, and would Mr. Jewell please stop the rain? Jewell had to wire back: "Can't stop the rain. The machine is wound up for ninety days." It was not known what happened to the calves.

Jewell returned to Wichita, but when he got there he found his detractors had been busy. He said he would turn Douglas Avenue into a canal. And he just about did, for an exceedingly heavy rain came which sent the rivers and creeks out of their banks. His believers were not at all surprised. Meantime, the Rock Island was flourishing; farmers everywhere were proclaiming it for its fine work; a farmer who shipped by any other road wasn't loyal.

Unfortunate incidents occurred. Aberdeen, South Dakota, was desperately in need of rain; but there was a schism among its people, also great secrecy. What should happen but two rival rainmakers were engaged and both began sending up their evil-smelling gases! The people became alarmed; they would be washed out and their crops drowned. One of the rainmakers was Captain Hauser; they tried to get him to desist; he said he had been engaged to make it rain and that if he desisted he couldn't claim the money. He kept grimly on working. The other was known as Professor Morris. They asked him to stop, but he wouldn't. There was the money and there was his reputation. But things worked themselves out, as they have a habit of doing, for it didn't rain at all. Finally the two embittered rainmakers moved on to new, pastures, taking care this time to go to different pastures.

The rainmaking business prospered. Sometimes the rainmakers hit it; sometimes they didn't. But it rained in adjacent towns and scoffers were put down. Human nature was at work. The companies got to cutting each other's throats; yes, lowering prices. Once the price had got up to $2,500, but finally it fell to $1,500. But still there was money in it. The three Goodland rivals worked industriously; the banks bulged.

In the midst of the successes of the Goodland rainmakers came the news that Kansas was suffering. They loyally rushed home, but, alas, could do nothing. Day after day they connected their electric batteries and sent up their gases, but no rain came. Their detractors increased. The rainmakers, who three seasons ago, had been so popular were now regarded with suspicion. In fact, one of the Kansas rainmaking companies had gone to Minden, Nebraska, but hadn't produced any rain at all. There was muttering among the farmers who became so stirred up that they seized the unfortunate man, tied him to a telephone pole, and turned the town fire-company hose on him and said, "Well, if you can't make it rain, we can." The man left town, dripping.

One of the famous men of Kansas was the Reverend Charles M. Sheldon, who had written the amazingly successful *In His Steps*. He was engaged by a magazine to go out and report how a rainmaker worked. He moved into a boxcar with one and was given a bunk. The end came rather suddenly, for the boxcar was left standing on a siding while a railroad strike was in progress. The strikers approached in the night, and not realizing the good work the car was doing, threw ropes over it and with poles sent the boxcar crashing on its side. The tank was overturned and gas began to escape. The Reverend Mr. Sheldon's eyes rained. He and the rainmaker shouted lustily; finally the strikers came back, chopped a hole in the side, and the Reverend Mr. Sheldon and the rainmaker crawled out.

The Reverend Mr. Sheldon wrote the story for his magazine, then quietly went back to his pulpit.

So widespread was the belief in rainmaking that Congress was convinced there was something in it. Senator Farwell, especially, was a believer and made such an impressive speech that Congress appropriated $19,000 for experiments in rainmaking. These were turned over to the Department of Agriculture and were carried out on a ranch in Texas. But even Congress and the Department of Agriculture couldn't make it rain; finally the experiments were given up and $5,000 of the money turned back into the United States Treasury. This was a pretty hard blow to rainmaking.

The Corn Belt wasn't the only place where belief in the powers of rainmakers prevailed. In California, a former sewing machine agent became famous as Rainmaker Hatfield; some of my older readers may recall him. He was more cautious than the men of the Middle West, for he said, "I only claim that I can induce Nature to release, by way of precipitation, the moisture which the air already has." He was successful. In March, 1912, he was offered $4,000, by the ranchers and merchants at Hemet, California, if he would make it rain. He got the money.

In 1916, sunny California was having more sun than it wanted; indeed, it was desperate for rain and was experiencing what it called the worst drought in history. Rainmaker Hatfield was sent for and was asked what his terms were, thus showing how implicit, at this time, was faith in rainmaking. He calmly made three propositions:

1. He would fill the Morena Reservoir (part of the city water system).

2. He would produce thirty inches of rain free of charge, but for all over that he would have to have $500 an inch.

3. He would deliver forty inches of rain free of charge, but for every inch over that he would have to have $1,000.

The desperate city council passed a resolution accepting his offer, but craftily did not mention which of the three propositions they were agreeing to.

Hatfield journeyed to the Morena dam, built mysterious towers, and sent up his gases. It turned out just as he firmly believed; in no time at all it was raining. But he must have been a little surprised, for 35.91 inches of it came down; in fact, it added up to the worst local flood in history,

California never doing things by halves. The city's losses ran into millions; the property owners became irate and threatened to sue the city for having produced such a storm. The harassed city council took it out on poor Hatfield; they said he had overdone it and that they hadn't ordered so much rain and flatly refused to pay. He said they hadn't set any limit and presented a bill for $10,000. The puzzled city council didn't know what to do about it, but finally agreed to abide by the written opinion of the city attorney. The city attorney carefully thought his way through it and announced that the whole thing was an Act of God and that Hatfield hadn't had anything to do with it. Hatfield said he had and demanded his money. Finally he offered to settle for $4,000; the city attorney said damned if he would. Hatfield came down to $1,400, but the city attorney, with God on his side, did not budge. At last the suit was dropped and Rainmaker Hatfield, for his outstanding job, did not get a single penny. The property owners stopped talking about their threatened suits and again California was sunny and lovely, and thus ended the most remarkable example of rainmaking in American history. The chief of the reference department of the San Diego Public Library, who gave me this information, told me that inquiries about this rainmaking attempt still arrive and that only recently a lawyer came in and said he believed that Hatfield still had a case and that he might revive it for him. The reference department hopes for the best.

Events, however, were moving against the rainmakers. One was the increased efficiency of the weather bureau; some of the detractors proclaimed that a rainmaker wouldn't undertake a job for a certain day unless he had seen the forecast. Drought, which had held the Corn Belt so long in its devastating grip, began to give way. Rain years came. No rainmaker was needed at all. Jewell was back at his old job of train-dispatching. Melbourne had disappeared into a cloud.

But the problem of weather remains and a vastly important one it is. Rain years and drought years—how much they mean to our farmers! There is now not a farmer in all the Corn Belt who believes in rainmakers; even during the Dust Bowl Days, no one was foolish enough to suggest getting a rainmaker. The idea now is to retain the water that falls instead of trying to coax it down. There is terrace farming and there are ponds and catchments everywhere; even grasses are planted to hold the water. Yet still the weather is the most important single topic that comes over the radio.

KMA, in Shenandoah, Iowa, known as the Farmer's Radio Station (you'll read about it in another chapter), sends out eleven weather forecasts a day, and the manager of the station told me so vital is its ten o' clock night forecast that many farmers remain up for it and pop into bed the moment it is over. (When you entice a farmer to stay up till ten, you've done all that human ingenuity can accomplish.)

It hardly seems possible today that I once went to town to see a rainmaker save our crops. But I believed in it then and so did most people.

ANECDOTE

Here's something to startle people with:

The word "tractor" was made up by a man in Charles City, Iowa. He was an advertising man by the name of W. H. Williams. The manufacturing company he was working for had a machine called the "gasoline traction engine." All this was too long for the ad, so he shortened it to "tractor."

Now go on to some other subject, as if you could tell interesting stories all evening.

Abraham Lincoln Once Owned A Farm in Iowa

It was not until I got to work on this volume I learned that Abraham Lincoln once owned a farm in Iowa. What? Abraham Lincoln had a farm in Iowa? But there it was.

I found, on closer study, that, as a matter of fact, he had had two farms in Iowa. Both farms had been given him, I learned, for his services in the Black Hawk War in 1832, for veterans were given land then, as in later wars. One was for forty acres, located near Dubuque; the other for 120 acres on the opposite side of the state. But he did not immediately turn the land Warrants in; he always said he was too poor to pay the taxes. In fact, he held the land warrants for the 120-acre farm until he was running for President before he felt secure enough to make use of them; they arrived in the midst of his campaign—just a week before he was elected President. He owned the land when he was assassinated. To my surprise I found Lincoln died without leaving a will. The land went to his widow, and, later, to his son, Robert Todd Lincoln.

I was eager to see the farm and, after a time, arrived in the little town of Denison, Iowa, and made my inquiries.

How simple a road can be to one who knows! What a problem to one negotiating it for the first time! And soon I realized my problem was getting me down. I passed a marker that said: "Vernon Voss Road. Killed in action in New Guinea, October 29th, 1942." And this, I thought, was an appropriate thing to do. He must have passed along this road many times...never dreaming some day it would be named for him.

And now I realized I was lost; I stopped to inquire. A woman came out the back door and stood on a little wooden platform that had a foot-scraper fastened to it.

"Can you direct me to the Abraham Lincoln farm?"

"Well, no, I can't exactly. My husband would know if he was here. But it happens he ain't."

I continued down the road and asked again. But got nowhere at all. Then I changed my question. "Do you know where the Martin H. Hansen farm is?"

"Yes, I do. There are two or three Hansens. The thing to do is to take Snake Road. When you get to the fork, ask."

I took Snake Road and, in no time at all, understood how it had got its name. How thin, gravelly, and eroded the soil was, this in almost-perfect-soil Iowa. There were hole-spotted Osage orange hedges, wooden culverts, and old wing-folding windmills.

Some way or other I missed the fork and was lost. I asked again. "Why, you're only a mile and a half from the Hansen farm. You'll pass a big stone under a barbed-wire fence. It has a plate on it. That's on the far corner of the farm. And now, on the alert for it, I found the stone and hopped out. On top was a bronze plaque and this is what it said: "Land Grant to Abraham Lincoln for services rendered in the Black Hawk War, 1832. Marked by the Denison Chapter of the Daughters of the American Revolution, 1923."

Here is the rest of the story as I got it from Martin H. Hansen: The Lincoln family owned the farm for thirty-three years. Robert Todd Lincoln sold the farm in 1892 for $1,300, or a little more than ten dollars an acre. Martin H. Hansen bought it in 1929 for $105 an acre.

I asked Mr. Hansen some questions about the farm. His answers are illuminating and show the cycle in changing land values:

"You say you paid $105 an acre in 1929. How much is the land worth now?"

"I wouldn't part with it for less than $120 an acre."

"How much have you in corn?"

"Forty acres. The rest is chiefly oats."

He told me about the abstract.

"It's quite a book! It would take a day or two to read it. The abstract shows twice where the land was given to Lincoln. In one place the abstract says, United States to Abraham Lincoln."

"For a long time the farm was 120 acres of trouble. It was sold twice for taxes. I think that sounds bad—Abraham Lincoln's farm selling for taxes. Nobody seemed to be able to make a go of it. I was born on the farm next to the Lincoln farm and I would look across at it and say to myself, "I'd like to own land that used to be Abraham Lincoln's. It would be a kind of honor, like. Also, I figured maybe I could make it pay. It didn't seem to me it'd ever been properly handled. Farming methods keep changin' all the time. What went ten years ago, wouldn't go now. In 1929 a chance came along, and I picked it up. That night I came home and said to my wife, 'I guess we own the Abraham Lincoln farm.' We both felt real pleased. I changed the farmin' methods and now its makin' me money. I'm real proud of that."

"Farming is about the best business there is to get into; it's a great deal, in this day and age, to be your own boss. Most people work for somebody else, but you don't when you own your farm. I read of people in the city having their furniture set onto the sidewalk. When you own land, you know nothin' like that is goin' to be your lot."

"Do you," I asked, "have many people coming here asking about the farm?"

Mr. Hansen smiled with pleasure. "I expect I have fifty a year! I'm always pleased to show them around. It's quite a nice thing to say you own the Abraham Lincoln farm."

"What question do they most frequently ask?"

"They all want to know if Abraham Lincoln ever farmed it himself. Of course he didn't. As a matter of fact, he never saw the land. I wish he had. I'd like to think he'd walked across it."

"Does it add to the value of the farm?"

"I expect not. Its only a sentimental value. Most people, when they put their money into a farm, want to know if it's going to pay out. But I've got sentiment toward the farm, always have had since I was a boy an' used to look across at it."

At last, I had to leave. I carried away with me the memory of the man who was proud to own the Abraham Lincoln farm.

Addendum: There is a little log-cabin museum in the town and in this is the original land grant which gave Lincoln the farm; on this land grant is Abraham Lincoln's signature. It sort of brings him back and makes his connection with the farm more vivid.

TRUE STORY

A young professor at Tarkio, Missouri (in the heart of the Corn Belt), taught classes by day, poked around alone in the college laboratory by night. His name: Wallace Hume Carothers. He developed a theory about fiber molecules and their arrangement. He was brilliant, erratic, moody; some said he should have been a musician.

The long arm of Harvard picked him up and set him teaching; then the du Ponts heard about him and soon he was in Seaford, Delaware, with his theory of polymers. He worked at a furious rate for nine years and finally completed a synthetic project. The du Ponts pulled a name out of a hat—Nylon—and got ready to advertise it.

One day the brilliant, moody organic chemist went to Philadelphia, engaged a hotel room, and sat around for some hours, smoking. Then he shook some powders into a glass, squeezed lemon juice into the glass, and swallowed the contents. In a few minutes he was dead…just before the success of his discovery became a world sensation.

Antonin Dvorak, the Composer, Lived and Worked in Iowa?

When I first heard that Iowa had made a notable contribution to music I was pleased; also I decided to "look into it." (Kansas had made one. I'll tell about this elsewhere.) I set to work and here are the facts as I was able to put them together:

The hero is Antonin Dvorak! Yes, Dvorak in Iowa.

In 1893, he was conducting the New York Symphony Orchestra, but this seems to have been a strain; and there was a great deal of social flinging around. He wanted to get away and create…. Who hasn't felt that urge?

In his orchestra was Joseph J. Kovarik who began to tell him about the wonders of his hometown in Iowa. It was all Bohemian, he said: Bohemian beer, Bohemian customs, everybody spoke Bohemian—a chip off the old block. And this was true; this town, I was surprised to find, was one of the oldest Czech settlements in the United States (1854).

Dvorak grew more and more interested. The upshot of it was that he decided to go to Iowa and take his family—quite an undertaking. When he put himself on the train, there were eleven in his party: himself and his wife, his wife's sister, a maid, six children, and the faithful hometown booster Kovarik. Dvorak fretted; too many stops, too little beer (but plenty of hell-raising by the children, I expect). At last, after four days and nights, they got off the train in Iowa. But this wasn't where they were going; it was merely the nearest town.

Two carriages were hired and off they went across what Dvorak always referred to as the prairie. It wasn't this at all, in 1893, for by this time it was a corn-farming section. It was chiefly Bohemian (later known as Czech). At last the carriages arrived in Spillville…. How Dvorak must have stared; for the town had only 300 people. But it was Bohemian, although named for a Swiss—a certain Spielman. At first it had been called Spielmanville, but that was a little too much; finally it shook down to Spillville.

The family floated into the house that had been engaged the biggest in town.

The people in the town were farmers, or in some way connected with farming. (And they still are.) But he did hear his native language and was able to get his native beer. He liked the change from New York; it was quiet and peaceful and at once, I'm told, he plunged into composing. He made even the early-stirring farmers blink, for he was up the next morning at four. He walked delightedly down the streets; here he would be able to compose. He went to the Church of St. Wenceslas at seven and to the organ loft, sat down, and began to play Czech hymns. The people had been waiting for days to see the great man from their home country and there he was, in the organ loft, playing! When mass was over, they hurried out to wait for him to pass; he spoke to them, touched by this mark of respect. "I will play for you many times," he said. How fortunate he was to have chosen Spillville!

He had no piano, but this was taken care of by loading Kovariks and bringing it to the big brick two-story house.

One of the things that pleased him was that there was a butcher in town by the name of Dvorak. This had been Dvorak's fathers work in old Bohemia. In order to distinguish the two men, the local people gave Antonin Dvorak the title roughly equivalent to Squire Dvorak. He liked it.

Through Spillville runs a cornfield stream called Turkey River. It's not much bigger than a creek, but river it was and river it still is. Every morning he popped out early, according to the people I interviewed, and walked along the banks stopping, now and then, to listen to the songs of the Iowa birds which were all new to him. Also he liked to listen to what he called "the wind in the prairie grasses." When I questioned this I was told that what he heard was, probably, the wind in the trees. But he always referred to it as "the wind in the prairie grasses."

Before he had left New York, he had been at work on what he later called his New World Symphony. My musical friends tell me that he was so impressed by the bird calls he heard on Turkey River that he made changes and put in this effect (in the third movement, I'm told). One put it this way: the symphony was born in New York, baptized in Spillville, then taken back to New York and confirmed.

And an oddity I picked up was the length of time required by different orchestras to play it. The time varies from forty to sixty-eight minutes. It all depends, it seems, on the conductor.

He set to work on his "String Quartet in F Major, Op. 96"; this went so well, due to his inspiring surroundings, that he composed a quintet for strings. This, I have been told, has not, in spite of its merit, been so widely received.

After the first few excited, work-filled weeks he wanted to see this thrilling new world he found himself in. He was told about the falls of Minnehaha, at Minnehaha, Minnesota, and there he went, all eyes and ears. It happened a tribe of Indians, that night, began a dance; and he stared and listened, too. Suddenly, in the midst of it, he tried to find a piece of paper, but he was not able to. But he did have his stiff white cuffs and he made notes on them. These he used in the second movement of his sonatina for violin and piano, Op. 100. This particular movement, later, was rearranged by Fritz Kreisler and published under the title of "Indian Lament."

Work was going so exceedingly well that he made notes for a piece he already had in mind—"the Humoresque." On the front of the brick house is a sign which says it was here that he wrote the "Humoresque," but this seems to be too self-boasting; he appears only to have made notes and sketches.

But the little corn town did do something outstanding. It arranged a music festival and played his "String Quartet" for the first time in this world, using the manuscript score. Dvorak himself directed the rehearsals. It is, I'm told, almost unheard of for a composer to conduct a mere string quartet in public.

I wanted to go to the very house where he had composed, but the woman would not let me in—"not for strangers," she said and slammed the door. But I did go to see his washwoman—Mrs. Anna Benda. She could not speak English, so an interpreter had to be used. But when Mrs. Benda understood what I wanted she advanced, put her arms on the yard fence, and smiled a smile that completely warmed my heart. "Ah," she said, "he was good, wonderful! Sometimes, when I come early for the clothes, I hear him playing an' I stand a little and listen. But he have one thing very badt." She paused and looked at me, even now pained to speak critical words of the great man. "He make notes on his cuffs and, no matter how I scrub, there is still a little there. But"—and now again the wonderful smile—"he was very good pay. Never do I have to wait."

How old-world the town seems; this feel is even in the buildings. Most of all it is in the talk. Everybody speaks Czech, except when they see a stranger. The old people have accents; I talked to only two young people—both boys but they did not have it; at least, during our brief conversation I did not notice it. There was, in the middle of what might be called a plaza, an honor roll of service men and women. About a hundred and fifty names were on it, boys and girls from the surrounding country. There was only one name I could pronounce easily. This, to me, was a good example of the different racial groups that have gone to make up the great, rich, colorful Corn Belt. I went to the organ loft where Mrs. F. C. Swella played for me. The ivory keys are ancient and they rattle, but it was thrilling to think that Dvorak had once played upon them.

I went to the Dvorak Memorial Park, the place where he had walked along Turkey River; there is an eight-sided pedestal, with the titles of eight of his compositions on it; and there is a bronze plaque telling of his days in Spillville. Iowa birds sing in the trees. But no wind in the prairie grasses. I am positive.

The summer passed pleasantly. He continued to work and play and drink his beer…then suddenly, almost in a twinkling, he snatched up his family and fled back to New York. I was told this hesitatingly, for Spillville is still exceedingly sensitive about it. It was, I soon discovered, one of those things one doesn't talk about. But what is a reporter for?

It seems that while Squire Dvorak had been in the clouds of composition, his oldest daughter had fallen in love with a local boy. Dvorak was appalled. He hired the teams that had brought him to town, and in four hours he and his family were out of the house and driving madly for the railroad.

"The man the daughter fell in love with still lives here," I was told. "But he will not speak. That is something that must never be done—mention it to him."

What was I to do? I did go to him—now a gray-haired, kindly-faced man. My heart gave a thump, for here was a man who had been part of a famous romance. And now that I was face to face with him, I felt tremendously self-conscious and ill at ease, but I finally got the words out. He did not like what I asked him. I suppose, I should not have gone at all. He did not wish publicity, he said, and wanted nothing printed. What surprised me most was how extremely sensitive he was after all these years. But it was his business and not mine and so I left. But I wished he had given me permission…ah!, those old reporters.

At last, I left the fascinating un-American, yet, somehow, still American town, the town which had helped give Dvorak an understanding of a new world. I stopped, as I passed Turkey River, and turned off the engine.

There the river was, except for the park, much as it must have been when he walked along it. And there was no wind in the prairie grasses. I listened carefully.

Addendum: I learn by correspondence, since I wrote the above, that the house is to be turned into a museum. Not a Dvorak museum, but a clock museum. Near Spillville are the Bily Brothers (also Bohemians), who have a hobby of carving strange and unusual clocks. Tourists from all over this section come to see the clocks, and now they're to go into the Dvorak house. That's the latest.

ANECDOTE

"St. Louis Blues" wasn't written in St. Louis, but in Memphis, Tennessee. It has nothing to do with St. Louis; the composer just happened to hang it on the place. At first, the people of St. Louis were mad and said it reflected on St. Louis. Now they say it exactly captures the spirit of the city.

The Story of Corn

How I hated corn! Work. That was all it meant. On mornings, when there was dew, the stalks marching under the cultivator arch would wet me from head to foot; in the fall, as I threw the ears into the wagon, my fingers would grow cold and stiff. When I got the cursed stuff to the crib, I'd have to scoop it. I tell you it was hell. And this was not just a teenage experience, for I plowed it and shucked it and scooped it until I was past twenty-one.

One day something happened. We had a Chautauqua. Its coming was the great event of the year; every farmer took a week off, except for chores, and drove in to hear the smart people talk and play and sing. We thought the Swiss Bell Ringers were wonderful and so was Blind Boone, the Negro piano player, and so was Russell H. Conwell, who, in a lecture called "Acres of Diamonds," told us thrilling stories about James J. Hill, Andrew Carnegie, and Weyerhaueser, the rich lumberman; he said if we were honest, worked hard, and saved our money we could grow rich. I decided, instead of trifling away the dime Pa had given me that day, I would take it home and save it.

I went with my mother and sat down on one of the plank seats, without a back, and waited for the program to begin. We were under a tent, with its sides rolled up; when we looked out we could see feet walking past. Around the tent was a ditch to carry off the water when it rained. (It always did, Chautauqua Week.) Palm-leaf fans were going, children had little slabs of taffy gripped in their hands. Outside, a man with a maul was trying to see how high he could knock a traveling weight. When it went *dong!*, it meant he would get a free cigar. Some day I would be knocking a weight and getting a free cigar.

The announcer came out and said the first number on the program this afternoon will be a lecture on corn. It almost made me sick at my stomach.

I wanted to get up and slip away, but I was trapped. I knew I could never get away from my mother and would have to stay and hear the man drone on about corn.

It was worse than I expected. A small man, with a large beard came out—Professor P. G. Holden. And danged if he wasn't holding a stalk of field corn, the last thing in the world I wanted to see. In fact, I'd come there so I wouldn't have to see that curse to humanity.

The little professor began to talk about corn. It was dull. My mind was out under the tent flaps and away. And I wished my body were the same. I began to wonder if I could say I had a headache and creep out, trying to look white around the gills. Then, little by little, I got interested in what the professor was saying. He held up ears and explained the difference between them and told how to select the best and finest for seed corn.

He began to talk about corn silk; I had seen millions of ears of corn silk but now, through his eyes and with understanding, I began to see corn silk in a way I had never even dreamed of. I began to understand the part it plays in corn reproducing itself. I was fascinated. I had been overlooking one of the greatest miracles in Nature. All the pollen that had got up my nostrils and choked the gizzard out of me, now meant something; this was nature's way of trying to raise more corn. A tiny pollen grain (a dozen could dance on the point of a pin), falling on a strand of the silk, would make one grain in the ear of corn, he said. I'll be doggoned! Never again would I look on corn as a back-breaker invested in a black mood by the Devil. Why, it was a gift from Heaven! I grew more and more fascinated; I was so enthralled I hardly breathed. Corn. Wonderful corn!

At last his exciting lecture was over and the little professor with his great beard gathered up his cornstalks and went creaking off the platform. I followed him with my eyes—this man who had opened up a new world.

We drove home in the hack. The story of the corn was still with me; I looked with respect at the fields of corn we jogged past.

The next day was cocklebur cutting. We went up and down the rows chopping out the burs with hoes—as hot work as there is outside of hell. But that was all right; the spell was still upon me. I tackled those burs with vengeance. They were enemies of our wonderful God-given corn. I slew them right and left. Indeed, I worked two or three days before I slipped back to normal.

But even if I did hate work, Professor Holden had opened up a new world to me. I still think corn is wonderful and I still think Professor Holden is wonderful. He is, as I write, still living and the place is Belleville, Michigan. I salute you, professor. You were a great pioneer. Henry A. Wallace told me that Professor Holden had been a tremendous influence in his life and that his first interest in corn had come from Professor Holden. Professor Holden has been an influence on endless people in the Corn Belt. Indeed, I would like to see a monument, when he is no longer upon this earth, lifted high and proudly in his memory.

Corn! It is truly a wonder crop. I can think of no other that yields so much for so little. Under favorable conditions it will hand back five hundred times the amount planted. In other words, a grain of corn will produce five hundred other grains. Nor does it take much "cultivation." Plow it three times and it's as happy as a dog patted on the head.

Indeed, I could tell you a dozen wonders about corn.

In all history no corn has ever been found growing wild. It always has to be cultivated; no plant in all the world is so dependent on man. Most plants, if left to shift for themselves, will manage to do so. But not corn. If man didn't cultivate it, it'd disappear from the face of the earth. One reason is that the grains are gripped in a tough husk; they would fall at the root of the stalk. The husk would rot, some of the grains would grow (weaker than the first ones), and these would spring up and topple down on the others. Vigorous wild grasses and outlaw plants would move in and soon that hill of corn would be no more.

It is the oldest cultivated plant. Far older than wheat or rice. A few years ago the American Museum of Natural History, New York, sent an expedition to Aztec, New Mexico, to delve into the ancient ruins. One day, one of the mules got loose and wandered around over the diggings. He was then seen chomping contentedly away; one of the museum men examined the morsel the mule had happened upon and was horrified to see that it was some of Aztec corn they had just excavated. The tree-ring chronology was applied and the mule's meal was found to date back to the year 1120. What is left of the animals meal is now in an exhibit at the American Museum of History. No mule is allowed to enter.

Yet more has happened to corn since 1910 than in all the ages since man began growing it. (More about that later in this chapter.)

I "read up" on the history of corn and here's something that struck me: the first "white man" to see corn was Christopher Columbus; November 5, 1492, he sent two of his crew into the interior of Cuba to see what they could find. They returned with some ears of corn. The natives showed how to cook it. Columbus ate and liked it so much that he sent for more. When he sailed he took some back to Italy and, later, to Spain. And that is the way, according to the historians, corn got across the ocean. But Columbus had applied the Indian word, as best he could understand it—*maize*. It seems the Anglo-Saxon word for wheat and all small grains was *Korn* and so ours came in under that. But we borrowed the name corn and began to employ it. In other words, corn was discovered in America but got its name from Europe.

A thing to be borne in mind is that the ears Columbus saw were not like the ones today. They were, it is pretty well established, the highly colored kind we call Indian Corn. This hard, flinty variety is still grown by American Indians on their reservations and by the people of New Mexico who grind it and use it for food. At railroad stops they sell it to tourists who bring it back home and hang it up for decorations. God help them if they ever try to eat it!

Historians don't know where corn originated, but it is generally believed that it must have been in Guatemala, although a good vigorous shove would land it in Peru. The state of Iowa is putting its money on Guatemala. This is more than an easy slang phrase, for Iowa is establishing a Research Center for the Iowa State College at Antigua, Guatemala. Test seeds, germinations, crosses, and double-crosses will be flown back and forth, thus being able to grow two generations in a year. Some of the corn will be tested at 3,000 feet above sea level, some at 5,000, and some at 7,500. Thus, whipsawed between Iowa and Guatemala, corn won't be able to hold back many of its secrets.

Another item I "read up" on was how greatly important corn was to the Pilgrim Fathers. They had little food, that first bleak dismal autumn, and the going was hard. Then Miles Standish and his men saw something they'd never seen before—corn. They found that the Indians had buried it in mounds. One account says they came upon a basket containing "six-and-thirty goodly ears." And I expect they were exactly that. "And surely it was God's providence we found this corn," says a chronicler of the day, "for else we know not what we should have done."

The Indians taught them how to grind and cook it. Next spring they taught them the best trick of all—how to grow it. The soil was thin, not corn soil at all; but the Indians had solved that. Into every hill of corn they put a fish. I think of these feeble, faltering first attempts to grow corn when I see the unending acres in the Corn Belt and my mind goes to Miles Standish and I like to think what would be his sensations if he could come back and see an Iowa farm. "Six-and-thirty goodly ears!" He would be popeyed.

As nearly as I can understand it, the Pilgrim Fathers would have pooped out if it hadn't been for corn; at least, the struggle for existence would have been tougher. I find in reading about Roger Williams in Rhode Island, that crows were a menace. They pulled the corn from the shallow soil; so watchtowers were built in the fields and here the older children were placed to scare away the crows. Roger Williams, in his journal, tells of the complication: the Indians would let the crows eat their heads off. The reason was that the Indians had a legend that crows had brought them the corn from the land to the South and that they must never kill a crow because of the good deed it had done. And now the corn authorities have found that wild geese, flying up from Guatemala, have grains of corn in their crops.

Corn became one of the principal foods of the colonists; wherever they went, corn went. Finally they got over the Appalachians and into Kentucky and Tennessee and Ohio and Indiana and corn faithfully with them. Indeed, I believe I could write quite a Saga of Corn. At last it hit the jackpot the great Corn Belt, the amazing black-loam section, the ten corn states I have mentioned. (Do you remember KNOWS?)

But it was the hard, flinty, enamel-cracking, eight-row Indian corn. Farmers wanted bigger corn, but all they could do was to save the most likely-looking ears and, next year, plant them. This was all right, but it didn't get the farmers very far. It was like having a BB gun but wanting a rifle.

One who selected earnestly and intelligently was a man in Brown County, Ohio, named Reid and spelled that way. He picked up and went to Delavan, Illinois, taking with him his biggest and finest ears. Now comes a lucky accident. The corn he brought with him was a reddish variety known as the "Gordon Hopkins"; it had been named for a person with that handle. He planted it, but it didn't all come up; so he got a local corn called "Little Yellow" and stuck that into the missing hills. That seemingly trivial matter proved tremendously important. Gordon Hopkins and Little Yellow lay down side by side and mated; a son was born with a dent in his head. Reid named him after himself, called him "Reid's Yellow Dent."

The elder Reid had a son named James L. Reid who became as great a zealot as the old man and even improved the variety by careful selection; soon everybody in the corn section began to raise Reid's Yellow Dent. It was the kind I grew up on.

James L. Reid began taking prizes everywhere; he walked off with the red apple at the Chicago World's Fair; in fact, for a time his corn was called the "World's Fair Corn." He doubled the number of rows that Indian corn had, an amazing feat.

I went to see his daughter Miss Olive Reid, in Delavan, Illinois, who gave me some of this information. The old gentleman died in 1910. He had put more money into the pockets of the farmers in the Corn Belt than any man who had ever lived.

I walked out across the farm and was touched to think this spot had done so much to enrich our country. He had a great beard...I could almost see him going up and down the rows, with a sack over his shoulders, selecting and sorting.

His fame spread; everybody in the Corn Belt knew James L. Reid. His farm was getting to be a show spot. One day an important visitor came-Professor Holden. They talked corn all afternoon and the professor stayed for supper. Mr. Reid began to like the understanding little professor and the two became chummy.

Mr. Reid paused and looked at his wife. "Do you suppose it would be all right to show him that *special* corn?"

"I think it would, James."

The bearded old zealot led the little professor into a room and pointed to the bed. Mr. Reid pulled back the covers, revealing that the bed had two mattresses. He lifted up the top one and there, between the two mattresses, were twenty ears of corn!

"Those are the best ears I've raised this season," said the old man. "My wife and I sleep on them every night so we can always know where they are and that nothing has happened to them." Professor Holden looked at them; they were the best he had ever seen.

"I'll give you one," said Mr. Reid and he did and Professor Holden was moved by this fine token of friendship.

But her father, his daughter told me, had problems. A jealous neighbor went into the cornfield at night and planted mongrel corn of various colors and sizes. It ruined the year's crop.

Reid was no business man; he was too much the scientist and experimenter to know how to capitalize on his talent. Instead of making money selling his corn for seed, he was losing it. He put a mortgage on his farm and it went the way of most mortgaged farms. He left his widow with hardly any money; in fact, for a time, she had to be taken care of by charity. The daughter is poor today and lives in a plain little house.

I looked through her scrapbook at the ribbons and medals her father had won. I asked her if there were any marker to her father and she said there wasn't; now and then some organization comes around and talks about erecting something appropriate, but that is the end of it. She told me how, as a young girl, she had helped him select his corn and how she had written his letters. When the interview was over, I stood in front of the paint-less old house and I was touched.

The torch that burned so brightly in the hands of James L. Reid was taken up and carried forward by Professor Holden himself. He, too, proved to be a zealot. Corn! Better corn! This the pioneers believed deeply and firmly and never did they depart from the idea; they made mistakes and went up roads that petered out, but always there was the search for better corn. Professor Holden started the corn shows in Iowa. Simple as that statement is, its carrying out meant a great deal to the advancement of corn. In no time at all thousands of boys were raising corn and were trying to win prizes. So important was this effort to grow better corn that it became a deep and moving faith.

Professor Holden also started the "Seed Corn Gospel Trains." I never attended one, but my father did and I have heard of them all my life. They were fitted up as traveling exhibits to show the planting, germination, and testing of corn—a corn fair on wheels. A train would pull into a depot and onto a siding; the farmers would be waiting. The windows were darkened, stereopticon slides were shown, and lecturers, with pointers in their hands, would explain what was being seen. Farm boys brought in ears to be judged and then, as the professors passed on them, the boys would ask questions. When the exhibition was over, the Seed Corn Gospel Train would roll on to the next town.

I would like to make as important as I can this stirring in the Middle West for better corn. One reason for this overwhelming interest was that corn production was falling off; yes, pocketbooks were being touched and when you touch a farmer's pocketbook he moans till you can hear him to the haybarn. The rich, unbelievable soil of the prairies had lost its youth—the days when my father chopped a hole in the sod and dropped in the grains. On top of this came insects; a dozen were attacking where once there had been no insect at all. The European corn borer was coming in, the meanest, most destructive pest ever to hit the Corn Belt.

Meanwhile, the farmers were selecting their seed corn from the biggest and best-filled ears in the field—still throwing them into the forward part of the wagon and hanging them in the attic during the winter so the rats and mice would not have a holiday. This was just what the professors had told the farmers to do. But they were on the wrong track. And now the story goes out of the Corn Belt to—of all places—Cold Spring Harbor, Long Island, New York, where you would think they wouldn't know any more about corn than an Eskimo about sunflowers. Meet George Harrison Shull! Also with a beard.

He was what is called a "pure" scientist. He is living, this minute, at 60 Jefferson Road, Princeton, New Jersey. (The idea suddenly strikes me: Are there any pure writers, artists, musicians, and so on?)

The year was 1904. The Seed Corn Gospel Trains were still rolling up and down the Corn Country. Professor Holden was still lecturing. James L. Reid was still keeping his choicest ears between the mattresses. I was thinking up ways to get out of work.

Professor Shull had known for a long time that a stalk of corn was both a boy and girl. He decided to do something about it.

His original idea was "to study the inheritance of the number of rows of kernels on an ear of corn as influenced by cross-pollination and by self-pollination." That sounds simple, but its result was penicillin to the Corn Belt.

The male part of the stalk is the tassel, which is away up at the top. The female part is the ear, halfway down the stalk. Their location is important.

He knew, as did many others, that pollen from the tassel drifted down and fell on the silk of the ear and started the works. Scientist Shull thought it would be interesting to see what would happen if he mated corn to itself; that is, kept it in the family—a sort of cornfield Jukes. So, in a patch of experimental corn, he put a bag over the tassels, and another bag over the ear of corn itself. Then, at the right time, he took some of the pollen from the tassel, opened up the girl bag, and poured this on her silk. Then watched to see what happened.

Disappointingly little. The children that came along were smaller than their parents but there was no noticeable defect of any kind; they weren't Jukes after all. Just undersized squirts.

Professor Shull said, "I wonder what would happen if I married them again for the second generation." The ceremony was pronounced and the happy couples danced off, hand in hand, on their honeymoon.

These children were even smaller, but retained the characteristics of the old folks.

But he wasn't content. He said, "Let's try it again."

These children were still smaller, just about circus-sideshow size. But they still looked like their Pas and Mas and their Grandpas and Grandmas.

Danged if he didn't do it the fifth time.

In the meantime, he was learning a lot about the ancestry of corn. He kept on till he reached a stage known as "purity."

Then he married these lines—and the children came out fighting. They were athletes and as vigorous as skiers. Professor Shull gazed in astonishment and when a scientist (pure) does that you can know that something has really happened down by the old mill stream.

He didn't know it then, but he had revolutionized corn-growing. He had produced what became known as "hybrid corn." January 28, 1908, he went to Washington, D.C., to make an address before the American Breeders' Association. He told them the revolutionary thing he had done, in scientific language, of course.

They looked at him impersonally. What did this have to do with them? They didn't know it, then, but he was changing their lives.

When he published his "findings," they created a ripple of the size caused by a feather falling into a coal bin.

In Columbia, Missouri, in January, 1909, he read before the American Breeders Association a paper entitled "A Pure Line Method of Corn

Breeding." This now is generally considered his most important paper; it really had the stuff. But it didn't attract much attention. A year later in Omaha, Nebraska, he again spoke before a meeting of the American Breeders Association. This attracted more attention; one of the leading farmers blinked several times in rapid succession. When the meeting was over, the farmers went home and continued to do exactly as they had been doing for twenty-five years. None of them dreamed that Shull would stuff gold in their pockets; if they had, they would have carried him on their shoulders and thrown their hats as high as a windmill.

And now a bit of irony: This was the year the old bearded patriarch James L. Reid died. He died without ever having seen an ear of hybrid corn—this man who once had revolutionized corn-growing. It was now Shull's time to spin the wheel.

I seem to indicate that George H. Shull did the whole trick himself, but this is misleading, for four or five other scientists were trying to surmount difficulties in the practical application; each contributed something. I could give their names, but in this brief space I could not tell anything worthwhile about them, for I am trying to put in a chapter one of the most important agricultural changes that has taken place in the United States. Indeed there is an entire book about the discovery and development of corn—*Singing Valleys*.

Little by little the hybrid idea worked its way west from the sandy soil of Long Island; the Middle West could hardly believe anybody from Long Island could teach it anything about corn.

The thing that delayed its acceptance was the staggering amount of work that had to be done to produce hybrid. At exactly the right time a swarm of people had to descend on the cornfield and tie nightcaps on the tassels and ears; also, at exactly the right time, they had to open these paper bags and throw pollen on the blushing bride; corn had lost its private life. Farmers said, "Nobody's goin' to do all that work; we're worked to death now. Why don't you invent something that takes less work instead of more?"

The question seemed unanswerable. But the scientists answered it: "It'll add ten bushels an acre."

That made the farmers ponder. Farmers always ponder when their pocketbook is touched.

One of the young men who had attended the corn shows and Seed Corn Gospel Trains was Henry A. Wallace. Wallace is an important name in Iowa; what Randolph is to Virginia, Wallace is to Iowa. He was the third generation of Wallaces. His father had been somebody and his grandfather had been somebody. He had been tremendously impressed, at the county and state fairs, by the long tables heaped with ears of corn. One day he listened to Professor Holden, just as the composer of these lines had done; only Henry A. Wallace did something about it when, alas, *all I did was to have a spurt of work for a few days, then lapse back to normal.* But Henry A. Wallace went home, took some of the ears of corn given him by Professor Holden and planted them. Indeed, he planted three acres on a plot of Wallace-family land outside of Des Moines, planted it himself by hand on what is called an "ear a row" basis and plowed it himself with one horse hooked to a Planet Junior cultivator, which is just plain hard work. When harvest time came, he gathered the corn as carefully as a mother taking her baby out of a crib. Then he compared the ears he had produced with some of the original ears he had saved. He was shocked to find the best ears he had planted did not produce the best children. He lost all faith in corn shows and became a corn cynic.

This was the year 1904.

In 1910, when he was a senior at Iowa State College at Ames, he happened to pick up the yearbook of the American Breeders Association and casually started to read an account of Shull's work on Long Island. He was fascinated; here was something new. Maybe Shull had something.

He decided he would try his hand at detasseling and inbreeding and this he did, not being a Croy. He did his first inbreeding work in 1913, but it was not until 1919 that he really got down to business when he began to detassel, inbreed, and cross-breed like mad. He enlisted the aid of several corn authorities; one was Dr. Donald F. Jones, of the Connecticut Agricultural Experiment Station, New Haven, inventor of the famous "double-cross." The first cross Wallace made was poor; in fact, he seemed to be slipping. But there was one thing about the ears of corn—sickly-looking as they were that impressed him: their uniformity. This was important and served as a kind of king-bolt to draw his running gears.

Doggoned if he didn't become a zealot just like the others (no beard); he was editor of *Wallaces' Farmer*, he wrote editorials, he made speeches, he talked to the farmers in the field telling them this new kind of corn (which was being called hybrid) was the real thing. He induced a few farmers to grow it and he, himself, raised this new honeymoon-controlled variety.

Scientific corn-yield tests had been started in 1922 and now Henry A. Wallace entered his crosses of inbreds and, for a number of years, walked off with the ribbons. The farmers got so mad they said that Wallace's hybrids would have to be entered in a separate class.

Corn-yield was vastly important, for:

400 pounds of corn will produce 100 pounds of bacon;

600 pounds of corn will produce 100 pounds of beefsteak. Oh boy!

There was still that problem of extra work—the detasseling and pollen-sprinkling business. But he had an answer to that; each year it showed in the corn fields. His corn yielded from three to six bushels an acre more than did the old-fashioned corn. Midwest farmers pondered that, too.

He grew more and more interested; something was on his side of the teeter-totter. And this was Erosion—the meanest, most dastardly devil that ever descended on the Corn Belt. Every time there was a goose-drowner, good corn soil rushed off to the Gulf of Mexico.

"The thing to do," said Wallace, "is to grow more corn and the way to grow more corn is to use hybrid. It will make up for the depleted soil. You can grow more bushels on less land and get the corn off the hillsides."

The farmers pondered that, too; but seed corn would cost more. The farmers groaned as if having molars pulled.

In 1916—twelve years after he had done his first corn tinkering—he bought a farm nine miles northwest of Des Moines. Ten years later, in 1920, he started to raise hybridized seed corn to sell. This was near a little town named Johnston. He took into partnership with him Jay J. Newlin who was a practical farmer and, finally, there was organized the "Pioneer Hi-bred Seed Corn Company"; surely hi-bred was the worst pun of the year. Why he doesn't call it simply the "Pioneer Corn Company" is more than I know. Also everybody knows he's selling seed corn, not buttered popcorn. No need to use the word seed.

I wrote to Henry A. Wallace. I was working on this book you bought and asked him if I could go out and see his farm and he fixed it up for me. I thought his farm would be representative of how hybridized seed corn is grown. It is not the largest; far from it. The DeKalb Agricultural Association has a larger turnover than its three nearest competitors put together.

I found that Henry A. Wallace and his wife together own about forty percent of the business; the rest is locally owned and by employees. He comes out to Iowa several times a year and goes over their problems with them. They are all strong for "the boss."

I was surprised at the size of the undertaking; there is a brick building in the country which looks like a consolidated school but it turned out to be his office and research laboratory. And darned if it wasn't air-cooled; I left the farm too soon. Another thing that surprised me was the number of scientists working there—six. One fascinated me; all day long he sits and stares through a microscope. I asked him what he was and he said a "genetic research botanist."

I asked him what he was trying to accomplish and he said, "I am trying to find a variable."

I pretended I knew what he was talking about.

When I left he again began to stare through the microscope, hot on the trail, I was sure, of a variable.

I think the thing that surprised me most was that this company has three times as many scientists working for it on the subject of corn as has Iowa State College. In other words, Iowa State College has two. I did not ask which group was better paid as I did not want to hurt the feelings of the college men.

I found that Henry A. Wallace's company has 1,200 acres of land here and has seven "stations," as they're called, in three other states—indeed it has under contract 35,000 acres of land. Hybrid seed corn is now big business.

I went from one department to another, absorbed by the details. One was the "cold room." This was as cold as a Laplander's bathroom, where the seed is chilled and frozen to find how it stands up against cold. Trays of corn were in it, each tray with a number like a convict. A tray could be pulled out, the numbers studied and the whole history of the seed would be revealed.

Another was the "rat department";' Pioneer has about five hundred rats it pets and pampers. (A girl runs this department; this made me blink, too.) Rats, I found, like the same kind of corn that hogs do; so the rats are fed different kinds to see how much weight they gain, or lose, for hybrid is now engineered—not merely to grow under adverse conditions—but to put weight on hogs and cattle.

I was there too early in the season to see the work of detasseling, but was told about it and saw the pictures. The amount of work is unbelievable... it made me feel that maybe I had been born at a better time than I had thought. Buses bring boys and girls and men and women out from Des Moines and from the surrounding towns and farms; they go into the fields and pull tassels off certain rows of corn and leave them on other rows. Its quite a trick. (I was told that the Garst & Thomas Hybrid Corn Company, of Coon Rapids, Iowa, would have 1,300 people working at detasseling; during detasseling time there's hardly a maid left in the kitchens of Iowa.) The Iowa papers go crazy getting pictures of pretty detasselers. The next day, after pulling off the tassels, the workers have to come back and do it all over again. Then they have to do it again the following day, for new tassels and new silk have come out. It must be pretty discouraging. Some of the fields are tramped over fifteen times. But it is not all footwork, for there is a giant rubber-tired behemoth that goes snorting and chugging down the field with half-a-dozen girls standing on platforms, snatching right and left...especially as the machine gets close to the photographers. Lunch is served to the workers on picnic tables; they have portable radios and sit around during the noon hour and enjoy themselves. It sure is an improvement over the way I used to go out in the yard and sleep, dog-tired, beneath a cherry tree with my hog-hide gloves under my head.

Another thing that surprised me at Wallace's was a scientist who did nothing else but raise monstrosity corn; his field looked like a madman's nightmare, for it had every conceivable kind of malformed, diseased, and distressed corn in the world; loathsome pests squirmed over it. The purpose, he said, was to test corn under "adverse conditions." The conditions were so adverse I got out as fast as I could.

I found the whole scheme behind hybrid is to raise it just as the farmers do; no coddling, no ideal conditions. They have even taken a poll as to the color that farmers like best and they "breed" it for that color. Farmers prefer dark green; they think it shows vigor but, as a matter of fact, there are other colors that are just as virile.

I saw more things than I have space to tell at any satisfactory length. One was a portable dryer; it made me think of the kind you see in beauty salons; it dries a bin of corn in no time.

The following is the most important quotation I got during the day and it came from Jay J. Newlin. I spoke to him of the great amount of science and research that goes into hybrid.

"Hybrid corn is still in the Model-T stage," he said. He went on to explain that corn research is just getting started and that amazing discoveries would come in the future.

Then he said, "It's not hard to get any one quality in a stalk of corn; for instance, to stand up against the wind or to resist root-rot. The trick is to develop a variety that has everything." In this I caught a glimpse of the possibilities of corn.

Indeed, hybrid corn is the only major improvement the white man has made since taking the grain over from the Indians. The widespread use of hybrid is shown by this: in 1939 only one acre in a thousand was planted to this variety; today all the field corn in Iowa is hybrid.

I must finish this chapter; it has run longer than I intended, but there has been so much to say that I didn't seem able to squeeze it into shorter space.

What will be the future of hybrid? I don't know. But that Model-T comparison stays in my mind.

DEPARTMENT OF COOKERY

Mrs. Virginia McDonald is the most famous restaurant woman in the Corn Belt. Her restaurant is at Gallatin, Missouri, and is called "McDonald's." She was once given up to die, but got out of bed and cooked her way to health. She is especially famous for her corn muffins. Here's her recipe, just as she gave it to me:

> *One pint meal*
> *One pint boiling water.*
> *(say boiling water and boiling it must be)*
> *One teaspoon salt*
> *Two whole eggs*

Four level teaspoons baking powder
One-half pint sweet milk
One tablespoon melted butter

Sift meal and salt, pour boiling water over same, add cold milk at once to keep from lumping, add eggs, beat well. Put in baking powder just before putting in oven, adding the melted butter the last thing. Bake in a very hot oven, 475 to 500 degrees. I use oven glass individual molds to bake my muffins in. Grease well with lard. Bake to a golden brown. This recipe makes 14 to 16. Take out of oven, split, put in a pat of butter, and they will literally melt in your mouth. Thousands have told me I make the best corn muffins they ever ate.

The Corn-husking Contests

My friends find it surprising when I tell them that the biggest-attended sports event in the United States is the national corn-husking contests. Such a contest makes a football game seem like a neighborhood picnic. The contest itself lasts an hour and twenty minutes and it's about the most grueling, hard-going, weight-reducing contest you can find on the calendar. As we go along I'll endeavor to explain why.

Also my non-corn friends find it surprising when I tell them the originator of the husking contests is Henry A. Wallace.

In "the old days" every neighborhood used to have a champion corn-shucker; and, of course, the neighborhood thought he was the best who'd ever banged a bangboard; tall stories flourished. It takes a good man to go into a field and fetch a hundred bushels of corn in a day; in fact, it takes an extraordinarily good man. (Note: The author of this book never got more than forty in his life.) These local men became so good (in the stories) that they could bring in two hundred bushels in a day; even two hundred and twenty bushels.

At this time Henry A. Wallace was editor of *Wallaces' Farmer*. One day in talking to a retired Norwegian fanner named Frank Falkenson, the latter said a man might bring in two hundred bushels of corn in a day but it would be slip-shucking. "Slip-shucking" means taking the big ears and letting the nubbins look after themselves; also not "cleaning" the corn. In other words, going into a field and grabbing the gravy.

After a bit of discussion the two decided to get the biggest liars and see what would happen. Editor Wallace wrote some pieces, the county papers shouldered the idea, and in December, 1922, at Ankeny, Iowa, the corn-huskers got together. Rules had to be laid down. The men were to be penalized for corn left behind; and for ribbons. Ribbons are the husks left on an ear. All agreed to this. Wallace served as a gleaner. A "gleaner" is a person who goes along behind and picks up corn that has been missed. Two other officials were H. D. Hughes of Ames, Iowa, and L. C. Burnett; these two served as weighers.

A shotgun was fired and, bang!, down the rows the champions started. The day was bitterly cold and the ears were covered with ice. The men shucked for an hour; from this could be judged how much they would bring in in a day. The corn was weighed, the penalties imposed—and it was found that, at the rate the men were going, the best man could average, under these conditions, only about ninety bushels a day. (I felt better.)

Instantly ears went up; human that is, not corn. Everywhere people were intrigued. How much corn, under favorable conditions, could be brought in in a day? The two-hundred-bushels-a-day men disappeared in the mist.

The next year the thing was better organized; the idea was to determine who was the best husker in Iowa. An Illinois man heard about it and sent word he could clean any husker in Iowa. The Iowans promptly sent word for him to clean. So the contest became an interstate affair. Again they started. The Illinois man was properly trounced and sent back where he belonged.

The idea of a shucking contest was tremendously appealing to all corn producers…but hard on the big huskers; their stories fell like dried corn silk.

The following year (1924) the organizers turned in an even better job. Nebraska had long been called the Cornhusker State, so sent word it had some speed shuckers; they were promptly invited. A new man from Illinois said he had what it takes. Word was sent for him to come and bring it—and the first National Corn Husking Contest was under way. Yes, Iowa won.

The idea took hold. Other states came trooping in, my own in 1926. New rules and regulations were laid down; one was that the contest should last eighty minutes—and what back-breaking, strength-testing, nerve-shattering minutes these are. A speed method had been worked out; I'll set it down in case you wish to use it. It consists of what is known as the "1-2-3"—that is, the three movements it takes to get an ear of corn off the stalk and on its way to the wagon.

1. The left hand flashes out and seizes the butt.

2. The right hand shoots out and, as it passes, rips open the husk. The left hand gives the ear a squeeze, forcing it out of the shuck.

3. The right hand returns, seizes the ear, and hurls it at the wagon.

That's all there is to it—just those three simple movements. Anyone can master them. I wish you luck.

Now and then, although it doesn't often happen, a husker will have two ears of corn in the air at once. And that is working with astonishing, almost incredible speed. But a champion will put fifty ears of corn in a wagon-box in sixty seconds. Another nice trick if you want to try it. Please report results.

In my time, in everyday, non-speed shucking (my kind) we used palm pegs. We speared a shuck and worried it off, like a dog at a bone. Then came along the thumb-peg. Old-timers said it was foolishness and would have nothing to do with it. I was with them. This thumb-peg fastened to the base of the thumb and had a hook on it as sharp as a spur. As it flashed forward it tore open the armament that surrounds an ear of corn; then the ear could be extracted and sent on its journey to the wagon. The thumb-peg was so much faster that it was not long before everybody was using it. The old-timers, who had said it was all foolishness, told how they had believed in it from the start.

We wore Canton flannel mittens. An innovation swept the Corn Belt; this was leather facing for mittens. My world rocked at the speed we were moving. Then came along something that made the leather facing as naught at all; this was a mitten with a separate place for the index finger. But this was not the end; indeed, it was only the beginning, for some genius came along with a corn-shucking glove. What wouldn't people think of next? The glove was such an improvement on the old flannel, leather-faced mitten that it almost made me want to shuck.

Meantime the contests were becoming more and more popular. A system had to be devised to select the men who were to represent the state. This was arrived at by a series of elimination county contests. The county winners competed in the state contests; then the two fastest were sent away to the National. The number of states increased until it was eleven. Pennsylvania is one. But Pennsylvania is not a corn state...(I'm sure going to get letters about that).

I attended only one national; and that was at Marshall. Missouri. It was more like a state fair. That's exactly what I thought of when I came in sight of the tents and exhibits, with planes buzzing overhead. Traffic officers on the highways, and, my gracious, stop-and-go signs. Streets were laid out in this canvas city with names of famous corn: Reid's Yellow

Dent, Golden Dent, Boone County White, Champion White Pearl, St. Charles White, Silver Mine, Early Huron.

It was a three days' fair, for that is the way the thing is arranged. The contests open on Saturday, people come on Sunday, and Monday the champion is crowned. And what a champion he is! Those hands! Steel. And when he is in action they flash so fast you can't follow them. They seize upon an ear, but before you know what is happening the ear is on its way to the throwboard. Each contestant follows, in main, the 1-2-3, but also he has short-cuts and secrets. A film company asked Irvin Bauman to allow it to make slow-motion pictures of his hands at their work, but he refused. No, indeed.

The people visit the exhibits, see the latest models in tractors and steel corn cribs and milking machines. And visit. Very much of this, indeed. You don't have to know a person to speak to him. Not at a husking.

Fashion shows! That, to me, is the most amazing of all. In a tent there is a wooden floor and girls come out and sway across the boards. What next? I think of my father and wonder what would have happened if the old gentleman had lived long enough to go to a corn contest and see a set of girls jiggling up and down a platform with no more on than roasting ears. I'm sure it would have shaken him.

The heroes are the huskers. People follow them about and ask for autographs. Looks funny to see a hand as big as a baseball glove sprawling a signature on a program. But it's what happens.

An item you might not think of is the importance of drinking water. The contestants bring theirs; in other words, a boy from South Dakota husking in Kansas has to have South Dakota water. For if they go upon strange water…well, it isn't advisable. Sometimes men, who have money up, tamper with the drinking water. So 'tis said.

Yes, and pickpockets. Not only that but plainclothesmen who go among the people watching for the light-fingered. We're getting to be real city-like.

The governor fires a warning gun, there is a moment's wait, then the starting gun cracks. The twenty-two men—state champions all—dart forward. They prefer to work bare-waisted; stalks that would jab the gizzard out of an ordinary person, they pay no attention to. They are surrounded by the officials; the number is amazing: weighers, sample weighers, weightmasters, gleaners, deductors.

A crowd moves out with the huskers, watching every movement and wrist-twist. A man drives the tractor which hauls the shucking wagon; behind the husker follow the penalizers…dreadful men. The contestant doesn't have to whoop at his team, as we did in my day, for the tractor driver takes care of that. Suddenly the husker stops and flashes to the wagon where his water jug hangs. He wraps the strap around his wrist, gives the jug an expert flip and gulps down the water. Sweat is upon him. And he loses weight just as a prizefighter does.

Not all the people can get out in the field and stick their noses in front of the thumb-hooks. They don't have to; a corn-husking contest is not a horse race. The head wagon isn't necessarily the winner. However, the people at the contest keep up with what's going on by the walkie-talkie which reports the blows ear-by-ear (not cauliflower).

The finish gun sounds and the contestants stop like ducks at a shooting gallery. But not one soul upon this planet knows who has won. For the wagons have to be taken to the weighing scales and the gleaners and penalizers and general enemies of mankind have to get in their work. Every ear left in the field counts against a contestant; and every shuck left on an ear is there to plague him. A hundred-pound sampling is taken and at last, by merits and demerits and mathematics, the judges arrive at the winner who is rushed to the microphone—the hero of the Corn Belt! But you'll be surprised at how little he wins. One hundred dollars. That's all. And a cup. But really that's not all, for there are prerequisites. He can go out and demonstrate tractors and combines and corn-pickers and motorized go-devils, if he wants to. He can be a judge in a hundred county fairs and plowing contests. And he can "endorse."

(Personal Note: I wrote a piece about contests for *Colliers*, issue of November 6, 1937. A film company saw it and thought corn-shucking would make a good background. Strangely enough I thought so, too. I was asked to concoct a story around a corn contest. The thing appeared on the screen, Twentieth Century-Fox. The studio in Hollywood brought some pale cornstalks and stuck them in the ground; the field where the contest took place was about as big as a calf-lot. Every person in the Corn Belt, who saw the picture, must have been profoundly shocked.)

The Carlsons, of Audubon, Iowa, are the corn-shuckingest family that ever lived. The father was the one to hit on the speed secret—1-2-3. He had him four sons and he started to make champions of them. The things the old corn king did are astonishing. He put up a prize of five dollars for the son who would bring in the most corn in a week. Corn-shucking depends chiefly on the power above the waist, especially in the shoulders and forearms. He fastened poles across the ceiling in the stable part of the barn and made his sons swing along these poles, hanging by their arms, like monkeys in a jungle. It paid out, for he developed two national champions, a tremendous, an astonishing record.

Carl was of a religious turn, indeed wanted to become a preacher. He took his prize money of fifty dollars (the amount at the time) and went to Chicago to attend the Moody Bible Institute. He still sends money to the institute, asking the institute to buy Bibles with it.

Once, after he had won the contest, someone asked him if he had prayed. Carl said, "I did."

When asked what he had said he replied:

"I said, 'God, please help me. But if you can't help me, don't get in there and help any of the others.'"

Odd things happen in the heat of the battle of the bangboards, as witness: in Benton County, Indiana, in 1928, a team of mules was drawing a contest wagon. The mules seemed to think the whole thing was damn foolishness, for they balked. Every second in a national contest counts, so the driver used all his powers of persuasion. But he didn't have enough; the mules calmly stood there, flicking their ears, and doing naught at all to tighten the tugs. The crowd entreated, the poor dumb animals, but they moved only their ears. Finally the mules were unhitched, men applied with their shoulders to the wagon and it was shoved along until a team of horses was brought on the run and shagged into place. In another contest a husker broke his thumb-hook. The timekeeper allowed him two minutes and ten seconds to replace it. The husker made the change within the specified time.

It's easy to think of this—the greatest day in the Corn Belt—as a man's day, but it's a family day and a church day, too. The churches have booths and serve chicken dinners; an all white-meat chicken dinner will set you back sixty cents. But there are booths where you can get a chicken dinner for forty cents; not all white meat, of course, but if you have the feel of the National in you, you won't mind.

I attended one Women's Corn Husking Contest; this was in my own county. It's small "punkins" compared to the Men's National; only one band, and no pickpockets, no white-meat chicken dinners. And they husk for only an hour. I hate to say it but they could shuck more corn than I could. I guess Pa was right; I didn't have it in me. Women are women, even in a corn contest, for two of the women wore high-heeled shoes. I think that made me blink more than anything else, for there, in the soft ground, were heel holes, like rabbit tracks in the snow. One more feminine touch: it is customary for the contestants to ride to the weighing scales on their wagons, sitting on their corn thrones so the world can see. One of the women, as she passed where I was gawking, whipped out a lipstick and calmly proceeded to beautify herself. This part of the world blinked.

How many bushels does a champion peel off? The record is 46.71 bushels and this was established by Irvin Bauman, already mentioned, for Illinois, in 1940. Other men have tossed more corn, but also they've tossed more shucks, so when came the ordeal by weight they lost.

Here's a word or two about the change that mechanical pickers have made in corn gathering. In my day it took a fiend to shuck a hundred bushels; he had to get out early and keep up the good work till the day was no more. But today a plug can go out with a mechanical picker and do his thousand. If somebody had prophesied this to my father, he would have telephoned the authorities a madman was loose.

The contests are rotated. The selection of a place is complicated, for there must be good roads and parking places and all that. A committee doesn't merely go out and look around till it finds a good corn-patch; indeed it takes two years to prepare a field. It has to be plowed and replowed and then—contest year—it has to be fertilized and tended as carefully as a blue baby. Then at last—after endless pains and plans—comes the Great Day.

The foregoing has been on the happy side; now for the sad. There will be no more national corn-husking contests. And for a surprising reason: Man has again gone down in defeat to the Machine. Yes, the mechanical picker. The farm boys today don't know much about corn-shucking, except how to guide a soulless machine. This means more than it appears, for, in order to have a state contest, there must be endless county eliminations.

Finally the state contestants are chosen and sent away to the national. This no longer takes place. No farm boy today is going to bother to get into shape and so ends the national corn-husking contests. I tell you, I hate machines.

ANECDOTE

One of the most phenomenally successful novels ever published in America was written by a preacher in Topeka, Kansas, In His Steps. *It deals with a group of people who try to conduct themselves as Christ would if He came back to earth. It was published as a serial in a religious weekly in Chicago. But the paper neglected to copyright it. Vulture book publishers discovered this and began to issue the story without paying royalties. Later, reputable publishers also began to bring it out; these paid royalties, although they could have dodged this. But for endless editions the Reverend Charles M. Sheldon received no money at all…makes a person a pessimist, or something.*

A Visit to a Farmer's Radio Station

I had never been in a farmer's radio station until I began assembling notes for this book. I don't believe I have ever caught the heartbeat of the corn states better than I did in Station KMA, in Shenandoah, Iowa. It is known as the "Farmer's Radio Station" and it is exactly that. Its whole appeal is to farmers; it hasn't any other interest.

The first thing that surprised me was the amazing number of letters it gets. Indeed, it is third among all the stations in the United States. The two that receive more are WLW, in Cincinnati, and WLS, in Chicago. These stations are 50,000 watts. The Iowa station has 5,000. The station receives on an average, a letter each year from 62 1/2 percent of the homes in its section. That's something for the city stations to think about.

The area it covers is only, as the station estimates it, 250 miles across. But how exceedingly well it does the job. The station was organized in 1925 and has been plopping along ever since. It is owned by the May Broadcasting Company, a sister firm to the Earl E. May Seed Company, and the late Earl May himself was its star. He had broadcast every day since the station gave its first peep. He believed he had broadcast longer, in point of years, than anybody in radio. I asked him if he hadn't ever got sick, or had something happen to him, so he couldn't get to the microphone and he said he had missed four times. He seemed apologetic.

"What do you find to talk about?" I asked in astonishment.

"The weather. Farming. Crops. What I am doing. I tell about the people who have been in to see me and I talk about my Palomino draft mares. There's lots of interest in Palomino draft horses. I discuss the livestock market. I never run short of material. When I go off the air I usually feel I didn't get to say all I wanted to."

I stared, for the few times I have been on the air I could barely think up enough to wiggle through one broadcast.

"I used to go on four times a day," said Mr. May, "but I found that was too much."

I blinked again. "How long is your broadcast?"

"Twelve minutes."

"Do you use notes?" I asked.

"Yes, I use a few notes. It helps tie things together."

I must have gulped here—me who has to rehearse and rehearse before I face a microphone.

He told me about the early days. His station had gone on the air of a morning at eight; it was believed that no farmer would listen before that hour. Then one morning Mr. May had to take an early trip to Omaha. As he drove along he saw the lights come on in the farm houses, some at five. By six nearly every house had a light.

"I thought maybe they would listen, in spite of what everybody said about early-hour radio. We started broadcasting to farmers at six. That is now one of the most popular hours in the whole day. If I hadn't taken that early morning trip to Omaha we might not have discovered that for some time."

"What is the most unusual thing you ever sold over the air?" I asked. He thought for a moment. "One day a friend I had known in Wyoming came in for a chin about old range days. I asked him what he was doing and it developed he had brought a car of wild horses to Omaha. But the horses hadn't sold once farmers had bought wild horses and had broken them to work. But they were no longer doing this—it was easier to run a tractor. My friend was down in the mouth. His wild horses were still in the stockyards in Omaha eating their heads off. I said, 'I'll see what I can do, Tom.' I sold them. I think that's the most unusual sale I ever made."

"To whom did you sell them?" I asked.

"I sold them to a firm in Rockford, Illinois. They turned them into soap."

And there, indeed, I caught a little of what goes on in a radio station in the Corn Belt. Grim, yes; but such things have to be.

Owen Saddler, of the station, is so saturated with the point of view of farmers that an outside point of view comes to him with a shock. Now and then a coast-to-coast network cuts in the station on a national program (sometimes it's international) "to find what the American farmer is thinking."

"One thing they always want," he said, "is to hear a cow being milked. We go out to a farmer and have him milk a cow with the actual sound effects. It seems pretty foolish to me, but that's what the networks want," said Mr. Saddler sadly.

This is the one station that does not believe in the exaggerated, overemphasized, inferiority-complex-arousing diction so much favored by radio announcers. Listeners want "farmer talk" and it must be genuine; they must feel the announcer knows what he is talking about and is one of them.

Once they hired "an Eastern announcer," whose diction was perfect; indeed, he had won a speech poll. He gave the Corn Belt farmers the finest, the most flawless language ever heard over their station. But one day, in reading the livestock news, he pronounced the word ewes—"e-wees."

"We had to let him go," said Mr. Saddler. "We couldn't have that kind of talk on our station."

Once the station thought it would "get up" a Farmers' Jubilee; it had in mind a small affair at which a few hundred farmers might drive in to town to spend the day. The response was instantaneous, in fact, grew so big the station had to get the governor to promise to speak; "the day" grew into a four-day affair. The biggest crowd in history poured into town, so many people the restaurants ran out of food. There were hog-calling contests, horseshoe-pitching contests, and milking contests.

"The most interest was in an event we hadn't given any special notice to when we had planned it," said Mr. Saddler, reminiscently. "It was a pancake-eating contest. It created much more interest than the governor. The winner ate twenty cakes in ten minutes! We then tried to put him on the air, but all he could do was to puff. You can never tell what is going to interest farmers."

I asked him what was the most important subject broadcast by the station. "The weather, he said. When they had first started they had put the weather on the air only once a day. Letters soon showed the almost overwhelming interest in weather; and so now the weather goes on the astonishing number of eleven times a day. It is really more complicated than that, for the station gets the Associated Press and the United Press weather reports and also those from its own United States Cooperative Weather station. "We are able to tell the farmers about forty-eight hours in advance what to expect. We never dreamed of that when we started. I guess the weather reports are the biggest thing we've got. We figure we save several lives a year by warning farmers where bridges are out. In winter we keep a good many cars from going off the road, by telling the farmers where the sleet areas are and which hills to watch. Storm warnings! That's where we shine. During storms we send out warnings once an hour; sometimes we interrupt programs to give the latest. More depends on the weather than you'd think; the farmer has a load of feeders he wants to market. So he watches the weather. He doesn't want his steers to go to market on a rainy day, so he listens to our weather and if things appear to be favorable, he calls the truckers and off the steers go. That one decision may mean the difference between profit and loss on his farm that year, so no wonder he wants to know all he can about the weather."

Stock markets next! What hogs and cattle are selling for. And corn. Always corn—field corn, shell corn, cob corn, soft corn, seed corn. But no shock corn, for that doesn't figure in the Corn Belt. Too inconsequential.

Here's what the farmers want:

1. Weather.
2. News.
3. Hillbilly music.
4. Religious music.

The contrast between the latter two is surprising, but that's what checking has shown. Another surprise is that dance music comes tenth and classical music sixteenth, something that city radio stations might keep in mind when they want to catch the ear of the Corn Belt.

The great difference between a metropolitan station and a farm station is that the farmer uses his station to help him make a living. This comes out in the letters the farmers write. I copied down some of them and, there it is!—this daily living problem:

From Kirkman, Iowa: "You recommend Butternut Flour and I want to tell you what it done for me. I had my wife make a plaster of it and put it on my back. In no time I was feeling better. I think it must be the vitamins and minerals in it. I am going to keep it on hand all the time now."

From Mound City, Missouri: "My husband was all run down and not much good for anything. I thought I might lose him and would have to look for another. I decided to try some of the vitamins you suggested. I fed them to him and shortly he began to improve. I want to thank you sincerely for keeping us together."

From Greenfield, Iowa: "Your plastic apron came today, but it is much too small. The waist hits me across the bust which is too high. I dislike to return anything, but I think I'll have to this time. Maybe you can send the apron to somebody built different."

From Sleepy Eye, Minnesota: "Our battery went dead and I am behind on things. I did not even know the Miller sisters had left your station, but I find on inquiry everybody else has known it for weeks. I am not going to be caught with a weak battery again. It makes me feel foolish when I go out socially."

Humorous—yes, but also, to me, they are infinitely moving, for I know how tremendously important such matters are to farm people. Since I copied this last letter I cannot get out of my mind this woman who was ashamed to go among her friends because she didn't know what everybody else knew. In my own world I've had the same experience, for sometimes I have gone where everybody else seemed so up to date and worldly wise that I felt ashamed of myself and became sensitive and tangle-tongued.

Another reason their radio station plays such an important part in the lives of the listeners is the "on-the-spot" broadcasts and interviews. The interviewer has a "wire recorder," sometimes a direct wire, and goes to the field where a farmer is working and asks him about his crops, when he plans to sell, and about any new twist in his farming operations. Other farmers listen eagerly, for they can learn. And sometimes there's a bit of comedy. Merrill Langfitt, the interviewer, told me that from the first of January to the middle of May he had interviewed 192 farmers—in their fields, barns, and homes. Once he ran into something he wasn't expecting. He was interviewing Colonel Chillcote, a dairy breeder at Bedford, Iowa, on the subject of Jerseys. The interviewer said:

"Colonel, what is the best calf show you ever saw?"

Farmer Chillcote gave it due consideration, seemingly anxious to be exact, then said:

"I guess it was at the State Fair once. A severe rainstorm swept down on the fair grounds—water covered the whole area—in fact, the water got up to the ladies' knees which made them lift their dresses exceedingly high. I think, everything considered, that was the best calf show I ever saw."

Subjects come up that city people know nothing about. At least, I don't suppose they do. One day Mr. Langfitt was interviewing Tom Surplus, at Maryville, Missouri. (Oh boy!) Tom is an artificial inseminator. During the course of the interview, Mr. Langfitt asked casually, "Do you have any nickname, or name which is a favorite in your community?" There was an awkward, embarrassing silence. Finally the interviewer asked it again, never realizing that lightning was going to strike.

"Yeah, I got one," said Tom, tremendously ill at ease. It's…Ferdinand."

That may not mean much to city people, but it means something in this section. Tom has never heard the end of it…nor the station, either, for that matter.

The station has a theater from which it broadcasts; admission is free. Farm families drop in, mothers hold sleeping children on their laps. Sometimes they open up boxes and eat home-packed lunches. The families stay a while, then go out and drive home, talking on the way about the good time they've had. On one occasion, according to Mr. Saddler, a comedian on the stage said he was hungry; a woman in the audience promptly got up, went around to the side, and handed him a piece of chicken. Of course, she really knew he wasn't hungry, but the audience feels at home with the entertainers and call them by their first names as if they were old friends. And indeed they are.

The "performers," as they are called, are content with their jobs; Leanna Driftmier has been on six times a week for twenty-one years; "Kitchen Klatter" is her broadcast. Others have been on ten years, some more. No one knows them outside their territory, but thousands upon thousands inside it know them and love them. They have no ambition to go to a larger station. "We like it here," they say. "We feel we do some good." And they do, I'm sure of that.

I visited the nurseries, seed sheds, and storing quarters; and the over-the-counter salesrooms, too, watching the men buy. For the most part the men were in blue coveralls and the women in chick dresses. In this section a chick dress is one a woman has made from a chicken-feed bag; sometimes, however, it's calf-feed, but chiefly it's chicken. It's not quite as primitive as it sounds, for the sacks are of good material, the advertising is printed in an ink that washes off indeed, a farm woman is proud to have a "chick dress" she herself has made.

At last the day was over, time to go. As I was leaving, a farm family came out of the theater; the father was carrying one child in his arms and leading another. The mother dangled a bag. They started down the street in what must have been the direction of their car, walking and talking happily. It had been a fine, wonderful day.

FOR LINCOLN FANS

Do you remember the story about Abraham Lincoln walking six miles to borrow a book, then six miles back? He was told about the book by his teacher Mentor Graham. Suddenly Mentor Graham disappeared; no one knew where he had gone. Nor today is it known exactly why. But he did leave, disappearing completely. He went, I found, to Blunt, South Dakota, a tremendous journey for those days. Even there he was still a teacher; he used to carry a book around with him and stop boys and teach them, so deep was his love of learning. One day the teacher—now an old man—started down the street with a book in his hand. Suddenly he was seen to be in distress; in a moment he staggered and fell. When they arrived, spilled on the ground beside him was the book he had been carrying. I would like to say it was a book he had used to teach Lincoln, but this has not been established. No one, at least very few, knew that he had been Lincoln's beloved teacher. The local paper did not seem to know it, for it had an obituary of only a few lines, with the casual heading, "An Aged Person Gone." The house where the old teacher had lived became deserted and the haven of hobos. I saw it in this condition...I'm glad to report that the house has now been acquired by the South Dakota Historical Society and will be kept as a public monument.

Fallacies About the Corn Belt

One of the strongest and most persistent fallacies about the Corn Belt is plowing a straight row. It is a singing expression, poets have soared on it, but, alas, there is no special virtue in plowing a straight row; it washes. Indeed, contour farming is exactly opposed to straight-row plowing. If a county agent today came along and saw a farmer plowing a gun-barrel row, he would crawl through the fence and talk to him.

It looks nice, but that's about the only purpose it serves. What is vastly more important is to set a straight fence. That takes skill and is admired by every farmer in the township. When a farmer sees a fine, straight fence going over hills and hollows and swales, he knows that the one who put it there was an exceedingly able man. I have seen my father hop out of the hack, go to a new fence, and sight along it to see if it were straight. If it was he would say with tremendous admiration, "That's a fine fence—true as a gun-barrel." If he saw a straight row he would probably have said. "He's spent a lot of time trying to run a straight row that would have been better spent coverin' weeds."

Another favorite is tall corn. I shudder to think about the thousands who have sung the glories of tall corn. It's mighty pretty, but no farmer in his right mind would want tall corn; strength all goes to the stalk instead of to the ear. And the ear is about fifty times more valuable than the stalk. Indeed, the hybrid experiments are chiefly bent upon producing short corn.

The tallest corn on record was grown by Lawrence Flander, Harper, Iowa. It was 23 feet and 2 1/2 inches tall and was exhibited as a sort of freak, as a circus would exhibit a giant. No farmer would want to plant it; it would draw the strength from the soil and would not be worth anything to him. Yes, go on singing (if you must) about the glories of tall corn, but, in the back of your mind, know that it's because you're out with the boys.

There are no red school houses. There may be back in New England, but not out where the short corn grows. I never remember, in all my life, seeing a red school house in the corn states. They're all white. (Now I'll wager I get a bunch of letters calling me an ill-informed dolt, but I can't help it; that's been my experience.)

There are, as I write, six thousand one-room schools in Iowa (my sampling state), but they're being done away with at the rate of about six hundred a year. Buses now whisk the children away to town, or to consolidated schools. Not a red one among them.

No barn dances. That's a favorite; I don't know what radio would do without it. But, as a matter of fact, there hasn't been a barn dance in the Corn Belt in fifty years. Indeed, there never were, to any appreciable extent, barn dances. They're an Eastern institution; there the barns are huge, with wide floors where people could really fling around. But in the Corn Belt, lumber was scarce; farmers were too poor to put up a barn with a middle section with mammoth drive-in doors. As a result, barn dances were almost unheard of. If the neighbors had come in and got out on that middle floor and had begun to skyhoot around, they would have scared the living daylights out of every cow and horse on the place. No, no barn dances. The next time you hear 'em yipping away on the radio, just realize this is an easy way for city people to earn a living. Turn off the radio and pick up a good book. (Suggestions for good books sent cheerfully.)

No husking bees, either. That's New England. I never even saw one in my life; my father and mother (who were from Ohio) used to talk about them, but they never went to one after they came to the Corn Country. Corn-shucking was too big and too elaborate a job to be pulled off in a barn. The bins were filled with scooped-in corn, not by the dribbles a few neighbors could produce in an evening. And no red ear. That meant poor farming. Indeed there were few red ears on a corn farm; if a boy had to wait till he found one before he could kiss a girl, he would have had to be wheeled up.

There's no "Giddy-up." This is a small matter, but it always riles me. This is what a farmer is supposed to say to a horse. I've seen it in countless stories and heard it in endless movies, but there's not a word of truth to it. When a Corn Belter wants to start his horse, he says, "Get up!" That's all there is to it. Very simple; anyone can learn it.

No piglets, either. Every now and then you read a story in which an honest, hard-working farmer comes to his wife and says, "Honey, we now have some piglets." No farmer ever said that; if he did, his wife would know she had a mental case on her hands. Pigs is pigs and that's all there is to it. Sometimes the children in a family will call 'em "piggies"; but they soon outgrow it.

Sometimes, in a movie, a farmer will say to his wife, "Mary, come with me out to the piggery." That's where I usually get up and walk out. He would in reality say, "Mary, come out to the pigpen with me." She would go with him confidently knowing he was all right in every way.

Another widespread movie belief is that farmers go around saying, "I'll swan." Sometimes it's, "I'll vum." It's interesting to watch farmers when they hear these expressions; usually it takes a few moments for them to figure out what is meant.

ASTONISH DINNER GUESTS WITH THIS BIT OF INFORMATION

The most important spot in the United States is in a former cornfield, in Kansas. Its no larger than a pinpoint and is engraved on a cross-mark on a bronze tablet. It is used as a survey center by the United States, Canada, and Mexico. What Greenwich is to the longitude of the world, this tiny speck is to the lines and boundaries of the North American continent. It's called the "Geodetic Center." But don't get it mixed up with the "Geographic Center." If you do, you're sunk.

Traits and Characteristics of the People of the Midwest

I think I would list first the Midwest's great *friendliness*. No doubt this comes from when the pioneer was glad to see anyone and to pass the time of day with him. And the Corn Belter is still that way; he wants to get acquainted with the new person who has moved into the neighborhood and promptly goes over and calls on him. *If there's anything I can do for you, you just let me know,* he says and means it. In no time at all the new arrival is part of the community. It always astonishes people from the Corn Belt that a New Yorker may not know his next-door neighbor and yet may have lived for years within a few feet of him.

On buses, at sales pavilions, and in tourist camps midwesterners immediately proceed to get acquainted. One of them holds out his hand and says heartily, "My name is Wilson and I'm in the real estate and abstract business."

The other seizes his hand and gives his name and business and soon the two are chatting away like twins.

Neighborliness. This, in a way, is an extension of the same quality. The people "neighbor" back and forth, help each other, sit up with each others' children, borrow from one another. A man will lend his car and not give it a thought; he knows his neighbor would do the same for him. In small towns the kitchen door is usually unlocked; a neighbor will walk in and borrow something, if the other family happens to be away; usually he will leave a note, or, when the other returns, immediately call up and tell him what he's done. I never heard of anyone taking exception.

They take more interest in politics. Residents of the great cities sometimes don't even know who their congressman is. In the Midwest this could hardly be possible; sometimes they have grown up with their political leader, or know him personally, or members of his family, or have friends who know him. His background and his actions are always before them; it's harder for a Midwest politician to get away with something than it is for a city politician; he's always under scrutiny. And this, it seems to me, is exactly as it should be.

Neighborhood opinion has more influence. Here the people live as units and the actions and deeds of everybody are known; a man hesitates when he realizes that he may have the whole community down on him. This serves to keep him from getting tangled up romantically and it makes him pay his debts more promptly and to pass up temptations that a city man wouldn't lose any time succumbing to.

A Midwesterner hardly ever pretends to be more than he is. In truth he usually is better off and financially more important than he appears. The reason may be that he knows he can be checked up; somebody'll come along who knows him. He has a kind of simple humbleness not to be found in the cities. I can't imagine a man from the Midwest pretending he is richer than he is, or that he occupies a more important place in the community than he does. A midwesterner is much more what he seems to be than a city man.

The Midwest is particularly free from the strange cults and weird beliefs that inflict Southern California. I suppose the reason is that the people of the Corn Belt are workers and are not semi-retired with time on their hands to develop crotchets. Indeed, the people from the Midwest are particularly sane; they may not always be right, but they hit a pretty high level.

The people are more truly religious than city dwellers. I don't know why this is, but no one going from country to city can doubt it. It may be because the beliefs of the people are simple; whatever may be the cause, faith in religion is an outstanding characteristic of the Corn Belt.

There is less "trying to keep up with the Joneses." Farmers do not compete with each other; nor do the people in the small towns, for they have known each other most of their lives; they do not have to depend on show to make an impression. The people are not pitted against each other as much as they are against the weather, crops, and natural conditions.

There is not so much fear of losing a job. One reason, I think, is that more people work for themselves; and a person and his background are pretty well known before he joins an organization. His next-door neighbor may be his employer; often the two meet socially. There is more "heart" in employment. Also a person who loses his job is not so distraught, for people in this section do not live on as narrow a financial margin. The fact that he has lost his job is not so completely overwhelming; indeed he may take a "trip," or go to visit kinfolks, before he casts around for another place for himself. In other words, he's not as near the financial edge as a city worker.

There is less suggestive storytelling than in the cities. This is true of men when they're alone; and it's true when there's a mixed group having a good time.

The people are more courteous. They have more natural, effortless courtesy. They do as they wish to be done by and that settles it. One reason may be that they may see the person again, may have the pleasure of meeting him. There is not the go-to-hell attitude of the cities.

Less communism. A reason, I think, is that the Midwest is the land of the small business man and of the man who owns his own home and who has a stake in affairs. Not so many people on the payrolls of huge industries who, when hard times come, are easy prey to hasty ideas.

A man is more sensitive to what "people think." He has known them most of his life, he expects to continue to live among them and wants them to have a good opinion of him; so he is less apt to indulge in strange fancies than the city dweller who probably privately scorns his neighbors, anyway.

The people belong to many clubs. They like to be friendly and to "engage in fellowship." They have all sorts of clubs—but not crackpot—which do a great good in the community. The number of children these clubs help educate is astonishing. Indeed there are few wholly sociable clubs; most of them do something to help somebody, or some worthwhile project.

Every farm boy is a natural mechanic. All his life he has been around machinery; he has earned his living with it; he knows what ails it and, what's more, in a crisis can repair it when a city man would be as useless and out-of-place as a whipsocket in a jeep.

Family life is more closely knit than in the cities. The reason seems to be simple: in a city the members of the family pile off to work early of a morning, get back late, see little of each other, and have many outside interests. In the Midwest they eat more meals together, come into closer relationship, and mean more to each other.

Fewer nervous breakdowns. The reason would appear to be that the people live under less strain than they do in the metropolitan centers;

there is not so much financial worry, for the people (as I've mentioned) are more secure in their future.

Clerks and sales people are more polite. Again I suppose the reason is that they may expect to see you again; you are not a nonentity. The time they will give you and the pains they will take to serve you is quite extraordinary. And this holds true for bus and taxi drivers. Especially is this true with the men who drive the inter-town, farm-to-city buses.

Children are better controlled. The reason, seemingly, is that the family exerts more influence on children than it does in the city.

These, it seems to me, are the outstanding traits of the Midwest.

MORE UTTERLY USELESS INFORMATION—READ AND FORGET

A stalk of corn has been known to grow eight inches in twenty-four hours.

The only bullfight ever held in the United States was in Dodge City, Kansas. Yes, when "Dodge" was wild.

Hogs root up pastures to get vitamins. In my day I thought it was pure cussedness.

It has always been said that there were a million acres in the Bad Lands. I questioned this and wrote to the Department of the Interior, Bureau of Land Management, Washington, D.C., and found the exact number to be 620,000. Quite a saving.

One-fourth of all the first-class farm land in the United States is in Iowa. Ask any Iowan. In fact, you don't have to ask.

Team-pulling contests at state and county fairs are extremely popular…in spite of the alleged passing of the horse. A machine measures exactly how much each team pulls and makes the amount visible to the audience. The machine is called a "Dynamometer." It saves arguments.

Ten Outstanding Men (and Women) of the Corn Belt

It seems to me these ten men best embody the traits and characteristics of the Corn Belt. Some of them still live there; all of them have either been born there, or have lived there during their formative years and who still represent the thought and the spirit of the section.

HARRY S TRUMAN. He made a living off a Missouri farm for eleven years and when you do that you come pretty close to the realities of life; still owns farm land in the state. His speech and his thoughts are true of the section. Wherever he goes, there goes a little of the soil of the Corn Belt.

HENRY A. WALLACE. Born of the third generation of Wallaces in Iowa. Early years spent as editor of *Wallaces' Farmer*. Was important in developing hybrid seed corn; indeed he has an interest in a seed-corn farm now in his home state. Has always been a storm center; yet in person is mild, almost bland.

GARDNER COWLES (pronounced *Coles*). He was born in Iowa of a second-generation Iowa family (one lap behind Henry A. Wallace) and followed his father's career as publisher. Is now publisher of *The Des Moines Register* and *Tribune* and of *Look* Magazine. (*Humor Note*: Had, in the basement of his home in Des Moines, the petrified body of the original "Cardiff Giant;" liked to show it to guests after cocktails.)

JAY N. DARLING (known as "Ding"). Has spent most of his life in Iowa, yet is an outstanding national political cartoonist. Still lives in Iowa, wouldn't live anywhere else, he says. If you want to know the Midwest, follow his cartoons (now widely syndicated).

WILLIAM M. JEFFERS. Born in North Platte, Nebraska, and has been associated with Nebraska most of his life. Left school at the end of the ninth grade and started as call boy and messenger for the Union Pacific Railroad; rose to presidency. Originator of the Challenger trains. During Second World War was Rubber Director.

THOMAS HART BENTON. He was born in a small town in Missouri; grand-nephew of Thomas Hart Benton who was Missouri's first senator. His own father was a congressman. Young Benton once deserted the Midwest and went to Paris to learn to paint like a Parisian. He got nowhere at all; came back, disgusted, and began to paint the Corn Belt. Had immediate success.

OMAR NELSON BRADLEY. He was born on a farm in Missouri, strangely enough only fifty-five miles from where General Pershing was born. He lived in his younger days at Moberly, Missouri; married his high-school classmate. Until recently had a home there. The airfield in Moberly is named in his honor. He, more than any other general in the Second World War, represented the thinking of the Midwest.

J. C. PENNEY. Lived all his early days on a farm near Hamilton, Missouri (still owns the farm). He did not start his first chain store in the Midwest, but in Kemmerer, Wyoming. Has done much humanitarian work.

ROY A. ROBERTS. Is president of the powerful Kansas City *Star*. Has been a newspaper man all his life. Is a director of the Associated Press and former president of the American Society of Newspaper Editors, and of the famous Gridiron Club, in Washington, D.C. Born in Kansas. Rotund, alert.

PHIL STONG. Is the section's literary spokesman. Born at Keosauqua, Iowa. Worked as newspaper man in the state; wrote editorials for *The Des Moines Register*. His best-known story is *State Fair*. Now lives in Washington, Connecticut, but keeps in touch with home.

I have eliminated from the list former president Herbert C. Hoover, as it does not seem to me he represents the section; he was born in Iowa, but left when he was twelve and rarely comes back. He was more influenced by California and by his mining work in foreign countries than by the Midwest.

Glenn L. Martin was born in Iowa, but at the age of two moved to western hardpan Kansas. Soon young Martin went to California where all Midwest influence was wrung out of him, like rinsing water from a shirt.

Four military men (in addition to General Bradley) have come from the section: Generals Pershing and Harbord of the First World War. General Dwight D. Eisenhower was born in Texas; lived briefly at Abilene, Kansas. All left early and had little to do with the section. The following are typical of this mid-section, but they are dead:

William Allen White. No other person, to my way of thinking, was so typically Midwest.

Walter P. Chrysler was Kansas-born, but represented Detroit better than he did the Midwest.

Dr. Arthur E. Hertzler, founder of the Halstead Hospital, Halstead, Kansas, and author of *The Horse and Buggy Doctor*. He himself gave it the title of *Forty Years a Country Doctor*, but the publishers (always wise men) changed it.

John Steuart Curry was born on a farm near Dunavent, Kansas, and became the state's greatest painter. Always a storm center himself, he liked to paint storms and cyclones.

George Washington Carver, famous Negro educator and agricultural chemist, was born near Diamond, Missouri. Famous for his experimental work with peanuts. Was once kidnapped and traded for a racehorse.

Grant Wood was born in Iowa and became its greatest painter. Two of his famous paintings are *American Gothic* and *Dinner for Threshers*.

Amelia Earhart was born in Atchison, Kansas; the house still stands. Became America's first famous woman flyer; was lost in the Pacific.

Ida B. Wise Smith did more than any other woman to put over Prohibition in America. She came to Hamburg, Iowa, at the age of two. Became president of the Iowa Woman's Christian Temperance Union and later vice-president of the national organization. Her greatest accomplishment: got Congress to appropriate ten thousand dollars toward paying the expenses of a world W. C. T. U. convention in Washington, D.C. The boys in the back room still talk about it. Has moved (as I write) to California.

Brief mention of other Corn Belt women: Amelia Jenks Bloomer (yes, the Bloomer Girl); Carry A. Nation, the Hatchet Woman. She made Kansas famous but is buried in Missouri. Sally Rand made Missouri famous without a hatchet or a pair of bloomers—almost without anything, I'm told.

Famous as a radio personality: Mary Margaret McBride. Was born in the Corn Belt, still has its point of view. The list is not complete; I've stayed away from movie personalities and politicians (except the ones set down) for they come and go... especially the latter. But I think the list is pretty representative; at least it gives a glimpse of some of the outstanding personalities of the section, past and present.

Small-town Possibilities

Many persons living in small towns become discouraged because, seemingly, there is so little to write about.[2] Everywhere, except in their hometown, the world seems to be teeming with life, but life as they find it drags a heavy foot. As a result they grow discouraged and think there is nothing within the radius of their observation that will bring them a literary penny.

And then, as a strange contrast, I, who have lived in New York, find writing friends complaining that the city is written out and wishing they were in small towns where life is fresh and the literary plums unpicked. It is the old, old story of the young man starting out to find the four-leaf clover and coming back an old man to find it at his own doorstep.

I have tried both; I have lived on a bleak and barren farm, and I have lived in literary Bohemia, and in my opinion it makes little difference where one's tent is pitched. The important thing is to have eyes.

Bigger than a diploma, bigger than travel, is that quality of the human mind which makes one interested in life and living. There is little hope for one who, of a morning, gets up with a sigh. The literary man's greatest asset is to get up each day as if on the edge of an adventure. To be interested in why a baby grips the bars of its crib with its toes, why a person turns in his thumb when he is unconsciously cold, why a person going into a restaurant naturally seeks a table against a wall, why the wheels of an automobile in a motion picture sometimes seem to be going backward are the rock and foundation on which a literary career is founded. If the writer's mind is eager, ever sifting life's little wonders, then the writer has what is more desirable from a literary point of view than a college education or a trunk with many strange stickers on it—they have the thrill of living in them.

---

2 From *88 Ways to Make Money By Writing* (The Editor Company, 1918); 55-58. "I" has been inserted in the second and third paragraph and subject-verb agreement made. In keeping with standard usage, the few instances where Croy uses outmoded and unwieldy references to himself such as "the author of this volume," or the "present author" have been excised in favor of the personal pronoun. The last sentence of this truncated piece appears appended from the final sentence in the original chapter, concluding on page 66.

The most remarkable literary man I know is a small-town man. He lives in and always will live in a small town. He was born miles from a railroad and at seventeen walked twelve miles to his first circus. He is not of the blasé type that loves to loll in Bohemian restaurants; instead, life to him is a constant adventure. He can get as excited over a blacksmith shoeing a horse as a literary dilettante over a subway explosion. Every time he does a new thing, or goes to a new place, or meets a new person, or reads a new book he is excited over it, as eager over it as a boy with his first air rifle.

He was the editor of a small paper in Marceline, Missouri, which was slowly dying in his hands, and there is nothing in the world quite so lifeless as a country paper in a comatose condition. During the day he fled with the local merchants to take advertising space in his weekly estate, while at night he composed stories and articles that he hoped would be welcomed by the editors of the far away metropolitan magazines; but rarely were his hopes justified. His quantity of outgoing mail was almost identically proportionate to the quality of his incoming mail.

He was promised a full-page advertisement by a local vegetable Croesus if he would get it in the next week's issue. Joyfully, he rushed to the case and helped the foreman set up the copy to catch the weekly edition, but as he was transforming it to the imposing stone he dropped the form, pieing the type. He went home, determined that he would sell the paper, even if he had to give it away, and so told his wife.

"What will you do for a living?" she asked.

"Write," he answered.

His wife, mindful of what his literary efforts had been bringing in, went to bed in tears, but in spite of her fears and protestations the paper was sold, sold being used technically rather than literally.

Stories, articles, descriptions he wrote, the greater part of his checks coming from David C. Cook Publishing Company, Elgin, Illinois, which remunerates at the rate of a quarter of a cent a word. In telling "How to Get a Choir to Practice on Time," or "How We Paid Our Pastor's Salary With a Pumpkin Sale," he made the words go as far as he thought consistent with the policy of the publications, always remembering that the current rate for adjectives was a quarter of a cent each. But even though depending on Elgin for his bread and butter, he kept hope and looked ahead. He was not content to get the choir out on time; he wanted to write fiction. After the grocer had been appeased he would give himself over to a literary effort of the first magnitude. It usually came back, but the next time he tried only the harder. He began climbing the ladder until one glorious day he opened an envelope and heaven was in it. It was an acceptance from *The Century*.

You may now see his name in *The Saturday Evening Post* almost any month. It was William H. Hamby.

As I study why Mr. Hamby has succeeded, two features stand out prominently—his ability to keep on and his great zest for living. To him nothing is prosaic. If he were confined in Robert Bruce's cave, he would come out a wiser man and in few weeks would be selling essays on spiders. This great interest he takes in everything he is able to impart to his work; to make others feel it.

Just what corner of the world the writer is living in makes little difference. A great part of the success of a writer is his ability to snatch up the broken sword—the hilt that someone else has thrown away and often is at one's feet.

The Perambulating Preacher of the Ozarks

The boy and the girl were not self-conscious about getting married, for their clothes were fresh and clean. The boy's overalls had been washed, his mother had made his chambray shirt for this special occasion, and his shoes had been blacked until they were as black as a crow's wing.[3] No coat, no tie. But it was all right. Summertime.

The girl looked even better than the boy, which is proper, for her dress had been made out of the Missouri Farmer's Association feed sacks, and printed here and there was MFA. She had chosen the sacks with the prettiest patterns she could find, and had scissored the dress herself. She had sent to Chicago for her shoes, so they looked nice, too.

But now the boy did look embarrassed, and lead the Perambulatin' Preacher of the Ozarks to one side so they could have a man-to-man talk. "I ain't got much money, but I want to do the best I can by you." An awkward pause.

"I don't make any charge for marrying people."

"I'm figgerin' to pay you anyway, because it's worth it." He looked at his bride proudly. "Out of our fall killin' I'll be givin' you a ham."

And so they were married by the Reverend Guy Howard, Schell City, Missouri, who has been marryin' and preachin' in the Ozarks for 10 years, come spring. The biggest sum he's ever received was from a hill Rockefeller who paid him $3. The smallest 50 cents. The most unusual, the ham.

He's the most famous—and the most helpful—man in the Ozarks. And the most loved, too. The hill people call him "Brother" Howard. Here's an odd thing: the Ozarks are mountains, but down here in the thick of 'em they're hills, and the people who live in them are "hill" people.*

[You should] see the people gathered beside a creek, waitin' for him to heave into sight. There he comes swinging down the trail, his hat off, a Bible under his arm, glory in his face!

---

3 From *Everyweek Magazine*, November 8, 1942. Occasional areas of illegibility in the microfilm of this rare article available from the Library of Congress are herein marked with an asterisk. Transcription resumes with the first legible sentence after incompletion.

Sometimes he has two or three Bibles under his arm. That's because he gives away about 100 Bibles a year. But the recipient must promise to read a verse a day for a month.

Funerals are hardest. He washes the bodies, dresses them, then helps carpenter a coffin. And for this, in all of his 10 years, he has never asked for a penny. "When you know these people you want to do things for them," he says.

Boys are boys and girls are girls. One night, close to midnight, there was a timid rapping and Brother Howard went to the door of his cabin and there stood a frightened young girl. He dressed and hoofed it across the ridge and got the boy out of bed, and when the license office in the county seat opened the next morning he had them both there. No ham this time.*

The things Brother Howard does are quite breathtaking. For instance, he walks on an average of 4,000 miles a year preaching to the hill people. He wears out six pairs of shoes a year. Sometimes he will walk 40 miles in a day. "That's the best I can do," he told me apologetically. "I'm slowing down." I didn't tell him the best I can do.

The churches he preaches in are churches that have been abandoned. The hill people know about the time he is due for preachin' and they come down out of the mountains and he lifts them to the heights. Just good old-fashioned religion. That's what he preaches and they like it.

It's no passing fancy, either, for he's been preaching among the hill people for 10 years, and expects to die with his walkin' shoes on. And for that 10 years he's averaged exactly $14.30 a month. "That's not much money, but it's a lot of satisfaction."

He never asks for money and never takes up a collection, but the people stand outside and put money into his hand after everything's over. That's where the $14.30 came from. Then one of them invites him home to a squirrel dinner. Squirrel tastes good after you've knocked off 40 miles.

In addition to his preachin' and perambulatin', he conducts funerals and baptizings. He does a big business in parolees. He has on an average of from 6 to 20 men and boys paroled in his care at one time. When a new one is turned over to him, he has a talk with him and makes him promise to go straight, work every day, go to church every Sunday, and read a chapter every day from the Bible.

It makes some of 'em cuss. But never in all his 10 years, handling things his own way, has he had anyone break parole. They're stronger for him when they finish than when they start, and'll shoot the warts off anybody who says Preacher ain't O.K.

On an average he preaches to 40,000 a year. But has gone to 70,000. And he's done it all on foot. Doesn't own a car to his name. I asked him if he wouldn't like to own one. His answer: "Naturally. Anybody like to have a car."

He is an ordained minister of The Christian Church, but has no creed but Christ, and his love of humanity, and he preaches in any kind of church, to any sort of believer, or non. "I try to follow what Christ meant when He said, 'And Thy Neighbor as Thyself.'"

"I am not on any church's mission payroll. I was once offered $1800 a year if I would join their creed and preach their particular doctrine. I wrote back the same day saying I was satisfied the way I was doing. Never, since I came to the Ozarks, have I had anybody ask me which church I was working for. People want Christ, not creed."

He preaches about God—and that's what he calls Him, not some vague phrase like Our Ever Ready Help—and the problems the hill people have to meet. Biographical note: He was born in Lucas, Iowa, where John L. Lewis hails from; knew the family but didn't know John. L.*

He has never owned a home of his own; his furniture is second-hand. Pays $60 a year rent. "Sometimes it's hard to raise, but I've never missed yet. My dream is to own a four-room log cabin that is absolutely my own, no mortgage. I want to have straight peeled pine logs, stained and varnished. Then I'd like to have an inside of sugar maple. If I could afford it, I would like to have oak floors."

A hard reality he has to meet is getting enough money to live on, since he never asks for a penny. But he has a way of taking care of that. Every fourth year he teaches school. But he has to teach only five days a week, so Friday afternoon he sets off with his walking shoes and his Bibles. Goodness knows how many miles he has streaked off by school bell-time Monday. They hold up their weddings and baptizings for him; even, a little, their funerals. The old mountain mother said, "I wouldn't feel right if I had any of my kin laid away by anybody except Brother Howard."

A spell back, quite a bit of excitement happened in the Ozarks. A long-distance telephone call arrived. Well, the town has no railroad, no telegraph office, and only one phone and that's the post office. And there Brother Howard took the mysterious call.

It was from a broadcasting company wanting him to come to New York and talk over them airwaves.

The people were tremendously excited. Preacher goin' to New York!*

The...boys talked to him and went off over the hills to their cabins and wrote a script, and managed to show it to him only shortly before he was to go on. He read its absurdities and was just plain, two-fisted mad, for it made his hill people long-bearded, ridiculous oafs, inspired, no doubt, by *Esquire's* conception of mountain people, and had them talking a language Preacher simply couldn't understand.

He refused to go on, and the broadcasting company sputtered around and said what they'd do, and he said go ahead and do it but under no consideration would he make monkeys of his mountain people. The upshot of it was that the company told him to stay another week, and that he could write his own broadcast. He did...and it was about as simple and as stirring a thing as you ever heard.

There he is today—this weekend—this Perambulatin' Preacher of the Ozarks. Maybe he's preachin' a funeral right now, or marrying a couple, or sampling his ham, or thinkin' about his cabin with an oak floor.

Jesse James Was My Neighbor

Jesse James was betrayed the year before I was born, but his memory was all around me. We talked of "Jesse"—and that's what we called him—as if he still lived. We never said the "James gang"; it was the "James Boys," or merely "Jesse and Frank." Or sometimes "the Boys." As a lad, I went around screeching at the top of my voice, "It was a dirty little coward that shot Mr. Howard and laid poor Jesse in his grave." And I meant it; it had seemed a ghastly deed.

Frank James, a few jumps away from my home in Maryville, Missouri, lived until 1915. His widow until 1944. Later I want to tell their love story. But it will have to fit in its place.

The stories that floated around us! Sometimes, at night, I could imagine the Boys were still riding. But of course they weren't, for Jesse was in his martyr grave and Frank was a horse starter at country fairs and with a circus.

Now as to some of the stories I grew up with. They happened in the county, one about five miles from our farm. I tell you it made us shiver—delightedly, of course. But late at night when we had to go out and pump up a drink of water just before going to bed...well, the shivers were pretty real, then.

I'll tell the "five-miles-away" one first. To freshen my memories, I went back, when I started this book, and checked up on my childhood. Most of my memories, I found, were correct. But how could a boy forget the big, the exciting, the thrilling deeds of Frank and Jesse?

The Carmichael farm! How many times I had ridden past it and stared like a grasshopper. Old Mr. Archibald Carmichael was living on it, then. But when I went back, he was gone. I had his son, John Carmichael, tell me the story. It was, surprisingly, just about as I had remembered it from his father.

We sat on the back porch and visited. He mentioned first what a good farmer my father was (very pleasing to me), then got down to the story.

"I was just a little sprout, but I don't have no trouble remembering it," said John Carmichael. "About dusk two men rode up, their horses showing evidence of having been pressed. We didn't know it, then, but they were

Frank and Jesse. Even if we had known it, they'd been mighty welcome to food and shelter. They said they were officers of the law, chasing horse thieves. That was perfectly reasonable, for the county was overrun with horse thieves. They asked if my mother could set them a bite. I went out with them while they were rubbing their animals down. I was too young myself to appreciate it, but my father said they were extremely fine specimens of horseflesh."

"We were always glad to have visitors, and, after supper, sat around and visited with the travelers. They were as pleasant men as you'd want to house. They asked about prices hereabouts, how the roads were and where the streams were fordable. My father gave out the information as best he could. This was the year 1871. Roads have changed considerable. You could bear across the country, then, any way you saw fit. Finally bedtime came upon us. My mother was assigning them to beds when the tall one cast a look at the short one and said he thought he'd patrol the yard and let his fellow officer get in what sleep he could; he said the horse thieves might pass and they'd know which way to pursue them the next morning. So we retired to bed, except the tall one I just mentioned. Sometime in the middle of the night, the tall one came to the window and tapped and the two exchanged places. The next morning my mother fixed them a substantial breakfast. After consuming it, the short one asked my father if he cared if he engaged in some pistol practice. Said some of the horse thieves they were pursuing were good shots and that it didn't pay to exchange shots with them unless you were in practice. My father said he could understand that."

"Well, I went out with the stranger to a spot behind our smokehouse and stood beside him while he got ready. There was a shellbark hickory about ninety yards off. Every time he fired, the bark flew. Lots of men with a rifle couldn't given him odds. Finally he put his pistol up, saying, 'It don't pay for an officer of the law to get rusty on his pistol work.' Then he went to the house and offered to pay my mother for their lodgment, but she wouldn't accept anything, so agreeable and entertaining had they been. Finally they rode off, us standing there watching and hating to see them go."

"It wasn't till my father went to Maryville, about two weeks later, that we found our visitors had been Frank and Jesse. We had considerable to talk about that night when Pa returned from the city. But we were glad to shelter them. They didn't ever cause farmers any trouble. Mostly they robbed banks and railroads and express companies that had plenty of money. On the whole we were real pleased we could provide for them for the night. Always when I see or hear about good shooting, I think of Jesse out behind the smokehouse, makin' the shellbark fly."

And that is the story as John Carmichael told it to me in August, 1948, substantially as I had remembered it.

Anecdotes featuring Jesse's persuasive way with shooting machinery are numerous and good, you can be sure they're true. Here's one told to me by Buck Darrell, who lives at 3207 South Seventeenth Street, St. Joseph, Missouri. When I talked with Buck Darrell he was eighty-nine. In the 1870s he had been a traveling gunsmith, going from town to town repairing rifles. He arrived one evening at Pattonsburg, Missouri, and was sitting in the hotel lobby, smoking and reading, when a .22-caliber pistol he was carrying dropped out of his pocket and fell on the floor.

A man seated nearby looked up with interest, then said, "You can't do much damage with that article, can you?"

"I've got one that will make up for it," said the gunsmith, and from a shoulder holster drew out a .45.

The stranger gazed with even more interest. "Do you fancy yourself as a marksman?" he asked.

Buck Darrell, who knew all about guns, said, "I guess I can hold up my end."

The whiskered stranger studied him a moment. "Would you like to do a little shooting?"

"I wouldn't mind."

"Let's take a walk," said the stranger.

When they got outside the town, the stranger took out a long-bladed, sharp-looking hunting knife and held it in his hand a moment. Then he cut a mark in a tree, and the two began to fire at it. Buck Darrell won.

The stranger gazed at Buck with more interest than ever.

"How are you on moving targets?"

"I guess I can hold up my end," said Buck.

"Did you ever see this?" asked the stranger. He proceeded to whittle out a stick about as long as his finger, which he drove into a tree. When he finished this, he cut a piece of string about the same length, pried a bullet out of a cartridge, cut a notch in the bullet, and drove one end of the string into the bullet.

He then tied the free end of the string to the peg in the tree, started the bullet swinging back and forth like a pendulum, and thrust the end of his hunting knife into the tree just at the point where the bullet crossed. The handle of the knife was pointed down, the tip of the blade up and the cutting edge out.

Then the stranger said: "The idea is to hit the bullet as it passes over the edge of the knife. If you do it right, you will cut, or shave, both bullets at one shot. We'll shoot from five paces."

Buck took his position and shot four or five times unsuccessfully.

The stranger stepped up, and on the third try hit the swinging bullet.

Then, with great satisfaction, Jesse James pocketed his gun and the two walked back to town together.

Of course, this was extremely good marksmanship, but at that time all men were marksmen. Some of their skill had come down from the trappers, Indian fighters, and the pioneers. Most of the men in the section had been in the Civil War and were accustomed to guns. Shooting matches were held frequently; in addition, there were turkey shoots at which the prize was a gobbler. A good shot was proud of his ability and he had a right to be, for nearly all men wanted to be marksmen. The Jameses were exceedingly good marksmen; they had always handled rifles and six-shooters and they kept in practice, which, everything considered, was a good idea.

Another childhood story. Just west of us was Quitman, Missouri, where Tom Bond lived. How we hated him! He was one of the Federal soldiers who had swept down on the James farm during the Civil War, and had been one of the men who had helped torture Dr. Reuben Samuels, Jesse's stepfather. It had been a dreadful scene. His stepfather had rope burns on his neck till he died. Jesse was fifteen; he had witnessed the cruel act, and went sobbing to his mother and said, "I'm going to kill every one of them." He didn't, but hate was always in him.

So one day he and Frank stopped in this town looking for Tom Bond. They walked up and down the street looking for him. They waited about two hours, then started on again, and then—plop-plop—in the middle of the road they met Tom Bond driving in a buggy with his wife. After they passed, one of them said, "I believe that's Bond."

Bond heard and knew who they were. He handed the lines to his wife and ran into the timber. Jesse and Frank sat on their horses debating whether to chase him or not; finally they rode on. They came back one other time, but Tom Bond was warned by old William Allbright, who knew the Boys by sight, and escaped. But it was too much for Tom Bond. He might not be so lucky the next time. He left Nodaway County. Only his close kin knew where he had gone.

Another farm we used to drive past—with me staring like a hoot owl—was the Richard Stafford farm, not so far from the Croy farm. A very exciting, yes, a very thrilling thing had happened there.

Washday on a farm! Do you remember the kettle of boiling water out in the yard, and the stove in the kitchen going great guns? And the way your mother used to take a damp cloth and run it along the non-rust metal clothesline to get off the rust? Some way or other it always rusted.

Anyway, on this Blue Monday, shortly before noon, Mrs. Stafford had just finished her washing and was ready to hang it out. She was cross; any woman would be, after doing a farm washing. It was then that two strangers cantered in from the main road and asked if they could feed and water their horses. This was nothing unusual, for men on horseback felt free to ask such a favor. And usually a farmer was glad to have them; company.

Mrs. Stafford didn't want anybody messing up things today. Not on top of a farm washing. But she told them they could water and feed.

In a short time they came up from the barn. "Where's your husband?"

She told him he had gone to town, which, then, was an all-day trip.

"Would it be askin' too much to ask you to cook up a meal for us?"

On washday! It certainly was; and Mrs. Stafford said so, directly and to the point.

"We'd appreciate it," said one, "and we wouldn't try to drive a bargain about the price."

"No," she said firmly, "I've got my washing to hang out." The men looked at the heaping baskets of clothes, then at each other.

"Ma'am, I reckon we could do that," said one of them. "You could spend the time cooking."

"There wouldn't be no quarrel about the price," urged the other.

"Well," said Mrs. Stafford, more agreeably, "all right, I'll do it. I'll run down a chicken."

She started to the chicken yard. One of the men left the clothes and asked her to show him which chicken she wanted. She pointed one out.

"There won't be any running down," he said. Drawing a pistol out of his pocket, he followed the fowl for a moment, then shot its head off.

"You'll have to help pluck it," said Mrs. Stafford.

The man mumbled something about getting more than he'd bargained for, but when she immersed the chicken in scalding water he began to pull off the feathers. The other man—having finished his job—came and watched the process, seeming to enjoy it hugely. "Get all the pinfeathers. You know you want to do a good job for the lady."

The other gave him a sour look, but plucked on.

"Get the little ones there on the wing. It pays to do good work."

At last the job was finished and the two men stretched out on the grass in the yard and rested.

When dinner was ready the two came in, and they ate heartily, according to Mrs. Stafford, who waited on the table.

When the meal was over, one of the men handed her a five-dollar bill—a tremendous sum.

"When your husband gets home, you can tell him you had the pleasure of having Frank and Jesse James for dinner."

Smiling, the two men rode away.

Another I used to gaze on in popeyed wonder was "Red Bob" Wilson. Why, it was almost as good as seeing Jesse! And lest my mind had done me tricks, I went to see him again in my hometown. He is now Robert E. Lee Wilson. But to me he's still Red Bob. And there, at 915 East First Street, you can find him.

He was a newsboy in St. Joseph, Missouri, on That Day. He chose the day to go catfishing in the Missouri River. When he came home that evening his mother said, "It's a pretty time for you to go skylarkin' around. This is the biggest day there ever was to sell papers. Jesse James was killed today!"

Red Bob was a bit flabbergasted, but he wasn't licked. He rushed to the office of the St. Joseph *News* and got a cartload of papers. Jesse was then at the undertaker's and a line of people was waiting to see him. Red Bob went up and down the line selling his papers.

"It was the best day I ever had," he said reminiscently. Then Red Bob went in and saw him himself.

"I wish I could say he had been one of my customers, but I can't. I had never seen him before."

Red Bob was the first person I ever knew who had seen Jesse "strapped to the board." I could shut my eyes and almost see Jesse, myself.

In questioning old friends and sons of the old-timers as to what they knew about the Boys, I came upon a new story, one I had never known before. It has to do with Don Alexander, now the dignified president of the Maryville school board.

One summer, between school terms, he had a job working in the house where Jesse gave up his life. Jesse fell upon the floor and died without speaking. His blood ran out on the floor. It was Don Alexander's duty to sell shavings from the boards to the morbidly curious—the grisly boards with Jesse's lifeblood upon them. Fifteen cents admission was charged, with another fifteen cents for a blood-soaked shaving. But tourists were many and sales problems were many. The owner of the house solved them neatly. Each morning he had Don smear the boards with chicken blood. Today, in America, there must be a hatful of shavings, all smeared with the lifeblood of ill-fated chickens.

Another hometown story new to me, til I began scouting around for this book, comes from Mrs. Stella Rankin, 1021 East Jenkins Street, Maryville, Missouri. Stella Rankin I have known a long time, but not the story. I believe the story is true, for I am not putting in this book any legends or folk tales. Only the truth as nearly as I can determine it. Jesse James has been a hobby with me for a good many years—long, long before I ever dreamed of putting him to paper. During this time I have sieved out a great deal of chaff. I believe what is left is wheat.

Stella Rankin's grandmother was Mrs. John Nanson. She lived in what was called the "Congrave-Jackson" house near Fayette, Missouri. One day Mrs. Nanson was canning peaches with the aid of "Easter," the family's "Mammy." Suddenly three men rode up. Mrs. Nanson recognized them, for they were neighbors and she had seen them before. They were Jesse and Frank and Cole Younger. They were restless and uneasy and showed signs of having ridden fast. They asked Mrs. Nanson if she would have Easter cook dinner in an hour. Easter agreed to try.

The men conferred, then asked Mrs. Nanson if she could suggest a place for them to hide their horses. In the rear was an old cave which some years before had been used as an icehouse. Around it had grown up a thicket of brush. Mrs. Nanson suggested they could use this; the men led their horses to the abandoned icehouse and put them in it, then came to the house. Mammy Easter was busily flinging about. Soon the meal was ready.

But just as the meal was about on the table, there was again the sound of horses outside—this time it was Federal troops. The soldiers were between Frank and Jesse and Cole and their horses.

Mrs. Nanson told the three to go upstairs, where she would hide them between featherbeds. She put Frank and Jesse in one bed, but Cole was so big he couldn't go in with them and had to have a separate bed. In they went, each between featherbeds; soon they were as cooked as the peaches downstairs.

The Federal soldiers came in and asked whom the meal was for. Mrs. Nanson said it was for her father and two neighbors. The Federals were delighted and sat down to a fine, leisurely meal. They complimented her upon her ability—and ate some more. Meanwhile Jesse, Frank, and Cole Younger cooked some more.

The Nanson family had a dog, Jo Shelby, named in honor of the great Confederate general, Jo Shelby. Inadvertently Mammy Easter called him by name.

Instantly one of the soldiers got out of his chair. "Anything with that name ought to die." Ordering the dog outside, he drew his pistol.

Mammy Easter begged for his life, saying she had cooked their dinner and they ought at least to do this for her, so the man relented, sitting down again.

At last the soldiers got up and left. Jesse, Frank, and Cole came downstairs again, dripping like hay hands. They looked at what was left of the sumptuous meal. Mammy Easter gathered up the remains, but they were afraid to be served downstairs. So they sat upstairs, where they could see the road, and nibbled at the leftovers.

Frank James looked up from a chicken neck and said, "If that man had shot Jo Shelby, I would have leaned out the window and shot him." Then he went back to the chicken neck. The others gnawed on in embittered silence.

This was not all. On August 29, 1903, Frank James and Cole Younger came to our town with a circus and had dinner with Mrs. Rankin in the very house where I was hearing this story.

It made the picture doubly vivid.

Oh, the tales I collected, about Frank as well as Jesse. Uel W. Lamkin of California, Missouri, told me the one about Frank James and the young intern. Later, Mr. Lamkin became president of the Northwest Missouri Teachers College in Maryville, but when he heard this story he was a boy in California, where it happened.

John Patrick Burke had grown up in California, become a medical student, been seized by wanderlust, and had gone to Texas where he became an intern. One day Frank James had been brought to him, a victim of typhoid fever. At that time Dr. Burke had not known who the tall, thin, rather hawk-nosed man he nursed safely through the illness was. But Frank was immensely grateful, and when he was ready to go he had identified himself and said, "If there is ever anything I can do for you, you let me know and its performance will be a pleasure."

Later young Dr. Burke returned to his old hometown and set up in practice, but he found it hard to get started. One day, as he was going to his office, he was surprised to see several horsemen moving slowly through the street, then doubly surprised to see that one was Frank James. The Moniteau County National Bank was on the corner, and immediately Dr. Burke put two and two together.

He did not hesitate, but went up to Frank, called him by name, and asked him if he were going to rob the bank. Frank appeared a bit embarrassed, then admitted that was his intention. Whereupon Dr. Burke said that people knew he had met Frank James in Texas, and would think he had served as a spy and had tipped Frank off about the bank, with the result that he would never be able to build up his practice.

Frank considered a moment. "There's something to what you say, Doc. When does the next train leave?"

Frank would not let his men rob the bank, for that would harm a friend. But the train was different.

Another story is Elmer Frazier's. Elmer is now dead, but I have heard him tell it, myself quaking pleasantly meanwhile. Marshall E. Ford of Maryville refreshed my boyhood memory of it. One day Elmer was sitting in Mike Hilgert's saloon watching the men at their pleasures. Mike's saloon had two pool tables. At one of these was playing a character called Omaha Charlie. He was a tough egg; no one wanted to play with him because he was so quarrelsome and insulting. Hardly ever did he get into a game but words were shouted and fists flourished. Later, indeed, they had to take him out and hang him to a railroad trestle. He had killed a man; many men engaged in the hanging went about it with great enthusiasm, so mean was Omaha Charlie.

On this day Elmer saw a rather handsome young stranger with a brown beard come in and seat himself. Omaha Charlie, unable to get anybody to play with him, approached the stranger. In no time they were playing and in no time a quarrel arose. The stranger was soft of voice and pleasant of manner. During the game, Omaha Charlie accused him of cheating. Not only that but came toward him with upraised cue. Instantly the stranger took on a deadly calm and his blue eyes became icy cold.

"Stop where you are. You are threatening the wrong man."

And so meaningly did the stranger say it that Omaha Charlie stopped, knowing that the stranger meant every word. Not only did Omaha Charlie stop, but he put up his pool cue and left the place. Later he said, "I could see hell in that man's eyes."

The stranger stayed a few minutes, then left.

It was not long before Elmer Frazier went, with a crowd of men from our town, to St. Joseph to see Jesse James at the undertaker's, and there, on the slab, was the mysterious stranger whose deadly coldness had made Omaha Charlie tread water.

No one ever knew why Jesse James was in our town that day, except that he had come "to look things over." His usual method was to go in a bank and ask to have a bill changed; while this was being done, he would cast his eyes about him, especially at the time lock, a subject that interested him profoundly. No one at either of our banks remembered him, or, at least, paid any attention to him. This happened just a short time before he was killed, when he was planning, with Bob Ford, another bank robbery. They settled upon Platte City, a town a short distance away. Our people always thought if he hadn't been frightened away by the pool game and attention drawn to him, Jesse would have robbed one of our banks. Sometimes I almost wished he had.

Part II
Middlewestern Memoir

At the conclusion of his most popular, widely-held memoir, *Country Cured* (Harper, 1943)—the first of Croy's two book-length autobiographies—the author declares, "The best qualities to be found in writing are sincerity and truth." *Country Cured* tells a full life story—describing the author's childhood, his ascent as a best-selling author and subsequent globetrotting man of letters, his midlife dark night of the soul, and his many midwestern homecomings, literal and figurative.

In *Wonderful Neighbor* (Harper, 1945) Croy relates the story of his people, the farmers and villagers of Corn Country, via the story of his native section in northwest Missouri and of the representative men and women who populated his world-in-miniature. In particular, *Wonderful Neighbor* pays tribute to Croy's boyhood hero and neighbor, Newt Kennedy—"big, brawny, fun-loving, tousle-haired, tenderhearted, boy-understanding Newt." He reminisces, "I walk down the road I know so well and look at the cornerpost and a miracle happens. Newt is there and I am there." Kennedy, the man who first wowed young Homer with his weekly "One-horse Farmer" columns for the Maryville, Missouri, newspaper, looms larger in the author's writing life than any other figure, including the author's father. Included in this section is Croy's poignant, tragicomic account of reaching adolescence, "I Lose My Manhood." Dubbed a "classic" by Croy friend and fellow writer Cameron Shipp, "I

Lose My Manhood" sounds, as Shipp puts it, "a note...likely to inspire any man to sentimental recollection." More than that, the remembrance testifies to the value of a quiet, nonjudgmental listener in a young man's life. In sum, Croy's memoirs evidence a happy if not impressionable soul grounded in a timeless place.

The first three readings in the section that follows appear from *Country Cured* while the last four, beginning with "The Beautiful Chip," come from *Wonderful Neighbor*.

An Aristocracy of the Land

We had an aristocracy, founded on land. Our people did not judge each other by clothes, or education, or family, even by money. A person may have been known to have money in the bank, or stocks or bonds, but we felt these would probably slip away from him and he'd end up living in an L with a relative. "If he has stocks and bonds, why doesn't he turn them into land?" we asked, and it was a question hard to answer. The only safe and enduring possession was land.

A man who had a quarter section did not stand as high as the man who had a half section. After all, people had to be weighed on some sort of scales, and land scales were as good as any.

We had a love of the soil, as have the peasants in France, but I don't believe ours was as deep, or as touching. For in France they lived generation after generation on the same farm, while ours was a changing country. Our people bought a farm, tilled it a while, then discovered what seemed to be a better "location" and moved on to that. A farmer might try corn-hog-and-cattle farming in our section, then feel he could do better in Iowa and move there. Or he might want to try the "hardpan" in Kansas, and so give that a whirl. Or he might want to try "Oklahoma red," and move down there where he would have to raise kaffir corn. To us, in our section, we considered kaffir-corn farming about as low as one could sink. Or he might want to try wheat in Nebraska, or South Dakota, so trade his land and take his chance on wheat. Or he might want "upland" farming and move to eastern Colorado. Now and then one of our people would pick up and go to Texas where it was not farming but ranching, which was something we didn't understand at all. One of the Sewells moved to Texas and bought an onion farm. No hogs, corn, or cattle. We felt it was a family disgrace.

One who, sooner or later, came up against aristocracy of land was the hired man. Our hand ate with us and nothing was thought of it. If a family poked its hired man off into the kitchen, everybody in the neighborhood would have been outspoken. Evenings he sat by the same stove and took part in the family conversation; if the stove wasn't going to suit him, he threw some cobs in; if it was going too briskly, he turned the damper and took care of that. There was a difference when "company" was heard outside. He might get up to his room but usually we'd say, "You don't have to leave, Dell. Stay and visit with them." Usually, he stayed.

But on Sunday, there was a decided difference. He would not dream of going to church with the family. And it would never occur to the family to ask him. In the first place, Sunday was his day off and he left early; he rode away on horseback. It was a kind of trust with a hired man to be back Monday morning by choring time. Sometimes by noon he was pretty yawny and when evening came he popped into bed as soon as the milk was strained. But he was there. You could depend on that.

One spring, Pa began to hunt around for a hand. We went to town and on the street he stopped the people he knew and told them he was looking for a "good, reliable man." He went to the hardware store and left word there; then to the bank and asked Joe Jackson if he knew of any changes in help. Then to the livery stable to see if the proprietor knew of anybody looking for a "place." But he didn't go to the pool hall; anybody who hung around a pool hall wouldn't be any good.

When he came home he said he'd heard of a man who seemed promising. His name was Renzo Davis, he said, a man from the east side of the county. A day or so later a spring-wagon with two men in it turned into our drive lot, but we did not connect this with our new hand, for usually a new hired man came on horseback with a couple of suitcases tied to the saddle. If he came walking across the field carrying just one suitcase, we regarded him with suspicion. A man with one suitcase wasn't going to stay long. Especially if he wanted to see his room first. Or if he asked how many cows.

It did not take long to see why Renzo had come in a spring wagon, for he had a trunk and, to our surprise, a violin case. He had got a friend to drive him over; soon the friend departed and Renzo, our new hand, was left with us.

It was exciting to have this break in our routine; in fact, it was exciting to have *anyone* come; and now here was a man with a trunk and violin case! I could hardly keep my eyes off him,

Renzo was thirty, rather on the small side, with a thin face and an indentation in his skin under one jaw, where something had been cut out. On a finger on his left hand was a ring made out of a horseshoe nail; and he had a silver watch, which later I discovered he wound with a key. He had a round braided human-hair watch chain. Every night he looped it over the bedpost and let the watch dangle from it.

We showed him to his room and got his trunk put away, then Pa took him out to let him learn how to chore. And I followed for the excitement of it, tremendously pleased someone was going to help us work. When milking time came, Renzo pitched in with a hearty will. But Pa was watching. He'd seen new brooms.

After supper we sat around talking, going through the process of getting acquainted. Renzo told about crops on the other side of the county and prices things were bringing. He told about a big farmer who had put in a "hay tedder." It was the first time I ever heard the word.

"I see you brought your fiddle," Pa said, finally. "Would you mind playing us something?"

"I'll try it," said Renzo obligingly, and began to tune up, plucking one string after another with his thick, work-hardened thumbnail. He got some rosin out of a paper box, and ran the rosin along the bow, then put his violin under his chin and drew his bow across the strings. In a moment his foot was going up and down and our living room was filled with the first fiddle music of its whole existence.

Renzo rested his violin on his lap and talked a while. Then back went his fiddle and again the thrilling, exciting sounds rang through the room.

When Renzo went off to his new bed, our room seemed lonesome. It was the best evening we'd had in months.

"We'll wait and see how he pans out," Pa said. I hoped to God he would pan out.

I am glad to say he did. He was a good worker and didn't rest his horses too long at the ends of the rows, and didn't mind pulling milkweeds. It was understood on rainy days a hand could do light work in the barn, such as greasing the harness, or cleaning out the cobs from the mangers. Renzo would do more than that. If it stopped raining, he would dart out to the woodpile and begin to split railroad ties. If it started to rain again, he would go back to the barn and climb into the manger with his cob basket.

We saw we had a treasure. But Pa still was skeptical. Now and then we would get a treasure; but some night he would come home as drunk as hell. Sometimes we'd have to go to town and bring him out. But if one ever got drunk enough to land in jail, Pa was through with him, no matter how perfect he was in other respects.

One day Renzo told Pa that if Pa would get him some traps he would see what he could do about the gophers. Never before had a hand volunteered to trap gophers, for it meant additional work; on top of this Pa didn't think he could trap them, gophers being what they are. So he gave him a steel trap and told him to see what he could do.

In a day or two, Renzo came in with a gopher tail. Soon he had another. So Pa went to town and got half a dozen traps. Renzo would dig a hole about a foot square until it crossed the run, then get on his knees and go through a careful process of covering the trap and weighting the tongue with just the right thickness of dirt. Then he would fasten the trap to the board and put the board over the top of the hole and cover it with dirt so as to shut out the light. In a day or two he would have a gopher.

Renzo became a most welcome addition to our family; he was cheerful and had a sense of humor and could tell the simplest thing that had happened to him during his day's work and make it absorbing. I began to realize, after a time, that he exaggerated. But that was all right; the element of essential truth was there; and by making allowances we could come pretty close to the kernel.

The neighbors came to esteem him and when we were invited to a party, Renzo went along as a matter of course. Sometimes I had the uncomfortable feeling that he was the most welcome one of us.

He developed a quality that few hands had. Of making money in addition to his wages. A horse belonging to a neighbor had been shocked by lightning and was considered worthless. Renzo traded for him, put him by himself in a pasture on soft ground and brought him out of his shakes. He traded him for a better horse and pretty soon bought a set of harness at a public sale. Little by little he began to "pick up" things.

Gradually, as his circle of acquaintances widened, there came a social problem. He wanted to "go" with the girls, and there the heart-wrench began, for Renzo, however deserving, owned no land. Personally he was pleasing and he was capable. But he didn't own land.

Saturdays he would stand on the edge of the sidewalk, on the west side of the Square, where the crowd was thickest, and when one of our farm girls came along, he would take off his hat (which some of our young men didn't do) and speak to the girl and make an excuse to walk down the street with her. Sometimes he would come to the back of the grocery where he knew the girl and her family were having dinner (trying to pretend this was accidental) and make friendly advances. This was all right, but he mustn't ask them to go anywhere with him. The girls who had spoken to him so friendly at the debates and spelling and ciphering matches, now, on the streets, could hardly see him.

He bought a black derby, which was the kind of hat the "city" men were wearing, and kept it carefully in the hatbox side of his trunk, but this did not change his social status. He got a new suit but even this made no difference. A fashion of white hands was going around, so he bought heavy pigskin gloves and wore them so they would sweat his brown paws white. He wore a red bandanna handkerchief drawn tight up against his neck, with the ends poked through a brass ring, so his neck would be white, too.

He never spoke to me about it except once. It was at the end of a corn row while we were resting our teams.

"I guess they look down on me. But someday they won't. You'll see!"

Most of the hired men talked sex almost continuously with the sons of the men they worked for. Renzo had a finer streak. He thought of girls and he talked of girls. But he didn't go past a certain point. Some innate fineness held him back, there. A girl lived behind our farm; to go to town she had to drive through our farm to get to the main road. Each time she went by, Renzo must have thought his thoughts, but he never said anything that told me what was going on in his mind. Once, as we were trimming hedge near her house, we saw one of her undergarments on the clothesline. It set my mind jumping and it must have fired Renzo's too, but he made only some mild remark and went on whacking.

The girl became aware of us, plucked the undergarment off the line and darted back into the house.

"I guess we can do a better job now," said Renzo and although I tried to lead him into more talk, when we rested, it was all he would say. It may have been he thought I was too young, or that my father would not approve; but on the whole I think it was a bit of fineness in humble Renzo.

He bought a buggy, with the spokes staggered in red hubs, spread his lap robe on the back of the seat, and asked the girls to try his new buggy. But they found excuses. He was too smart not to understand and, at times, had depressed spells—Renzo who had always been so cheerful and the life of our fireside.

He became secretive and wrote letters and took them down to the mailman and handed them to him personally. On the day he expected an answer he would manage to meet the carrier before he got to our box. But in spite of this, now and then there would be a nice neat little envelope addressed to Lorenzo Davis among our farm papers and incubator catalogues. He would put the letter into his hip pocket, as if it didn't amount to much. Sometimes, at the barn, I would see the ends he had ragged off.

In the meantime he continued to trade, In a big businessman this would have been called "financial shrewdness." We called it "dickering."

On the Fourth of July he put in his lapel a celluloid button which said GIRL WANTED and walked slowly from one group of girls to another. Other boys were also wearing the button, but his really meant something to Renzo.

Finally he said he had been offered a job in Holt County; when he left he had two horses and two or three pieces of farm machinery, and some money in the bank. We hated to see him go. It was lonesome that evening without Renzo and his violin.

Two years later, possibly, he drove up in a spring-wagon, a girl beside him. "How do you like her?" he asked proudly. He stayed for dinner and we talked over old times, delighted to have Renzo at our table again. The girl, we found, was a hired girl working for a farmer who had a sickly wife. We liked the girl. She was all right. But the one we really liked was Renzo. We telephoned the neighbors and several of them came in. He introduced her proudly. Once there was a slip, for one of the neighbors pretended that Renzo had sparked every girl in the neighborhood. I think this hurt Renzo a little, for the real truth of it must have flashed before him. We went out and had a stock weighing and Pa let him guess the closest so Renzo could impress his girl.

When time came to leave, Renzo drove away with his own team, waving to us as he whirled out of the lot. A bit later he sent us a three-line newspaper item, pasted on his letter with white of egg, saying that Lorenzo Davis and Miss So-and-So had been married and had rented such-and-such a farm where they would soon move and set up housekeeping.

Two or three years passed. Now and then we would get a letter written by his wife asking us how we were and, as she put it, "expressing my husband's best wishes." One day we were surprised and delighted to have Renzo swirl up in our drive lot with a very dashing team covered with expensive fly nets. He could hardly wait to tell us the news. He had bought the So-and-So farm in our neighborhood! And he exactly had. He hadn't had much money to put down, but he had made the deal and maybe with good luck he could pull through. Well, Renzo pulled through.

He lives in the neighborhood which once wouldn't have him, and is one of its leaders. And so is his wife. She is a member of the "Knabb Country Club," she "entertains," and does it very well. The favorite kind of home entertainment is the "covered-dish luncheon." Which means that the women arrange to meet at a member's home and each member takes along a "covered dish"; this is usually a hot dish. These are put on the table and luncheon is announced. The women go in and someone says grace and the lunch is served. Well, Mrs. Renzo has as good a covered-dish luncheon as anyone, and is as well thought of as anyone. And the very girls—now women—who once turned up their noses at Renzo now accept him fully and so does the neighborhood, for he now belongs to the land aristocracy.

Inferiority Complex

Our farmers felt immensely inferior to "city people," as we thought of those who lived in town. There was good reason for it. For when we clunked in our mud-spattered wagons, the "city people" were dashing around on vitrified brick paving in carriages with high-stepping horses and with buggy whips that stood up straight. As we would pull up in front of the grocery store and get out our half-bushel measure of oats, the city people would smile superciliously. Sometimes, as we stood in the back part of the grocery fishing the eggs out of the oats, the city people would come in and purchase things we couldn't even dream of buying.

When we went in to trade, the merchants wore fine clothes and had elegant polished manners. When we wanted to buy a pair of shoes, we would feel sensitive because of the milk stains. One day Pa took me in the Bee Hive and said, "I'd like to get a pair of Sunday shoes for my boy." The man said, "Sit right down. I'm sure we can fit you out with any dress shoe you want." We noticed such things.

It was understood that Saturday afternoon belonged to the farmers; so the sleek city people kept off the street. But at half-past four or five, the farmers would have to go home to chore. Then the surreys and high-stepping horses would appear. One elegant city man had an Irish jaunting cart on which he sat sideways; it was pulled by one horse with a ribbon around his tail and his head reined high. It gave us something to talk about clear to the water tower. The man never saw us and we would no more have dreamed of speaking to him than we would to God.

There wasn't any common meeting ground on Sunday, either. The farmers went to their country churches, and the city people went to theirs. Except the Catholics. They all went to the same church. Nobody could understand them.

All of us country boys felt a dreadful sense of inferiority and, when we met on the street or walked together, we didn't laugh and joke and have a good time the way we did Sunday afternoons on the farm. We could spot a town boy coming a block and we could see him nudge his friend and make funny remarks. We'd pretend we didn't see, or slink out of sight on the stairway going up to a photographer's, and talk in low, constrained tones. Sometime he would meet at dinnertime in the back of the grocery store and talk together as we ate our cheese and crackers. But not the hearty way we did on the farm.

The town girls would sweep down the street, three abreast, arms locked; when we saw them coming, we would swing over so they could pass.

In the paper was a department called "Society," where we would read about the people as if they were titled foreigners. No farmer ever got into society. On another page was a department called "Selected Jottings." A farmer could get into that, but usually he had to top the hog market, or have a two-headed calf.

But there was one place we felt at ease; the Pavilion. This was the arena where, every other Saturday afternoon, horses and mules and cattle and sheep were auctioned off. Sometimes household plunder. The farmers would stand around in their muddy boots and their caps with earlaps and feel at home; no city man ever came there unless he wanted to see us queer people. Sometimes, however, the city boys would come. But his was a different world—our world—and they didn't monkey around long.

Beyond our city people, there existed another world—the faraway world of New York—the rich whose names we saw in the papers. One day as we were going to town, I said, "Pa, how much would Vanderbilt pay for a buggy whip?"

He thought a moment, and said, "Twenty-five dollars."

I nearly fell out of the hack. Hired hands were getting $18 a month.

As we rod along, I kept thinking why some people could pay only $1.25 for a buggy whip, and others $25. All my life that has been a puzzle; I still don't understand it.

There had been developing in my mind the idea that I wanted to go to advanced school. Books were becoming more and more fascinating. The spell that words weave. The thrill of a new idea!

I spoke to Pa about it.

Only one other boy from Knabb had ever gone to the high school at the county seat; no Croy ever had. It was a new world for Pa to think in, but he said, "If you want to go, Homer, I'll manage to send you."

I knew how much was behind this. Someone must do the work I had been doing; some way must be provided to get me back and forth, six miles twice a day. When I had gone to Uncle Will Sewell's to visit, it had been twelve miles, a tremendous distance. Now I must travel that far each day.

Ma drove in to town with me to see the professor and I was enrolled. As the day approached, I became more and more concerned. Could I hold up my end among the smart city boys? On top of this was another millstone: all my life I had been shy and self-conscious and I had the feeling that all the country boys in our section had: inferiority. And I was awkward and ill at ease and gulpy-throat when I met new people.

There was the problem of clothes. And the problem of money to buy them with. "You can wear my Sunday pants, Homer."

I protested and yet I *did* want to wear them.

"You go ahead and wear them. I've been thinking of getting a new pair, anyway."

Pa must have sensed the violent change that was coming into my life. "Homer, I'll drive you in Monday morning and bring you back. I've got some things I want to do in town."

I knew that was a polite lie, but it made me like Pa. Sometimes he seemed so indifferent and impersonal and hard-driving that I almost hated him; then he would do something that made a warm flash come in my heart.

He drove me up in front of the schoolhouse and I climbed down out of the hack. "I'll be up around the Square at noontime." Then he shook the lines and drove slowly away.

I did not speak to a soul I didn't have to. I was taller and older than the boys in the freshman class, as I soon discovered, and knew nothing about the ringing of the classroom bells and the constant marching here and there. At noon one of the teachers sat down at a piano and played for us to march out. I thought I had just about reached the top in education.

Pa was standing in front of the grocery where we always met.

"How did you fare, son?"

"All right, I guess."

"Well, I guess we'd better eat. We'll go to the short order today." No eating in the back of the grocery today.

It was where the farmers went and where we felt at home. He said proudly to one of the men, "My son's just startin' a term of school."

The man looked me over. "Ain't he goin' to be a farmer?"

"Sure he is," said Pa confidently.

At the end of the meal he said, "You needn't hurry when school dismisses. I'll be around the grocery." There he was, when school was out, patiently waiting.

The next day I was on my own. In my ill-fitting clothes, I moved about in this new and complicated world in a sort of daze. When I arrived each morning I hated to go in, and when school dismissed I darted away to where I had my horse stabled and clunked off for home as fast as I could.

Mornings were worst. As I rode in on old Dave, I would have to pass students on the way to school. I felt horribly ashamed of big-footed Dave who had a way of making distressing noises. I was the only one who had to clump in on horseback and when Dave rumbled by, the students would turn their eyes on us, and it seemed to me I would die.

I soon discovered the streets most frequented, and veered my course so I wouldn't be seen by so many students. Now and then a boy would come out of his home, fresh from breakfast, and fall in with friends on the way to school. It seemed to me the very epitome of luxury to be able to live in town, get up late, and have gay friends to walk to school with.

At noon the boys and girls went to their homes, but I went to the widow's stable where I kept Dave. I would water him and put his feed in his box, then sit down near him and the two of us would eat.

The barn was so gloomy and fly-filled that I wanted to take my paper-wrapped lunch somewhere else. But there was the problem of the other students who always seemed to be smiling at me.

I began putting my lunch in my pocket and going behind the Methodist Church. But now and then someone would come through the alley and stare. Finally I hit on a new plan. There was an area way back of the church and I would lower myself into it and unwrap my lunch.

I would go back to the school ground where the other boys were playing, and would stand around, wanting to play but not knowing how to go about it. Now and then one of the boys would make a friendly advance, but I would be brief with him to show I was getting along all right.

With the secrecy of youth, I said nothing to anyone. Even when Ma asked me how I liked the city boys and girls I said, All right. I had no friends, yet I liked people and yearned desperately to make friends.

I wore shoes, except in stormy weather when I wore boots, as I did on the farm. One morning, as I was saddling Dave, he bumped my foot. That day at school my foot was sore and I quietly slipped off my boot. "Colonel" Cox, who sat behind me, saw that I had it off and got it away from me. In a few minutes the teacher told me to come to the board and explain something. I said I didn't know how, but she told me to come and try. I limped up, one boot on, one boot off...a humiliating moment.

People were fascinating to me. But I had seen very few, only our relatives and neighbors; now suddenly there was a whole new world. I listened to the students recite, intrigued far more by them than by what they were saying. I would discover some item of interest about one of the students; the next day I would discover something else. Every day I added to my collection of facts about each student. No longer were they a formless horde, all lined up against me, each was an individual; each had traits and characteristics a good deal like my Knabb neighbors. The discovery just about floored me.

I began to feel a bit more at home and made a few shy advances, so stimulating were people to me. Little by little I accumulated a few friends, like a tree making rings. I pulled up out of the area way and began taking my lunch to the schoolyard and eating it on a bench. Sometimes some of the very boys I had slid down the areaway to avoid would rush through their lunch at home to come and sit on the bench with me.

A change had taken place. But I did not know why.

I became acquainted with a farm girl from another part of the county. It seemed to me she was wonderful and I began to "go" with her. I knew her father owned more land than mine, but I didn't realize how important this was going to be.

One day, when I happened to mention that my father owned a quarter section, she said, "I know that."

I was surprised, as I knew I hadn't mentioned it before. So I asked her how she knew it.

"I looked it up in the plat book."

My ardor fell off, and a young man whose father owned far more land than mine succeeded, later, in winning her. Another example of the aristocracy of land.

Little I Knew

In New York I met writers who seemed to have read everything and to know everything, while I realized how little I had read and how little I knew. They all seemed to have traveled abroad and to have very firm opinions on things I didn't know about at all. A vast feeling of inferiority had me. Maybe I shouldn't continue to write. Maybe I should go back to the farm. Well, that wouldn't be so bad. But some inner propulsion sent me forward and kept me trying. It all seemed so good when I was at it; so poor when the words were cold. Everybody seemed to be succeeding but myself. Sometimes I would look at them, or their pictures, and think, "Why can they make a success and I can't?" One night I went to a reception given by the Authors' League of America. I went up in an elevator and when I stepped off I beheld men and women in evening clothes, with Winston Churchill (our American author), Laura Jean Libbey, and Ella Wheeler Wilcox at the head of the receiving line. They all looked so successful and so important that I did not check my hat, but slipped out.

But I kept on trying, and, some way or other, made a living.

And, some way or other, I found time to write another novel which got good reviews and another faint ping.

I became engaged…did I dare undertake marriage when I never knew from one month to another how much I would make?

As a boy I had listened to an entrancing train whistle at night, coming in over the sloughs, and wished with all my heart I could get on a train and go somewhere. And now an exceedingly bold idea laid hold of me. I would try to go around the world! One editor looked at me sternly. "That's a fine idea. It must be a fine one, or so many people wouldn't present it."

I kept on until I got *Leslie's Weekly* to agree to send me. When the letter of agreement was drawn up, I found that it bound *Leslie's Weekly* as loosely as a twin string around a shorthorn. I was put down by this, not yet having fathomed the ways of magazines, but I was so eager to go that I entered only a mild protest. Then I did something I'm still astonished at. I went to a number of advertising companies and announced that I was going on a trip around the world and that I would be pleased to represent their clients. My youth, or enthusiasm, or eagerness, or something—I'm not sure what it was—made them sign up. I was to smoke a certain kind of pipe tobacco, use a certain kind of toothpaste, and chew just one kind of gum. I still blink as I remember all the things I was to do. When I got back I was to write of my experiences going around the world smoking, chewing, and tooth-cleaning.

Encouraged by my success (so far), I hit upon another bold idea. I would take motion pictures! I singled out Universal Film Company as being susceptible, and tripped gaily in. Here again my tremendous confidence must have been on my side, for I was passed along until I came before Carl Laemmle himself. He was a short man, a German Jew, with a wide space between his two upper middle teeth which seemed to make his accent more pronounced. He had a kindly, almost fatherly, attitude; in fact, his office name was "Uncle Carl." He hesitated when I told him my fine idea. "How ya goin' to make pichers when you don't take photographs?" he asked.

"You'll have to send a cameraman with me," I announced. "I'm going to direct the pictures."

He studied me, and I knew my fate was being weighed. "How many pictures have you direct'?"

"I haven't directed any yet," I said, sensing that victory was coming my way. "But I can do it all right."

He looked at me, meditating....

It was finally agreed that I was to see him in Hollywood, but when I arrived there I found ten thousand others were also trying to see him, for these were the wild, gold-strike days of motion pictures. I shadowed him, not only at his office but also on the lot, every time the poor man left his door. But all the other pursuers were after him, too, some of them far more bloodthirsty than I was. One day in his office, I happened to overhear in a conversation that he was going to the bank. I waited to pounce on him, for I had by this time grown desperate, but he used an unexpected side door. I started across the lot feeling everything was lost, then spied him getting into his big, open-topped car. I dashed for him, leaped on the running board of the moving car and plopped down beside the astonished man. For a moment he did not know me and seemed to think he was the victim of some wild plot.

I talked as I had never before talked in my life. By the time we reached the bank he had said Yes.

His publicity department had widely publicized something it termed "Laemmle Luck," and I'm sure the old gentleman believed he had it. I hoped to God he was right.

A cameraman was assigned and I started out with my smoking tobacco, chewing gum and toothpaste to go around the world. I found a Universal film company working in Honolulu, making what they called "authentic" South Seas pictures, and learned a little about handling film and chemicals and drying racks in the subtropics.

The first place I photographed, after Honolulu, was Japan; and the first "shot" (I was learning fast) was a silkworm factory. The Japanese government sent three men and they never got farther away from me, I'm sure, than ten feet. And demanded to see every inch of film.

I won't stop to set down all my adventures, except this one point.

I was on the China Sea, on a North German-Lloyd ship named the Francis Ferdinand, sitting at the captain's table, one noon, when a man from the wireless office came, said something in German, and handed the captain a message. The captain read it, then reread it, and, to my astonishment, arose slowly and, without a word to anyone, faced the end of the dining room where there was a painting on the wall of the Archduke Francis Ferdinand. He saluted the picture gravely, and sat down. Then he said, "He has just been assassinated at Serajevo."

The whole thing meant little—how could the assassination of someone thousands of miles away affect me? His getting up and saluting the painting was just a funny German quirk, I thought.

But it did affect me, as I soon found. Singapore—England's stronghold in the Orient—was filled with German spies. And soon, at my Dutch hotel, I heard nothing but war. But it would be over soon.

On the way to Rangoon, later, four or five English "clarks," who had been assigned to duty at home, walked up and down the deck giving an imitation of the goose step and roaring with laughter. I laughed, too. It all seemed vastly amusing.

One of the clerks said, "It'll all be over before we get home and I'll have to turn around and come back which'll be just my luck."

At Rangoon a shadow fell across us. We were transferred to another ship, one much smaller. Gradually matters grew worse and I felt myself struggling against something powerful and relentless, as one does in a troubled dream.

I had no passport of any kind, for at that time passports were not required. But I did have a personal letter from William J. Bryan, Secretary of State, which the publisher of *Leslie's Weekly* had got for me.

I got on the train one night in Calcutta with a Pennsylvania Dutch young man of my age. We were in the compartment alone together; the engine was smoking and breathing heavily, and people were going up and down the platform in a last-minute excitement of departure when suddenly the door was opened by two British officers. One said, "Are there any Germans in here?"

The young man with me answered, "*Nein.*"

He was hauled out and was, I learned later, kept in Ceylon as a prisoner for three months.

I made newsreels and travel pictures across India, but even here, miles from any British stronghold, I felt the war roaring toward me like some gigantic but invisible force. In Bombay my camera was taken from me and I had to see half a dozen officials to get it back. I ran out of money, and the Majestic Hotel ejected us, but kept our cameras, chemicals and equipment. I moved into the YMCA where, for three weeks, I was without a shilling to my name. All I could do was to smoke and scour my teeth and chew gum. At last money came through. I claimed my cameras and equipment, and got on to Egypt. The shadow had grown darker. I could fill pages with details of what happened, but I must forego that, for I don't want to make my book too long. Only just one point: I was questioned at the Second Cataract as a spy. William J. Bryan saved me.

At last I got to London and cut the film. It was released as half reel subjects under my name. I thought it was, for the most part, pretty poor. But when the Universal house organ came out, it had this as a banner line: "UNIVERSAL SCORES AGAIN. LAEMMLE LUCK STILL HOLDS." I felt better.

I went to the advertising companies with my pictures and the pieces I'd written. The chewing gum company said No; and wanted none of what I had to offer. The others bought some of my "still" pictures and some of the material I wrote, at a price which I thought was pretty good, but which I now realize was ridiculously cheap.

And now I had enough money to get married. Oh boy!

When we were married, the Universal Newsreel made motion pictures of us coming out of the church and getting into a cab; the pictures were shown on the screen in and around New York. Thus we became the first couple in the world to be put into a newsreel. The church was the Swedenborgian, near Madison Avenue, New York, and the time was February 7, 1915. Until then the newsreels had dealt with burning buildings, street accidents and other calamities. Then they discovered love. It just shows how they were progressing. Later, in the British Museum, London, I was pleased to find a write-up of the wedding and the statement (very British) that an American couple had chosen to throw modesty to the winds and be photographed for the cinema actualities. The write-up didn't think much of the brash American couple. Well, they're still married. (And they still have the negative of the film.)

When I went home I told Pa about my marriage which, of course, he had already known. I told him that my wife was from Florida; he had known that, too, but he wanted more details. So she was a southerner? he said, not quite approving of the idea. Well, he supposed it would be all right. Was she a farm girl? When I told him she wasn't, he was disappointed. "Well," he said finally, "all right, just so she makes you a good wife." She has.

And now, with my outside point of view, I became aware of differences between the East and my section. It seemed to me I could meet someone I had never seen before and say, almost in a moment, "He is from my section" or "Why, I know him already!" First, there were the external differences. Certainly the people of my section didn't dress as well; did not have the tailored look of easterners. Nor did they have the education. These grammar lapses were not true merely of the farmers; they also were true of the professional men, the so-called "educated classes." The judge on his bench said "ain't" and nothing was thought of it. It was the language of the majority of the people, so he used it. The only ones who scurried away from it were the new law school graduates who weren't sure of themselves. By the time they got to be judges they'd probably drop back into it. One of our most revered judges chewed tobacco on the bench; in fact, our prosecuting attorney himself chewed tobacco. And so did the jury; between every two men was a cuspidor. I know it seems shocking and I suppose it is, but it was not shocking to us. I suspect our juries brought in about as fair verdicts as the more sophisticated juries.

I began to see that our people had the look of people who lived out in the sun. Not only the men but also the women. Their faces were leathery and wind-tanned and there were deep cracks in the necks of the men. Their hands showed it at a glance; for the hands of our men and the women were thicker; pads of muscles were in the palms; the fingers had thrown out protective thicknesses. Even the nails showed the difference, for the nails of the men-and the women, too, were thick and heavy and the color of hazelnuts. And nearly every hand carried a scar; sometimes across the back of a man's hand would be a jagged whitish line. Barbed wire. Our people walked differently. Their feet, when they put them on cement, turned out as if they were still meeting the problems of plowed ground; the people bent forward and looked at the sidewalk more than did the city people.

But these were only external differences due to their occupation and the daily problems they had to solve. I felt there was a deeper difference, a difference in their very thinking, their approach to life. This difference, as I sensed it, goes back to the Puritans. I can put this direct relationship in one specific illustration. The first women, traditionally, who stepped on, the granite boulder at Plymouth was Mary Chilton. Our banker is named for her, his name being Chilton Robinson. As the Puritans moved west, they took a piece of the Rock in their covered wagons. Some of our settlers came by way of Ohio and some by way of Indiana, but they had started from Plymouth. Some differences developed on the way, but essentially it was the same thinking. I find it hard to pin down this difference in a word. I suppose the old phrase "rugged individualism" comes as near it as any. They had lived and pioneered as individuals and they thought as individuals. One phase of their Puritan influence that had been lost somewhere between Massachusetts and Missouri was the "town meeting." I never have seen anything in my section even remotely resembling the New England town meeting I had heard so much about. Why this should be dropped as the people moved west, I don't know. Issues were discussed on every corner, but our people never went into an assembly and fought it out. Candidates, for and against, were put up and, when they were elected, they voted and settled matters. A situation that rocked our town to its foundation was the agitation to pull down the hitch racks around the Square. From the days of the pioneers the farmers had hitched there; on Saturday you saw a red brick courthouse with teams tied clear around it. The merchants said this must be no more; the farmers said it must. The farmers threatened to trade in surrounding hitch-rack towns and the merchants told them to take their trade and get. For something like two months this warfare went on—and a very real one it was to the farmers; then the matter was put to a vote. The farmers won. Time also won, as time so often has a way of doing. For the hitch racks came down, finally, and now cars stand where horses once stood by the grace of God.

I think the deepest and most significant trait among our people is self-dependence. The depression didn't affect us, in the same proportion it did the population centers, for there was still the pioneer belief that each tub must stand on its own bottom and that it was now, as always, root hog or die. Our people were self-employed; each man was his own boss. He conducted his own business and made his own decisions—and his own mistakes, too. He never tried to blame them on someone else.

Our problems are not man against man, but man against nature. Crops, weather, that ever-present—that powerful factor—"the market." The market, of course, is the grain market and the livestock market. The kind of market they talk about in New York is as far away as last week's dream.

Like the Puritans we believe that idleness is a sin. When our women go visiting they take their work along. Even after our "covered dish" parties, the women get out their sewing bags, or their knitting equipment; no one suggests cards. Cards are a waste of time; and that is exactly the way I feel even today. Some of our "city women" play cards of an afternoon. But the farm women—the backbone of our community—never dream of such a thing. There still clings to card playing the feel of wickedness, but only a little. Our preachers won't jump on card players but once a year.

Some of the contacts I had, as I returned home from time to time, were disillusioning. I think the greatest was to realize how average our town was. Why, there were ten thousand like it in the United States! But our papers, or our orators, had never let us believe it was average. Especially our Fourth of July orators. No Fourth of July orator could be brought in from the outside and begin his speech without telling us how delighted he was with our town and how truly fortunate we were to live in such a beautiful, hustling community. We believed it. Once, when I was home, I got a shock. I found, according to the last census, that our town had lost thirty-two. It was so preposterous that I asked one of my friends, who knew far more about local conditions than I did, and he said it was true. I felt as if our town had been disgraced.

Another disillusionment was to find how little the boys and girls I had grown up with (now men and women) cared about what was going on in the world. And how narrow their intellectual interests. The world of ideas seemed to have no appeal at all. They seemed to believe as they had in high school and to be perfectly content with these beliefs. At first I tried to argue and to try to show them glimpses of a world that I was experiencing, but they looked on me as being set up and trying to show off, so after a time I gave up.

But in spite of these disillusionments, I liked the town and could hardly wait to get home. Pa still met me at the depot, but it was getting harder for him to swing my grip. Phebe would be standing in the door of the house south of the water tower, just as she had stood in the door of the house on the farm. After a visit, there would come the ceremony of going out to the farm, always a happy time for Pa and for me, too, for that matter.

Under his direction the farm was prospering, but, for that matter, so were all the other farms. The easiest and surest way to tell if all is well with a farm is to look at its buildings and at its fences. If the buildings are painted and the fences are taken care of, then that farm is doing well. Pa and I would walk slowly across the field to where the tenant was working, talking more intimately than we could anywhere else, for something seemed to bring us together, when we were on the land itself. Now and then he would throw out a sly hint…was I calculatin' on comin' back? If I got tired of city life, I'd find a mighty good piece of land waitin' me. Also he seemed to know my answers before I gave them. But he still threw out the hints, as if still hoping.

The ditch that he and I and Mr. Shannon had made with our tiling spades was now a great angry gash, so wide and so deep that two bridges had to be put across it. Every time it rained, some of our black soil slipped away, like blood from a wound. And now the tenant had to work almost as hard as Pa and Mr. Shannon and I had in order to stay its progress. Straw was staked down and junk iron tossed on it; willows were planted. But the black loam kept slipping away. So much slipped away that our farm, and endless other farms, were to pay for our mistake with the Dust Bowl.

Pa talked of "the old clays." He spoke of the first time I had brought him a jug of water. I had no memory of it, but he pointed out almost the very spot. He spoke of the time I had tried to drive a hay frame through a gate and had banged the frame into one of the posts and had given the frame a wrench. I could remember that and I could remember how provoked he had been. But I didn't mention that.

We had dinner with the tenant and his family. Pa didn't sit at the head of the table now, but part way down. There was the pained, self-conscious moment when there is doubt whether a blessing is to be asked or not. "Will you ask the blessing, Mr. Croy?" Pa's head, very white now, bent over his plate in this moment of thanks and appreciation that never left him, no matter how tired, or worn, or weary he was.

His hand was slipping. Bad days he didn't go out; he contented himself by talking on the farmers' telephone to the tenant. Instead of knowing all the endless details, he knew only the important ones. More and more he was leaving the little things to the tenant. He would pass a milkweed without pulling it up. But some days his old-time energy and work-spirit would leap up, and he would get the wire stretchers to repair a fence, or a water gap, or he would brace a cornerpost, or get the scythe out of the granary and fly into the dog fennel. Then he would come to the house and sit on the porch where he had sat so many years, leaning against a post; his weary eyes would close; his mouth would open a little. When he woke he would pump himself a drink, turn his back on the old farm, and start toward town.

He talked about the past. The weather was changing. Why, in the old days the snow was so deep and crusted you could drive over a four-wire fence! Say, the grasshopper year was bad! You could see them in the sky like clouds. At first the turkeys lit into them with gobbles of delight; but it wasn't long till they were so sick of them they wouldn't eat 'em.

They used to have some hot horse-thief chases! There was the time that him and Newt Kennedy and a couple of others chased a horse thief as hard as they could. But the thief had turned the horse's shoes around and they were chasing him backward! Pa laughed with a little of his old-time relish.

The old settlers were going. He and Phebe would get in the buggy and join the procession. When there was a G.A.R. funeral, he would put on his old blue uniform and stand by the grave; then he would come home and hang the uniform in the closet till next time.

He wrote no more at all. Phebe's letters always ended, "Your father says to come home whenever you can."

The inevitable happened. One day I got a telegram. "Your father is failing. Phebe."

No one came to meet me at the depot; there was no one to swing my grip. But when I got out of the jitney, Phebe was at the door to meet me, looking old and worn, her eyes still framed in the gold glasses. "He's been asking all morning when you'd get here."

The old gentleman was in the north room, in the house south of the water tower, in the walnut bed he had brought in from the farm. His knotted, misshapen hands were on the outside of the covers. He held his hand out to me and said in a faint voice, "I'm glad to see you, son. I guess you got in on the 8:10."

At the foot of the bed, next to the south wall, was the old tin, camel-back trunk I had taken to the university. It was now covered with a horse blanket, and I sat down on it.

His face was drawn, but his eyes were as blue as ever. The same spirit of mutual understanding we always had when we got together, after being separated, leaped up.

All the questions were about me. "How is your wife, Homer?"

"What kind of weather have you been havin' back East?"

It was not long before he began to talk about the farm. "Homer, you've got a good farm there." The poignancy touched me. He was releasing his hold on the farm. "Some of them laughed at me when I got it because there wasn't any timber on it, but it worked out pretty well!" A gleam in his eyes there, for now he had the best farm in the neighborhood. "Your mother was always awful fond of you." He was not one to pay compliments himself, and I realized that he was also saying this for himself.

He spoke of events of years ago as if they had just happened. Once a dashy-dressed drummer for a nursery had come to our house, driving a high-stepping livery team, and asked me to drive around with him and introduce him to the farmers. For which he would pay my father five dollars a day—a fortune. And now my father spoke of it.

"I'm glad I didn't take it."

He had to rest and I crept out of the room for a while. When I looked in again his blue eyes were still open.

"I wish you'd pare my fingernails."

And now I realized something that touched me. He had never been a man to show open marks of affection, such as putting his arm around me, as I have seen so many fathers do to their children. But now...in these last hours...he wanted the feel of his son. I had sense enough to make the paring of the nails last as long as I could.

"I've got my G.A.R. suit hangin' in the closet. I've always been proud of it."

His eyes closed; after a while they opened. "Do you remember the time I bought the buffalo robe for Christmas for your mother?"

I nodded, choked with feeling.

He wanted to do something for me, as if it was some final fatherly touch.

"Phebe and I have got a good feather bed upstairs we're not usin'. How would you like to have it?"

I explained as gently as I could that people in New York did not use feather beds.

"I suppose not," he said with a sigh.

It was not long before he was back to the farm. "It's all free and clear. It's been my ambition to leave it to you that way and that's what I'm doing. Don't ever put a mortgage on it. They eat like a cancer."

The time came when I must go back, and I went in and sat on the camel-backed trunk for the last time. Finally when the moment came, I shook his gnarled hand. "Take care of yourself, Homer." It was the last thing he ever said to me.

After I had been back about a week, I got word that the end had come. I could not go to the funeral...only in my thoughts.

The Beautiful Chip

In our section we hardly ever used the word "love." We said "like." A person might "love" his country, or he might "love" God, but he never said he "loved" his wife. He said he "liked" his wife, or he "managed to get along with her pretty well," but he never bleated out he loved her. We said a boy was "going" with a girl, or "keeping company," or "calling on her regularly." But we never said he was in "love" with her. I suppose it was some sort of Puritan influence.

Yet the attachment husbands and wives had for each other was deep and abiding. And the attachment parents had for their children was deep and moving, though they didn't put it into words. We thought of such expressions as being "soft" and out of place. In fact, we were always a little embarrassed when someone said something tender about another person, or spoke openly of affection. Life was hard; in many ways it was cruel. No time for mush.

I'm sure men married, had children and died without ever using the word "love" in relation to their wives. But that was all right; it was our way. Yet secretly the wives must have yearned for it.

In this way Newt was like all our men. He didn't go around saying he "loved" his wife; sometimes, in speaking of her, he called her "the woman." Our women said, "my husband," but our men said "the woman." Never "my" woman; it was always "the."

Then, one day, Newt, for our section, did something extremely unusual.

When the pioneers had first arrived a most important matter was fencing. There was little or no timber; snake fences impossible; and there was hardly any barbed wire. So the early settlers had planted Osage hedge. It grew rapidly but was not a very good fence. Winter freeze would get it and there would be thin spots that would let the stock out. So, bit by bit, this hedge was coming down and wire was going up. August was hedge-killing month; if it were grubbed up and the roots salted, then the hedge might die. But if it wasn't grubbed at the right time, it had a dozen lives. The yellow chips were beautiful; and they made the best firewood we could get.

On this special day, he picked up an unusually smooth, orange-colored chip and stood admiring it. Moved by impulse, he carried the chip to the woodshed. Here he had a flat, thick-headed carpenter's pencil. With the pencil he wrote on the chip, "I love you," filled a pail, put this chip on top and carried the pale down to the house.

"Here's some chips," he said with an effort to be casual and set the bucket down by the door. Then walked away hastily, almost guiltily.

Mrs. Newt was touched when she saw this humble tribute. Actually using the word "love!" She wanted to thank him. She arranged the pots and pans, thinking just what she would say, then went out the kitchen door looking for him. By this time Newt was grinding a sickle bar; he was sitting astride the frame, pumping away with his feet and holding the sickle bar at the correct angle. A tin can, filled with water, was fastened above the flying stone; a hole had been punched in the tin can and a burnt match plugged into the hole; a trickle of water followed the match down.

"I got your chip," she said.

He pumped a moment; a gray froth of sand particles and water raced along where the blade engaged the stone.

"Did you?" said Newt, immensely pleased.

"I liked it."

His feet continued to fly. "Did you?"

"I'm going to keep it."

"I didn't think about you doin' that," he said, even more pleased.

"It was nice and thoughtful of you."

"It wasn't anything," allowed Newt, a bit embarrassed now. "I just happened to think of it."

The matter of the chip was dropped; there were other things to talk of; there were always things to talk of on a farm and in raising a family. Finally she turned and started back toward the kitchen door. Newt looked up from the stone and gazed at her, pleased with himself and with her. "I ought to do those things oftener," he thought.

She placed it on the center table in the sitting room for everyone to see—this beautiful, orange-colored Osage hedge chip. If company came in and if they didn't seem to notice the chip, she would pick it up and say, "See what I found!"

Then she would tell the story. There would be silence among the women, for each was thinking that her husband hadn't done anything so sweet and lovely.

Sometimes she said, "I wouldn't take a great deal for that chip." It became a kind of symbol of their love.

She had another way of showing her affection for him.

Newt wore high-topped leather boots. In bad weather they became soaked. When the day's work was over, he pulled them off with his bootjack, then hung the bootjack on its nail in the kitchen; there were half-moon marks on the wall where the bootjack had swung back and forth. It would not do to let the boots dry when they were wet, for they would become hard and misshapen, would crack and soon would be leaking. So he kept a bucket of drying oats. The oats, when poured into the boots and allowed to stay there overnight, let the boots dry slowly, remain soft and pliable and hold their shape. He should have poured the oats in himself, but she always did this for him; it was a kind of token of her love. She never asked the children to do this. She didn't mind doing it, she said; this was as close as she would come to expressing her love for him.

She believed that Newt grew lightheaded when he oiled the windmill. He had once said he had felt dizzy up on the platform. She had never forgotten it; each time he went out to oil, she went with him. There she would stand, apprehensively watching him as he mounted higher and higher. Of course if he had been seized with lightheadedness, she could not have done anything. He wished she would not come, for the neighbors joked him about it. It was a reflection, indeed, on a man when his wife had to come out and watch him so he wouldn't fall off the windmill! But he couldn't tell her not to come. When he was up on the platform, he would look toward the road to see if anyone were passing. He hoped no one would be.

As soon as he came down, she would go to the house.

The children laughed at her, and so did Grandpa. But nothing kept her from going and standing by the windmill when Newt went up to oil. Sometimes she complained about living on a farm; city was better, she said.

Newt Writes "The One-Horse Farmer"

Monday night was hell night. For that was the night Newt wrote "The One-Horse Farmer." We all dreaded for the night to come, yet we wouldn't have missed it for anything. It was hell while it lasted…a nice exciting kind of hell.

He was "neighborhood correspondent" for our county weekly. For this he received a free subscription and fifty cents a week. There, in a little square pasteboard box on the center table for everybody to see, was the pile of stamped and self-addressed envelopes furnished by the newspaper. It was an honor to have such a pile of envelopes on a center table.

I was thrilled to be so close to someone who could put words on paper and then, a few days later, have them appear magically in print. It made me wish I could do that, too. Maybe sometime I would.

Monday was the night the neighborhood news had to be written; this would give it just time to get in that week's paper. When ours came, I would snatch it open and there would be those shining words.

He was the best correspondent in the paper, for he not only told the news but put fun into the items. He had a vein of true humor and managed to get this into his neighborhood news. Most correspondence was stodgy, but not Newt's. At the end he put a poem; everybody remembered them and quoted them, for they expressed just what we believed. One was:

> *A bull unpenned*
> *Is a danger no end.*

Another was:

> *Fretting over weather's lack,*
> *Never filled an empty sack.*

Another:

> *Keep away from trees and fences*
> *When a thunderstorm commences.*

All correspondents signed names; they used such names as "The Listener," "Aunt Polly," "Blue Eyes," "Sunbonnet Sue," "Ben-Hur," and so on. But not Newt. He signed himself, "The One-Horse Farmer"; this made everybody laugh, for it would take three horses at the very least to operate a farm; five would be better. Delinksy could never make it with one.

Newt's correspondence made him important in town on Saturdays. People would come and tell how they had read something by the One-Horse Farmer. He would stand, pulling at his big brown hands, immensely pleased, but pretending he hadn't written the item. "That sounds interestin'. I'll look it up when I get home." When the Kennedy family went to the back end of the grocery store to eat dinner, there would be other families sitting at the tables the grocery furnished. Everybody smiled and looked at Newt in a friendly, laughing way. Sometimes the people hardly noticed Mrs. Kennedy at all. Mrs. Kennedy was always the first one to want to leave.

When it came time to write up the neighborhood news, a dramatic ceremony would take place. All the family would be in the sitting room, Grandpa in the corner, his gnarled hands in his lap. Newt would turn up the wick, haul out his pocket knife and sharpen his pencil, then carefully arrange his writing tablet in front of him. There he would sit looking at the tablet. Then he would gaze up at the ceiling and down in to the coal scuttle and at the floor, all the time scowling fearfully. "Dog-gone it! I can't think of a thing. I tell you nothing's happened. Nothing a-tall," he would say mournfully. "I wish I hadn't ever started this One-horse thing."

He would get up and go to the kitchen; the tin dipper would rattle in the cedar bucket.

Coming back, he would sink dejectedly into his chair.

"I'm goin' to give it up. There's nothing this week, absolutely nothing."

"Has anybody died?" Grandpa would ask. He was always thinking about people dying.

Newt would shake his head. "Not a soul," he would say mournfully.

"Has anybody gone anywhere?" Mrs. Kennedy would ask.

Nobody had.

"Is there anybody sick?" Grandpa would ask.

Newt would shake his head again. "There hasn't been a doctor in the neighborhood all winter."

"Is there any news about the teacher?" Mrs. Kennedy would ask. Mrs. Kennedy had once been a teacher.

"Not a thing," Newt would say in the same gloomy, despondent voice.

"Has anybody got hog cholera?" Grandpa would ask. Again Newt would shake his head. "Not a case in the neighborhood."

Grandpa would unlock his hands, then lock them in a new position, "Any Bang's disease?"

"I want to get something a little more cheerful than Bang's disease, Pa." Any marriages?"

Ida would sit up here. "I know one that's going to be."

"Have they announced?"

"Not yet."

"Can't we say they're going together?" asks Ida. "Everybody is interested in people going together."

"Engagements and marriages, that's what we've got to stick to. Lucy, you're supposed to be bright, so give a little evidence of it." Even Lucy couldn't think of anything.

Newt would get up and put some coal in the base-burner, then sit down heavily and despondently.

We would all get gloomier and gloomier; the clock on the shelf would tick very loud.

Newt throws down the pencil in disgust. "I'm goin' to write and tell him there is no news. I shouldn't ever have undertaken this damned job anyway."

He runs his hands through his hair; he squirms in his chair, going through the tortures of the damned. "It's the hardest money I earn," he moans. "I wish to God I'd never got in it."

"Newt!" says Mrs. Kennedy. "The children."

"I don't care," Newt mutters; "that's just the way I feel about it." .

The dog gets up and lies down in a new place.

"I know!" Harlan suddenly exclaims. "The wolf hunt!" We all look at one another in astonishment. Why hadn't we thought of this before?

Once or twice a winter a wolf hunt was organized; men with dogs and guns went across the hills and draws until a wolf was turned up. The one who shot him got to take his ears to town.

"Of course!" cries Newt, delighted. "That's exactly it."

"Who's goin'?"

He begins to write as fast as he can; no hair rumpling now, no scowling, no muttering.

"The shivaree!" Ida calls out.

Her father looks at her admiringly. "Of course! Why didn't we think of that? I can get in some funny touches there. Any window lights broken?"

His pencil flies across the paper…he is stuck…goes on again.

Ideas are leaping in the room; even Grandpa can think of something besides who is sick. "Wait! slow up!" cries Newt. "You're goin' too fast for me."

He pauses, reads aloud. We all laugh, for no one had the touch he had. Newt beams with pleasure. "I got a good scald on that one, didn't I?" He turns to Mrs. Kennedy. "Minnie, what is that tricky way for spelling fellow, meaning the inside of a tire?"

"F-e-l-l-o-e."

"Webster must have had some fun when he thought that up." He turns the pencil end to end, rubs out a letter and writes in the correct one.

At last Newt is finished and reads the items aloud; they are a day-by-day history of our neighborhood; and there is his own humor and philosophy and there is life as he sees it. His voice has an excited, resounding quality. He pauses. "Is that word just right?"

We discuss the word. I am thrilled. Oh how wonderful—how completely satisfying—it is to have the only word that will do!

He lays down the pages, almost tenderly, so proud, so vastly pleased. "I think that's the best 'Farmer' I ever wrote." He beams. "A lot of people are goin' to mention it."

"You mustn't get your head turned," says Mrs. Kennedy.

"Oh pshaw! I guess I won't," says Newt modestly.

Eats now, cookies and apples. There we sit, looking into the isinglass, an apple in one hand and a cookie in the other, eating as hard as we can. It is nice.

The dog gets up and stretches, first one hind leg, then the other.

Mrs. Kennedy is the practical one. "Are the soapstones warm?"

We all look at the soapstones.

Time for me to go. Newt puts the pages into the stamped and self-addressed envelope. "Homer, do you mind pushin' this into the mailbox?" Mind? Why, it would be an honor!

I start out across the snow. Rabbits go hopping through the moonlight. Sleep sounds come up from the barn; the mules are at it again. The weathervane creaks.

There is the box on a post in the snow. I push the letter into it with my own hands.

Our Hat-tipping Problem

My world was an expanding one. The D. Ward King road-drag was performing wonders. Sometimes I went to the other side of the county to Uncle Will Sewell's and stayed two or three days. He had a fringe of beard that ran around the edge of his jaw like brown lace. He had to walk with a cane, dragging one foot. So many of our farmers had rheumatism. Arthritis, I suppose it would be called today. At night he would take his electric insoles out; next morning he would put them back in again. He would move slowly across the barn lot; sometimes he would stop, rest on his good leg, and edge a corncob out of the way with his cane. Then would start slowly and cautiously on again.

Not only was my world expanding geographically but also intellectually, for there were the debates, the spelling schools, the ciphering matches and our wonderful chautauquas. I can still see the great tent and the rows and rows of foot-wide planks which made the seats. They just about broke our backs, but we were learning things and were hearing about a world we had never seen. Thrilling talkers stood on that platform. One was P. G. Holden, of Iowa, who told us how to raise better corn. He had a table with ears on it and, as he talked, held them up so we could see with our own eyes. One man lectured on what was announced as "The Immortal Bard." This turned out to be Shakespeare. He was pretty dull; most of the farmers went out behind and talked crops.

It seemed a long time since Harlan and I had looked out the knothole to see Mr. Willhoyte's mare being served. Or since Ida had sent off her bust developer; or since we had seen Harlan's mother's union suit hanging on the clothesline and had gaped at the two cups.

We looked down on girls and womenfolks, as everybody did; it took men to do work and run things. Women were necessary but not up to our standard. But now—suddenly and mysteriously—girls were becoming tremendously fascinating. Sometimes we even said we'd like to attend a strawberry festival, go inside the church where the girls were sitting, and ask one to come out and eat. But mostly it was talk; we could hardly get our courage up to that.

Girls were divided into two classes; country girls and city girls. We stood completely in awe of city girls. They lead dainty existences; they were unapproachable. Never in their lives had they put on a pair of gum boots and milked a cow on a rainy night. Yet, now and then, we did get acquainted with one. Sometimes it was at the grocery; sometimes we managed to work up an acquaintance on the street. But not often as the girls' parents didn't want the girls to have anything to do with farm boys.

The best time was Farmers' Day. On this day, the city men and women had to cook a rabbit dinner for the farmers and serve it in the basement of the church. We didn't have to work; just sit there and eat and have the city people wait on us. It was nice. The city girls waited on the table and sometimes we got acquainted with one. But mostly we were so tongue-tied we couldn't think of anything new to say. We would just eat. The next time we would look at her hopefully; sometimes she would speak to us and our hearts would give a thump.

Harlan and I even talked about "going" with city girls. But it was only talk; we knew we would never get that high up

One day as Harlan and I were out cutting hedge we began to talk about hat tipping. City men were doing this all the time; and so were city boys. But no farmer in the world ever yanked his hat off just because he met a woman. And no farm boy ever swooped off his hat just because he met a neighbor girl. She would have thought he was daft.

Harlan said, "Let's tip our hats to a girl."

Harlan had a great deal more confidence and self-assurance than I had. He was the "sport" of the neighborhood.

"Do you mean to one of the girls around here?"

"I mean," said Harlan firmly, "to a city girl."

The idea was so exciting that we had to stop and sit down and rest. There we sat, with the long sharp blades of our knives covered with sticky juice from the hedge sprouts, talking it over. The sun beat down; grasshoppers hopped here and there; around us was the soft rustling of the corn. Hedge is cut in August when the farm work is slack; this makes it about the hottest work on a farm. But the hat-tipping idea made us forget the weather.

"Do you think we'd dare?" I asked.

"Of course we can." Harlan made it seem nothing at all.

"Suppose she snubs us?"

"She won't snub us," said Harlan.

I looked at him admiringly, wishing I had his confidence and his dash. "Suppose we don't see a girl we know, what then?"

"We'll keep on till we do," said undefeatable Harlan.

A tumblebug came along. His back was black and shiny, with flecks of gold toward the end. We buried him, then watched him work his way out.

We took our whetstones out of our pockets and sharpened the knives. Anything to slow up work.

"We could try," I agreed.

"We'll do it," said Harlan, the confident.

We got the jug out of the shade and swigged down a drink. Pretty soon the knives were slashing again. Harland worked on one side of the hedge and I worked on the other. The fallen sprouts made two green paths. As we slashed we talked back and forth.

"If she snubs us, people will see and laugh," I said.

"She won't snub us," said Harlan.

We decided to go to town Saturday and try the idea. We met dressed up, but were not quite so confident. There was a vast difference between talking a thing over along a hedge fence and being in town with the thing right on us. Rigs were pulling in at the hitch racks and tying to the log chains. Farmers went by taking jugs to the hardware store to get them filled with linseed oil. Heat beat down on the sidewalks and shimmered over the streets. Pigeons flew lazily in and out of the belfry. I was delighted to see that Harlan was willing to put it off a little. We went to the drugstore and had a vanilla milkshake with cinnamon on top, certainly the finest drink in the world. Five cents for a little one, ten cents for a big one, but worth it if you have the money.

"We could walk past the jail," I said. Country people liked to walk past the jail and see desperate criminals looking out the windows.

"We're goin' to hunt up a girl an' tip," said Harlan, the slave driver.

City folks walked on the west of the square; farmers walked on the other side of the street, next to the horses. We made for this side of the street, me hoping to God there wouldn't be a city girl on the farmer side. There we walked, our hearts thumping and us feeling that everybody in

182

town was watching. Farmers stood here and there, talking crops and when to turn their hogs. As we passed they nodded casually, not realizing what a tremendous adventure we were on.

Plenty of farm girls; we spoke but we didn't tip. I began to wish to heaven we had never got into it. "Harlan," I said, "let's put it off till sometime when there're not so many people around."

"We said we would and we're goin' to," announced Harlan.

We marched back again, me peering ahead and hoping no city girl would be on this side. Thank God! there wasn't. Maybe Harlan would weaken.

But he did not weaken. Nothing under the sun—as we clunked up and down—seemed to have that power. Then he did seem to weaken…

"Well," he said and my heart gave a happy thump.

But too soon.

"Let's go on the other side and try it there," he said.

Among all the city people who already seemed to be staring at us! I would as soon have walked on coals.

City people here, talking of things we knew nothing about. Harlan and I walked briskly among them. And then we saw coming toward us a city girl—Grace Langan who worked at the library. How pretty she looked, how fashionable. Inferiority laid hold of me and a sudden desire not to be seen by her gripped me. I wanted to edge over to a store window and pretend I had suddenly discovered something overwhelmingly interesting. But Harlan would not let me and we plunged straight toward this exquisite creature. A craven thought came to me; maybe I could discover that one of my shoes had become unlaced and make a dive at it. She came closer, she saw us, and then—oh, then—she smiled and spoke. For one terrified moment I stared at her, paralyzed; then my hand shot up and I snatched my hat off and murmured "Howdy-do."

We walked on, still trembling a little. But we had done it! Actually gone through with it exactly as we had said we would.

For some time after this, I was still self-conscious when I met a city girl, but I always managed to get my hat off.

I began to tip to our farm girls and women. But the neighborhood men didn't. No such foolishness for them.

I Lose My Manhood

In every farm community there is somebody that people like to "talk things over with." In ours it was Newt. Sometimes it was about buying feeder steers, sometimes when to turn the hogs. Sometimes it was more than that; sometimes it was personal problems and family situations. I can still see him sitting with gravest attention, his elbow on his knee, running his fingers through his hair, thinking. Sometimes a neighbor couldn't wait and would walk across the field to where he was plowing to get what the neighbor called "Newt's ideas." There Newt would stand, the lines over his shoulders, leaning against the plow handle. "I dunno, Earl. Let's figure into it. You don't want to stretch your wire so tight you break it." (Everybody knew what this meant, for if wire stretchers were pumped too tight the wire would break and there would be all kinds of trouble.) "Always think before you cut your grass; once it's down it's hard to stand it up again. Well, Earl, everything considered it seems to me if I was in your place, I'd do thus and so."

Earl nods. "Maybe you're right, Newt. It gets goin' round in my head so I don't know what to think."

"That's what I'd do, Earl," repeats Newt.

Earl starts back, Newt speaks to the horses, the tugs tighten and the plow begins the strange whispering sound a turning plow makes.

I was growing older; it seemed a long time since the vaccinating; and a long time since Harlan and I crept up into the haymow to watch Mr. Willhoyte's mare. Yes, I was growing, but also my problems were increasing. I was extending beyond our tight, intense little neighborhood into a new world. For I had started to high school—six miles in to town on old Dave's back—twelve long weary jolting miles on the slowest, biggest-footed, worst-mannered horse that ever plopped down a city street. I was at the "secretive age." There were certain things about myself that, almost, I would rather have died than confide to any other living human being. Yet how many suggestive stories I had heard in the hayfield, at public sales and at hog scalds. How exciting, how titillating those stories had been. How they inflamed and set my imagination on fire. But some of the stories were too strong; sometimes I felt ashamed to be in a group listening to them. However, riding back and forth on old Dave I would think of the stories and go over every alluring detail. Then, almost within the same moment, I would feel ashamed.

I come slowly upon a point. Saturdays we went to town, tied the horses to the log chain hitch racks, then went from store to store, trading. As choring time came upon us, Pa would say, "We'll meet at the hack." In a few minutes we would be clopping home; the water tower would fall away behind us. Sometimes I would turn and look back. There it would be, the demarcation between country and town. Sometimes it would seem wonderful if I could leave the farm and move to town; people in town appeared to have so much more fun than we did; and to do so many more things. Go so many more places; travel on trains. I had never been out of the county. Nor, for that matter, had any of the other boys or girls in our neighborhood, except Bertha Scott who had gone back to Cadiz, Ohio, to see her kinfolks. When she got back to our school, the teacher drew a map of Ohio on the board, and Bertha made a speech about her trip. She said that General Custer had been born in Cadiz. It made us feel small, for nobody famous had ever been born in our town, or, for that matter, even in our section of the state. Jesse James had been in our town once to see about holding up the bank; that was as close to fame as we could come.

I got there first and in our hack I found an advertising booklet. Town boys had contracts with advertising and mail-order medical firms to put pamphlets and booklets in farmers' rigs; the boys went from wagon to wagon and buggy to buggy tossing the booklets in. The booklets were usually for Radway's Ready Relief, Grandpas's Wonder Tar Soap, Dr. Pirces's Golden Medical Discovery, Piso's Consumption Cure, Lydia E Pinkham's Vegetable Compound, Horseford's Acid Bitters, Cascarets—they work while you sleep, Dr. Kilmer's Swamp Root, Hostetters's Bitters, Dr. King's Gargling Oil, or others we knew by heart. But on this special day there was one I had never seen before. On the cover was the picture of a man suffering the tortures of the damned. Written slantwise across the booklet, in handwriting, were the dreadful words: Lost Manhood.

I didn't know what lost manhood was, but I knew I didn't want it to happen to me.

I had time only to glance at the booklet before my father came. But I saw that it dealt with something I could not possibly discuss with him—private affairs. In fact, I would almost rather have died than mention such a subject. And this was true of all the boys in our neighborhood. Women were women, and babies were babies. We would grow up to understand such things in due time, our parents held.

I got a chance to read some of it while we were choring and what I read alarmed me thoroughly. It was addressed to men, as the booklet said, "between the ages of sixteen and the married state." That took me in. It said that men—especially young men—between these ages were apt to have bad dreams at night and, as a result of these dreams, have their priceless manhood drained away. I gave a jump, for that was exactly what was happening to me.

I read more while Pa was breaking corn for the steers.

The booklet said that those who had their priceless manhood drained away were doomed to end their lives in misery. I gave a start there, too, for I did not want to end my life in misery.

I raced through milking and after my father had started to the house with the pails, I took another squint. The little gray booklet said that all over the land were men who were drifting into an abyss of torture and self-negation. I was not quite sure what self-negation was, but I knew I wanted none of it.

I got another whack at the heartbreaking booklet after supper; that was my study time. I had a special coal-oil lamp on a little table and, by putting the booklet inside my schoolbook, I found out more about the abyss. There were words I had never heard before; one was titillation. I looked it up. It was dreadful. Another was titivation. It was almost as bad.

I turned to a chapter that had the heading: "The Results of Lost Manhood." I was horrified. It was a curse that befell all men who had their precious manhood drained away by what the booklet called "nocturnal seminal emissions." I turned to look that up. I knew before I read it that it was going to be bad, for, by now, I realized that everything—*everything*—in that cursed booklet was bad. One phrase was: "the terrors that come by night." I read the phrase again and my heart sank. For that booklet had found my secret soul, a part of me I had bared to no one in the world.

Another chapter was entitled: "How To Tell if the Curse of Lost Manhood Has Descended Upon You."

I knew, without reading, it had. I discovered one thing that led to my lost manhood was that one's mind dwelt on what the booklet called "the attractions of the opposite sex." It had me there. Also it said that there were yearnings—best left undescribed—that came to young men who were losing their manhood. There I was again. Another symptom of a young man losing his manhood was that he felt a lassitude of a morning at getting-up time. That, indeed, went home. I had had this most of my life. But had never suspected the pitiful condition that was causing it.

Pimples, the booklet said, were a sure sign. No need to look in the mirror, for I knew I had the dreadful telltale marks.

It seemed to me I could not bear to read another paragraph. But I could not stop. I must know the evil end that awaited me. This booklet that understood my case so well said that at the end of a day a person who was losing his manhood was apt to feel "unduly" tired. There I was again. I not only felt unduly tired now and then, but practically every night; sometimes I was so unduly tired that I would fall asleep twenty seconds after my head hit the pillow. And there I would lie, dead to the world, dead almost to myself, until five the next morning when Pa came in and shook me.

As I rode back and forth to school, I found that I did not grow as hungry as I used to. Always, when I had got home, I had dashed out to the pantry and had got some bread and butter and apple butter. I didn't need it now. Even when suppertime came, I did not feel hungry.

The booklet told what would happen to man, afflicted as I most certainly was, when he entered the "married state." I would wreck not only my life but the life of the trusting helpmate who had given herself to me to love and cherish. I was profoundly shocked. For I did not want to wreck the life of any woman. The booklet said that if the reader would study his case he would find that this tired feeling was slowly growing; also his lassitude. The next step was loss of appetite. *Spang!* that went home.

The next was what the booklet called "unwarranted irritable spells." Sometimes, as I brooded over my approaching fate, I found that I was irritatedly kicking old Dave in the sides and yelling at him...another downward step.

"Wandering attention." I knew the moment I spotted the words that they were meant for me. For, as the class droned along it was all I could do to keep my mind on what the teacher was saying. Not only was this true at school, but also at home. My father would tell me to do certain chores. I would not think of them again until he discovered they hadn't been done.

"Homer, why do I have to tell you twice? It seems to me you would take interest in your work. Don't you want to help?"

I would look at him, agonized. I wanted to do what he wished, but my mind was slipping. "The insane asylums," said the deadly little gray booklet, "are filled with men who have lost their manhood." I writhed. For Number 2 State Insane Asylum was at St. Joseph and in it were over three thousand inmates. Half of them were probably men... Someday I might be there; my poor father and mother would come to see me and would find me throwing up feathers and trying to catch them. For once one of our neighbors had been taken away, and this was what he was doing the morning they came for him.

Day by day I brooded on what I had read. I wanted desperately to talk to someone. We had a hired hand, but he was so coarse I could not quite hint around to find if he had ever been troubled with lost manhood. I could not ask Harlan. I liked to talk to Harlan about girls and their possibilities, but never—never in this world—could I even hint that I was slowly losing my manhood.

The nights of anguish and days of terror went on. Every few nights I lost some more of my precious manhood.

There was a way I could save it. I had read it that first evening, but I could not possibly meet the necessary requirements. This was to send five dollars to the company, Lansdowne, Pennsylvania, and their priceless remedy would promptly be forwarded to any sufferer from man's greatest scourge. Not only did I not have five dollars, but I had no way of earning it, or getting that much money without attracting attention. Each year I planted onions and sold them; each year my father gave me a pig; when the pig went away, the money was mine. But I had spent my last pig; I could not possibly go to my father and ask him to give me money. In fact, it was only on the most urgent need that I could bring myself to ask my father for money at all. Certainly, nothing so large as five dollars. He might have given it to me, but I could not possibly have asked. Once, when we had gone to town to celebrate the Fourth of July, he had given me a half dollar. "Spend it all, if you want to." And, for a moment that morning there on Main Street in front of the grocery, I worshiped my father. But that was when I was much younger. Before my manhood was being taken from me.

In the back of the booklet were what the booklet called "Our Unsolicited Testimonials." There they were, with the names of the men and the names of the states where the men lived. But not the town, or city, or rural route. But I did not doubt, for the letters were in print and what was in print surely must be true. I looked at the names and the states of the men who had been saved from a fate worse than death and wished with all my heart that I could be saved.

On the last page, in a little box, it said: "Free! If a sufferer will write us, we will be glad to send additional information free of charge." Maybe I could find some ray of hope in this additional information.

I was shocked, some days later, to get a printed postcard from Mr. Staples, who ran our express office, saying that a package was being held for me with five dollars due. I knew instantly where it was from; and I knew I had no chance in the world of getting the money. But I *had* to get it or the firm would make trouble for me. I might be sued. Then *everybody* would know. I would be dragged through court. If only I hadn't written for that additional information.

I counted up my money, as I had many times before, and I had a little over two dollars.

I thought of Newt. If I could get the money from anyone in the world, it would be from understanding, kindhearted Newt, the man I loved most dearly of anyone in the world outside my family. I would go to him; I would get the money. Newt would not fail me.

I hated to go, as I had never hated anything in my life. Would I have to confess? Surely he would not make me do that.

In no time at all I was at his house. He was making gambrels. I stood watching, putting off the dreadful moment when I must brace him.

He stood one end of the Osage hedge stick on the block and shaped it with neat strokes, for Newt did everything well.

I kept putting off the moment, yet knowing that I must—I *would*—ask him. Always I called him Newt and never with embarrassment, for he was Newt to me and to everybody.

"Mr. Kennedy," I began, "what would you say if I asked to borrow three dollars?"

Three dollars! A day's wages for a man with a team.

He laid down the hedge stick and looked up at me—with that cast in his eye—puzzled. "I don't rightly know what I'd say, Homer. I suppose it sort of depends like."

"Well," I said, trying to be very grown and man-to-man, "if you can do it without inconveniencing yourself too much, I'd like to have it. You'll get it back all right; you needn't ever worry about that, Mr. Kennedy."

"Did you get into a betting game with those older boys?"

"No, sir. I—I just happen to need it."

He pointed a gambrel. "Did you speak to your Pa?" I moved uneasily. "Well, no, I haven't."

"Haven't you got any hides?" This was a reference to my trapping.

"It's the wrong season."

The unusualness of suddenly being braced for so much money seemed to grow on Newt. "Is it anything you can tell me about?"

I stood agonized, looking at him sitting on one end of the chopping block, wanting to tell him and yet unable to reveal my secret. "I'd rather not."

He seemed to catch something in my tremendous—my almost overwhelming—earnestness. "You haven't got yourself into a situation with a girl, have you?"

"No, sir."

Grandpa, came slowly out and stopped to watch. "Point 'em a little more, Newton. It's hard to engage them in cold weather, if you don't."

"Yes, Pa," said Newt patiently. He chopped a few more strokes.

"Now you're gettin' it," said Grandpa. Satisfied, he turned and scuffed slowly back to the L.

Newt looked up at me and I knew the very moment had come. "I'll do it, Homer. I'll go in now."

My heart gave a joyful leap. Newt—the best man who ever lived!

He came back with three silver dollars. "This is just between you and I, is it?"

"Yes."

"I'll abide by it."

Mr. Staples laid a brown package on the counter; the package was tied with heavy cord and on the knot there was a blob of red sealing wax.

I opened it, when I got home, and found a box a little less in size than the palm of my hand; when I took the lid off I found three compartments, each with a layer of cotton on the bottom, and each containing a dozen or so small colored pills. Each compartment had its own color. Pasted on the side of each compartment was a slip of instructions for what the slip called "the suffering patient."

> First Day of Treatment: Take a pill of this color. Second
> Day of Treatment: Take a pill of this color. Third Day of
> Treatment: Take a pill of this color. Now go back to the
> beginning and repeat treatment until relief is secured.

I gazed with an outpouring of thankfulness at the magic pills—the wonderful, the God-given pills that were going to save me. And so deep, so complete was my faith that I knew the pills would cure me and make me whole again. There was a small printed slip inside which said that the sufferer would not immediately experience any change in his condition, but, if he continued faithfully to take the pills, he would begin—little by little—to feel better: One thing was very important and this was that the sufferer must have faith in the sovereign remedy and he must stop worrying. By doing this, the slip continued, the sufferer would aid the work of the marvelous pellets. In time, the sufferer would be returned to sturdy manhood. This I wanted above everything else in this world.

I hid the box in the hayloft and began taking the pills with faith and gratitude.

The little printed slip was exactly right. At first I did not notice it change, but I continued faithfully, each color in its proper order. Indeed, so deep was my faith that I stopped worrying; the little pills would cure me. I began to sleep better; my appetite returned; old Dave and I continued to jog back and forth. But I was gaining. The possessive dreams returned, but I did not worry. I knew I had them licked. In fact, my gain was so remarkable I did not have to finish the box of colored pills.

At last I earned the money and at last I started down the hedge-lined road I knew so well. Fear laid hold of me. Would Newt make me tell, now that it was over, why. I had so desperately wanted the money? He was nailing up a gate where a hay frame had jammed into it. We talked, as we always did, about everything. *Bang! bang! bang!* went the hammer. Most farmers talked of things around them—the crops, the weather, neighborhood news. We talked—Newt and I—about things we had read in the papers and things I had studied in school and the items he was going to write next week for the county paper.

I hauled out the money.

"There it is, Newt!" I said—no "Mr. Kennedy" now. "Here's the three iron men I borrowed."

He stopped hammering and looked at me intently, that strange, hypnotic cast showing. "Did it serve you?"

"Yes."

The moment had come. Now he was going to ask me why I had wanted the money. The disgraceful thing was still too close upon me. I could not tell him.

"So everything is all right?" he asked invitingly.

"Yes, sir," I said, dropping back into *sir.*

"Are you and me the only ones who know about our deal?"

"Yes, sir."

He looked at me again; I was turning red and beginning, under his deep scrutiny, to fidget. "All right, Homer. I'll never speak of it."

My heart soared away. Never was there such an understanding friend in the world. I flew into the work with him and soon we had the gate fixed as good as new.

Part III
Humor and Commentary

As a humorist Homer Croy enjoys his most enduring legacy, as the following samples attest. Prior to the publication of his breakthrough bestseller *West of the Water Tower* in 1923, Croy put food on the table mostly with his homespun, freelance humor writing, examples of which are included here for the first time in print in over seventy-five years. In "A Kiss and a Red Ear," "How to Treat a Cow," and "On Meeting Cyclones," all written for *Collier's*, Croy cuts contemporary pundits, professors, and pressmen down to size, countering academic inanities with episodes from his own down-to-earth middle American upbringing. The exception is "Six Years Out of College and Still Broke," which, while it references Missouri boyhood chums that made it big, locates itself firmly in the young author's present, jobless moment. Somewhat fictionalized, "Six Years" features some trademark Croy biographical revisions, as the author mentions graduating from college (Croy's graduation from the University of Missouri was thwarted, ironically, by a failing grade in English) while positioning himself as a budding scientist rather than the struggling ex-liberal arts student he was in real life. It is likely, too, that the names of childhood friends as they appear here are pseudos. Beyond such comedic inventions, however, the piece closely mirrors Croy's post-University experience, as his insider's reference to St. Louis washrooms makes evident. (Croy eked out a living as a newspaperman in St. Louis after leaving the

University.) More autobiographically revelatory is the seemingly offhand line "In getting my first job after leaving college, I walked 1,345 miles"—at first blush hyperbolic, but, on further examination, an exact reference to the distance from St. Louis to Boston, where Croy headed after his stint at the St. Louis *Post-Dispatch*.

The humor and sentiment Croy wrote for *Leslie's Weekly* resembles, in tone and subject matter, the *Collier's* work, and shows Croy solidifying a style. In the articles "Seventy-Seven Times Thankful" and "The Joyous County Fair," wherein a then-thirty-something-year-old Croy writes in the voice of an older nostalgic, the author leavens his verifiable farm past with the use of a narrative persona. Likewise, "Making Maple Sugar" sticks closely to Croy's farm past, though certain details—for instance, the use of the appellation "father" instead of Croy's usual "Pa" and the reference to "we children" to suggest brothers and sisters or a neighborhood gaggle of kids—hint at embellishment.

"The Uses of Obesity" from *Life* magazine turns the notion of the "starving artist" on its head, satirizing a superficial literary fashion toward writing about weight loss and the vogue of "authors [writing] about themselves" more generally. In such a world, how, Croy wonders, could a thin, farm-born, thoroughly "normal" writer pay the gas bill? Tongue in cheek, the bittersweet piece nevertheless makes passing mention of the burdensome mortgage on the Long Island house Croy would eventually lose to the bank.

The concluding selection from *What Grandpa Laughed At* represents the author's attempt to distill the quintessence of middle American humor across the decades—what he calls the "Six Gold-medal Jokes" of all-time. Taking as its thesis the notion that "the history of this country could be told by its jokes," the 1948 anthology attempts to do just that. While the "Gold-medal Jokes" may seem quaint to twenty-first century ears, it should be noted that American comedy finds its wellspring in the "good clean joke," a Croy calling card, not coincidentally.

"A Kiss and a Red Ear"

I see in the papers that the scientists are doing all they can to eliminate the red ear. They say that this shows that the breed of corn is running out, and that the red ear is good for nothing.[4]

I beg leave to differ with them. It is good for a kiss.

And there is nothing better than a kiss—unless it's a hammock.

Old Mr. Taylor, who lived on Clear Creek, had a large family of girls, and it didn't take him any time to get his fodder shucked out. Along in the fall he would spread his fodder on the hall floor of the barn and have a shucking bee. Every time you found a red ear you had to kiss your partner, and I certainly loved to shuck corn. It is my favorite recreation. The work never galls on me. I'm not much on standing corn, but when it comes to fodder I dearly love to strip the ear bare of its ensheltering, fibrous coat.

I could shuck best when sitting next to Fannie. So could Lafe Stamper. Lafe was as thick through the shoulders as a pantry, and was fast making a reputation for himself as a blacksmith. I was more of the kitchenette order of architecture, and addicted to the use of poetry. Lafe didn't know a poetical foot from a last winter's overshoe, but he had arms like laundry bags.

One night at Mr. Taylor's husking bee I was the first one to find a red ear. It occurred to me at once what to do next. No one had to remind me that my work wasn't done. I leaned over toward Fannie and went at it painstakingly, and when I had finished I felt that none could call me slipshod. But when I had finished I heard Lafe calling me something under his breath, and I surmised that it wasn't slipshod.

Pretty soon I chanced upon another red ear. This time I displayed more technique than ever, and, when I returned to my husking, Lafe was still mumbling under his breath words that I could not catch.

Strange as it may seem, I found another red ear. I could get hardly any work done for finding red ears, but I got other things done. I got them done with *éclat*. I used *éclat* because I knew that Lafe's *éclat* crop had winter killed. Not once during the evening did Lafe find a red ear, while my *éclat* held out till the last shock was shucked.

---

4 From *Collier's*, July 26, 1913

That night on the way home I found Lafe waiting for me by the side of the road. I had not asked him to meet me in the glen, but he seemed anxious to spend a few moments with me alone. I noticed that he had his hands tightly closed. I tried to excuse myself on the plea that I was tired after shucking all that corn, but he would listen to none of my excuses.

"You are so fond of red ears that I am going to give you two to take with you," said Lafe in a high, determined key. I tried to expostulate with him, but he came up and thrust his chin into my face. I withdrew my face and tried to use my *éclat* on him, but I found that it wouldn't work in a glen. I looked around for some place to retire to, but Lafe advanced upon my ears and tried to hammer them into my head. This aroused my indignation, and I spoke to him bitterly, but he only renewed his efforts. When he had finished with my ears he opened hostilities on my face, and finally climbed up on my stomach with both knees and worked steadily away with both hands and feet, using words that I do not care to repeat. After at time, he withdrew, and a kind neighbor took me home in a buckboard. I did not thank the neighbor, as I did not know that he had taken me home until the next morning.

But it was no time until I was out and myself again. In a couple of weeks I could sit up, and in three weeks I could walk to the front porch.

But there was an inner injury that stung me worse than where Lafe had been on my features. He publicly said that I had used the same ear all evening!

Still, I wish the agricultural scientists wouldn't do away with the red ears. I wish they would leave just one anyway!

Swimming on Sunday

Governor Major of Missouri says that the happiest days of his life were when he was a boy on a farm and ran away, swimming, Sunday afternoon.[5]

I have been a boy on a farm and have run away, swimming, Sunday afternoon, but my great love of truth keeps me from saying that these were the happiest days of my boyhood.

One Sunday I invited two boys to come home with me after Sunday school. At dinner Pa told me not to go swimming in the creek that afternoon, as I might get the yellow jaundice. Yellow jaundice becomes very few people. Yellow jaundice makes a person look too much as though somebody had dropped an egg in full possession of its powers on him and then had maliciously hidden the towel.

We boys wandered out to the creek. We looked into the cool depths of the water, but we couldn't see any yellow jaundice. We felt that it had been a backward season for the yellow jaundice, and that probably all the spawn had been killed. For some reason or other, I forgot all about what Pa had said, and in a fit of absent-mindedness took off my clothes. When next I noticed what I was doing I had water in my ear.

We swam down the creek and made a slippery bank, where we would go up to the top and coast down on the lower end of our spinal column. Tiring of this, we began to throw mud at each other, lifting our voices in light-hearted laughter. I had just planted a large, pliable handful of mud in the ear of one of the fellows, and was laughing at his plight, when I saw Pa coming down by the creek with a long, shapely hazel brush sprout in his hand. The plight had thickened. Then it suddenly occurred to me what Pa had said at dinner. I felt nonplused at myself for having forgotten it, and decided to go to some quiet spot and think it over alone. With me to think was to act. I reached with great celerity; it was the best brand of celerity I had ever come across.

I darted out through the underbrush toward my clothes, but some unthinking person had removed my raiment. The person had left no clues. I would have been more content if he had taken the clues and left the clothes.

---

5 From *Collier's* September 13, 1913

I must have clothes! What would people think if they met me on the moor with nothing on except a mud bath? I wanted to save these people all the embarrassment I could, so I streaked it for the house of a neighbor. Here I intended to bathe in the water tank and get enough clothes to return home. But the neighbor's dog did not know this: he misunderstood my plans. He thought I had designs on the house. But I hadn't on a single design. All I had on was a layer of gumbo and a friendly mien. I had no place to put my hands. The pockets on my friendly mien were missing.

The dog was a large, quick-tempered creature and rushed at me impulsively. Without my trousers I kept wondering what he would find to set his teeth into. He came at me rapidly, as if it wasn't worrying him. It worried me greatly, although I said nothing to him about it. When he came at me I withdrew. I withdrew so fast that I did not stop to open the gate for him.

Although I was not hampered by any wearing apparel or finery of any kind, I did not make the speed I desired. The dog was good at running. I don't know whether he was bred for running or not—I did not stop to cavil. I had left all my cavil in my other clothes. The dog snapped at my calf. I removed it as rapidly as I could, and spoke to him in a deep guttural, but he paid no heed to my wish to be left alone. Finally I reached the high wooden gate behind our barn and mounted it. Once I was safe, the dog turned and withdrew in the direction whence he came. No effort was made on my part to detain him. Just as I drew in a sigh of relief I heard a step. It was Pa with the same hazel sprout in his hand.

Our greeting was short and our conversation desultory. When I came down Pa told me to turn my back to him, although I felt that this was not manners. But immediately I felt something else. I stood with my back to him for a long while, first on one foot, then on the other: part of the time I spent in midair. When Pa and I had finished with the hazel sprout it was about worn out. So was Pa, and I myself felt that we had accomplished enough for one day.

That night at supper mother looked at me and exclaimed: "Why, son, it beats me where you got that mud!"

"It beats me where I got it, too!" I answered fervently, but mother thought mine was just a fill-in answer.

Governor Major's happiest days may have been the ones when he ran away and went swimming on Sunday, but his father must have patronized in a different hazel patch from mine.

How to Treat a Cow

Some scientific expert engaged in farming has just discovered that a cow should be treated as a lady.[6] Sometimes this is difficult, as often this depends on her early training.

We used to have a cow back home, a large roan with a low, retreating forehead, who had a way of stepping in the bucket that lost her many friends. No cow can endear herself to a person when she is standing with one foot in the bucket. No cow with the right kind of early life will do this.

When a person is thrown into the society of a cow it does not take him too long to find out what her early life has been. It she stands with one foot in the bucket for any length of time, one can feel morally certain that her mother was not of the highest type.

Our cow's name was Clarice. I was often called on to milk Clarice. I was loath to do this, and she was just as loath to have me. We were never what might be called fast friends.

Once, with a bucket on my arm, I approached her on the subject of milking. Clarice was standing in the milk lot with a sad, far-away look in her eyes, as if all her dreams had not come true, going over her supper for a second time. Clarice was always going back and putting a few finishing touches to her supper.

I placed the pail under her body, well toward the rear, and seated myself on a one-legged stool. I had not asked her if I could do this but I felt that all would be well. Clarice had a window weight on the end of her tail, that she had picked up fighting flies down in the creek. I did not know that she was armed. I had just turned my attention to the pail when she hit me with the window weight. She was a good hitter.

I did not say anything but gave her a significant look. Fitting my shoulder into her side I again took hold of her. I put my hands around the parts mentioned and squeezed them. While I was trying to get the milk running she again hit me with the window weight. I gave her another significant look, followed by a lowering glance, and again placed my ear in her flank and reached for the source of supply. My hands had barely closed

---

6 From *Collier's*, November 1, 1913

over the source of supply before I felt the muscles in her flank gather and become taut. Still suspicion did not strike me—but something else did. The last I remember distinctly was having my ear in her flank; the next thing I knew I had it in a pillow. From that time on there was a certain coldness between us. Her charm was gone. She now had feet of clay.

One evening I was crossing the meadows just as night was stealing out of the woods and blowing his black breath over the countryside, when I heard an angry voice behind me. I immediately turned around. It was Clarice's husband.

He was coming at me in high dudgeon. He had his nose close to the ground and his eyes on me. I saw that I was not needed, and I turned and started away as fast as I could. The husband came on apace. When I turned I found that he had come on several of them.

I headed toward a tree. When I arrived at the tree I took hold of a lower limb and started to ascend at once. I was out of breath, but I felt that it would be best to wait until I was at the top to regain it. I felt a shock, and in a moment saw the seat of a pair of trousers on his horns. I felt that they were mine. I kept on climbing. This did not deter me a jot or a tittle. Not a jittle.

My pursuer stood under the tree, and, placing his nose near the ground, said things that I do not care to repeat, for I do not know how many may be reading these lines. He stayed a long while under the tree, while I remained in it. I had no desire to come down. I would wait until my caller had gone. I was glad that the tree had selected that spot for its nativity. I was thankful that it had not seen fit to cast its fortunes a quarter of a mile farther on.

At last the unpleasant creature left. I did not try to get him to stay. I was tiring of his company. One or twice I yawned openly. Finally, in the gloaming, he joined Clarice, and the two strolled off.

I did not feel favorably disposed toward either party. Try as I might, I could not help picking flaws in their breeding. Clarice had not lived up to my ideal of a lady, and her better half had fallen far short of my idea of a gentleman.

On Meeting Cyclones

A Kansas man says that he as invented a simple house that is cyclone proof.[7]

I do not wish to attack the man's character without knowing more about him, but he is a liar. That is a harsh word, but I went though a cyclone once, and feel deeply on the subject. I, for one, don't believe cyclones will ever be successfully domesticated. I cannot picture a full-grown cyclone eating out of anyone's hand.

A large Clydesdale cyclone visited our parts once, and when it moved on there was only a ragged hole in the ground where the well had once stood, and a deep-rooted feeling of animosity in my neighborhood against strange cyclones. Our family saw the cyclone coming, but we had no idea that it was a rude, uncultured cyclone without any trace of bringing up. We gathered on the porch to watch the spectacle. We had never had a cyclone perform for our amusement before.

It drew itself up into a funnel shape and advanced boldly toward us. Before any greetings were exchanged we saw that it was not a friend of the family, and withdrew into the cyclone cellar to let the cyclone knock at the door, unheeded. We heard it muttering under its breath, and when we looked out later the door of our house was gone. Then we missed the porch where we had so lately stood; soon, to our astonishment, we saw that the whole house had been removed. The cyclone had left no address.

One Kansas cyclone that I knew in a passing sort of way blew a cow away and came back two days later for a calf.

One day I was out alone on the lea, driving Light Horse Harry to a buckboard, when a cyclone came along. Although I gave no sign of recognition, it came up and accosted me. I tried to wave it aside, but it grew coarse and abusive. It gathered me up by the waist, took the buggy out from under me, and whisked it away. It left me lonely and morose in the air, with the earth far removed. I always like the earth near me, but I thought better not to take up the matter with the cyclone just yet. I would wait until it had a full stomach and its house slippers on. I could not see Light Horse Harry and the vehicle, but I felt all was not well with them.

---

7 From *Collier's*, August 2, 1913

Although I had only a speaking acquaintance with cyclones, I saw that this cyclone was of low caste and coarse-mannered, and felt that there could be no real sympathy between us. While I was turning this over in my mind the cyclone was busily engaged in turning me over, although I had expressed no such desire.

I saw the buggy going by with large footprints on the dashboard. I surmised these belonged to Light Horse Harry, although he was no longer with the rig, but I did not stop to examine. I would let the mystery go unsolved until some other day when I was not so pressed for time.

In a few minutes, I awoke to the realization that I was surrounded by a coalmine. I didn't know whose coalmine it was, so I thought I had better get out. I climbed up the rope on the windlass and peeked out. The cyclone had not missed me and had gone on in search of pastures new; I made no effort to call it back. I climbed out and looked around for the buckboard. At last I found half of the whip socket, torn and mutilated—all that was mortal of my buckboard.

Light Horse Harry got back in a couple of days, but he was never the same horse again. He had a low, hacking cough, and every time he felt a zephyr from the northwest he would crowd under my arm and whinny for protection. I tried to explain that I would be of little protection to him, as I had lost my ability to look a large-boned, dapple-gray cyclone in the eye and cow it, but his faith in my cowing ability was unlimited. So I traded him off, that he might never know what little influence I had with a large, sixteen-hand, stall-fed cyclone.

Cyclones are all right to read about, but they are poor company.

Six Years Out of College and Still Broke

After I had personally seen to the framing of my degree, I sat down and wrote a number of dignified letters to different prominent firms, telling them that I had just finished my college career and would be willing to entertain a proposition from them provided that I had Saturday off, an assistant that I could depend on, and a capable stenographer to look after the detail work.[8] I enclosed a list of my grades, calling particular attention to my work in invertebrate anatomy and to my thesis on "The Cellular Structure of the Amoebea." The firms wrote back and said they had all the stenographers they needed, and that they preferred girls anyway.

Experts on the life and habits of the amoeba were not in as high demand as I had thought. I had imagined that a person who could write a whole thesis on an animal the size of a pinhead would have little trouble in naming his own figure. The amoeba market was poor. It was sickening the way the world could get along without knowing anything about our simplest manifestations of life.

The ignorance among successful businessmen was appalling: some of them said they had never heard of the amoeba and wanted to know if they had any specimens at the zoo.

Writing to different firms whose addresses I took from the magazines didn't get me anywhere, so I began answering the ads in the paper. One advertisement in particular caught my attention. A junior partner was wanted in the leather-belting business. The word junior caught my eye. That suited me to a T. That was where I belonged. Then I could work up to senior partner, and after a time come to own the concern. I hadn't a very clear idea what leather-belting was—weather it was to go around the ladies' waists or around flywheels, but it wouldn't take me long to master the details. It wouldn't be long until I could write a thesis on "The Tissue Structure of a Leather Belt"

The more I thought about the business the surer I became that the leather-belting business was profitable. When you come to think of it, nearly everybody wore a belt—even little schoolgirls were wearing them—and somebody had to supply the demand. If flywheels were meant, think

---

8 From *Collier's*, June 21, 1913

how many machines in the world had flywheels! It was a pretty poor machine that didn't have some kind of flywheel. With the tireless energy that I would put into the concern, I would organize a combine and form a leather-belting trust, so that not a flywheel in all the land could turn without my permission.

It seemed strange that no one had ever thought of cornering the flywheel business of the country. Still, it is the simplest things that are always being overlooked. It was not until the year that Shakespeare died that the circulation of the blood was discovered. Up to that time they had thought that the arteries had air in them, for they were always empty when examined after death. In all history of the world, in ten thousand years, no one has had discovered why the blood circulated until William Harvey announced it in 1616. I easily understood why no one had hit upon the idea of cornering the flywheel-belting business.

I went to see the people who had the leather-belting business. I found them on a side street away up on a dark floor with a lot of power shafts going and wheels turning. It seemed a bit strange that a business with such large possibilities should be lost in such an out-of-the-way place.

The manager had to look over three chairs before he could find one for me with a bottom. When I told him that I was a college graduate, he seemed very much impressed, and when I imparted to him, with all the modestly I could command and still be businesslike, that I had specialized in the life and habits of the amoeba, he was delighted. When I gave him a copy of my pamphlet, "The Cellular Structure of the Amoeba," his eyes shone and he said he would take it home to his wife. It did me good to see a man in the sordid world of business who appreciated a college education at its true worth.

"You have just the spirit we want," said the manager. "You seem to be honest, conscientious, sober, industrious, and capable." I wondered how he had found out about these qualities. "You have a mind for detail, and at the same time you have a broad grasp of affairs that will soon make you a valued officer in our organization." I agreed perfectly. He was putting into words my own ideas, but I couldn't help thinking how he knew all these things. "You have a highly trained brain and one that should make a revolution in this business. It seems too good to be true that we have been fortunate enough to meet you.

Then he brought in the senior member, and we went to lunch together. They began telling me little things about the business they had not mentioned before. The business was doing well—oh, yes, indeed— but they needed just a little more capital. Of course, I had understood that from the heading of the column under which I had found the advertisement—"Business Chances"—and, of course, was willing to invest money in the business. If I invested $2000 or $3000, of course I could expect to become merely general manager, but if I put in $5,000 I could become vice president. The money was sure to double in three years—oh, yes, absolutely.

Here they were asking me to invest $5000 when I had been doing my own socks and handkerchiefs for two months and using a kneaded rubber on my collars to save the wear and tear of a laundry. You know how hard laundries are on collars. You can take a bright, young collar to steam laundry and it comes back a haggard and toothless wreck.

A kneaded rubber to erase the soiled marks costs only five cents and will last a year.

When I told him that I did not care to invest at the present they both looked at me in astonishment. Then they gave me to understand that I was no gentleman for trying to trick them into believing that I meant business. I had been coolly deceiving them and was probably some kind of confidence man. They would not turn me over to the authorities this time, but I must never show my face in their establishment again. Hurt and sorrowed, the two men got up and left me to pay the dinner checks. I did and walked home, and on the way bought a small pair of scissors that could be used for either manicuring or trimming cuffs.

I quit looking for a position and began hunting for a job.

When I still was in English A., I scorned $25 a week and pitied the poor man who had to support a wife on $50 a week. In getting my first job after leaving college, I walked 1,345 miles. It paid $12 a week, with night work only on Wednesdays, Thursdays, and Fridays, and an occasional Sunday. My greatest responsibility was to let down early, open up, and see that the fire buckets in the halls were kept filled. I was so glad to get my week's wages that I divided it in three pockets before I went out on the street and wondered aloud how a man with only a wife could fritter away $50 a week.

A dollar looked as big to me as a washbowl in an East St. Louis hotel, and it was fall before I could cross my legs without being afraid the top of my socks would work out of my shoes.

I began noticing queer things as the years slipped by. The fellows who drew down the big grades in school and who were expected by everybody to be in the Cabinet the day after they were thirty-five were still helping father with the grocery, because he hadn't been feeling well lately, and the men who didn't know enough in class to tell a dithyramboid from a pterodactyl were now the ones who talked about demountable rims.

There was Puss Fleming. He was as strong as an ox and had the wide-awake expression of a double blank domino. Puss had muscles like the colored chart in the front of a physiology, but he was as out of place in the classroom as a maiden lady at sixty-three at a structural ironworkers' convention. If you shook your finger at him suddenly and asked who was Gutenberg, who invented printing in 1450, he would say: "The man who found Stanley in Africa. He suffered many hardships." He could name off the Presidents of the United States down to Jefferson glibly enough, but after that he would be pretty sure to have Captain Lawrence and Paul Revere taking turns sitting in the first chair of the land, with Kit Carson in the Cabinet.

Just the opposite was Charley Eglehoff. Charley had a head the size of a globe in the primary department showing Coin, Iowa, and had the general tendency of a bed slat to put on flesh. His forehead was as high as your hand and he cried all night if he got below 98 percent. He could repeat off the kings of England like a poem and worked plane geometry in his head. He said that the atomic theory was more interesting than Ben Hur, and had learned the encyclopedia by heart down to *Carthorse–Everglades*. He pressed his suit by putting it between the mattress and bed springs every night and had a theory that knocked the nebular hypothesis all hollow. Before he was a senior, every boy in college had promised to vote for him for President. We called him by his first name so it would feel natural when we dropped in to see him after the fourth of March. We would slap him on the back in the East Room in a few years and say: "Hello, Charley, old boy—you remember the time Hud Phillips put molasses on your chair at the club? Looking well, Charley. Guess you must be pretty busy, Charley. We're proud of you Charley, old man. Well, remember me to the missus, Charley. So long. Charley."

We did hope that he would give Puss Fleming a job around the White House at something like putting seals on legal papers or covering the canary at night.

How things change! Charley Eglehoff is now superintendent of schools in a town so small that you have a map the size of a horse blanket and put one finger at the letter P at the top and another finger at the figure four on the side of the map and bring your fingers together to find the place. He is well-liked and has five children. He is now as far as *Ulysses–Wubb*, and rusty circles show on his trousers, as if he were too absorbed in knocking the nebular hypothesis hollow ever to put papers over them.

The other day I heard that Puss Fleming was in Chicago, and dropped in to see him. I wondered aloud what he was doing in a big city all by himself, and decided that I wouldn't go around until after lunch so that Puss wouldn't feel embarrassed. An office boy in uniform met me, with reading on his collar. It said, "The Fleming Company." The name Pendleton Fleming was on a door that lead down an aisle, and under his name were two words: "Private Offices." I thought that was going a bit too far. A porter in uniform was prowling around with a feather duster, three kinds of patent dustless cloths, and a chamois skin, trying to find a flyspeck.

"I'd like to see Mr. Fleming," I said, thinking how funny *Mister* sounded.

"Has he an appointment with you?" asked the boy.

I almost laughed in the boy's face—the idea of Puss Fleming being of enough importance to make an appointment with anybody.

"No, I just dropped in to see him. How long has he had a job here?"

"He organized the company five years ago, I believe. I'll speak to one of his secretaries and see if you can go in."

A girl came out to see me, looked me over suspiciously, and asked a few questions. She explained as diplomatically as she could that Mr. Fleming—*Mister* again—was a very busy man, and as so many got in to see him under some pretext or another and then tried to sell him authorized histories of the Balkan War or mines in Peru, she had to be very careful about callers she granted interviews to.

"Have you known Mr. Fleming long?" she asked.

"Grew up with him and lent him a towel the week he couldn't get back his laundry. We're old college chums, don't you see?"

"Yes, his old college chums drop in every day—to sell him something," returned the girl suspiciously. "You're the third one this morning. The last one had the only autographed edition of the writings of Woodrow Wilson, President of the United States, complete in twelve volumes, half morocco, including a handsome photogravure of the President himself and a full oak bookrack, all for the price of the books alone. When did you see him last?"

"Not since the time he went to sleep in calculus and his elbow slipped off the chair arm and he landed on the floor."

Finally, I worked into the girl's confidence and was let inside Puss's private office. Puss was signing papers with seals on with one hand and holding the telephone to his ear with the other. He hadn't slapped me on the shoulder until two telegrams were put on his desk for an immediate answer. While he was ordering a new propeller for his yacht, I looked at my watch and remembered about that important engagement. He started to see me to the door, but had to stop to give orders to three assistants and answer a cable from his London office.

I couldn't believe that this was the sleepy-headed Puss Fleming I had known in college: Puss who in college hadn't known enough to get off his hand when it was asleep. No one had ever expected anything of him, and we had all hoped that his father could take care of him if the struggle for bread became too bitter, and now any of the rest of us could light a cigar and call the crumbs from his cake a full meal. At college there had been some doubt if Puss would ever get far enough along to put the eyes in candy mice, and now he hardly had time to send the chauffeur back to get the name and make settlement if he ran one of us down.

Here was Puss traveling with the yacht crowd and telling the make of a car by the way it coughed, and in college he hadn't known an amoeba from a decimal point. On the other hand, Charley Eglehoff had always been a ready-reference library with a course of reading and memory training in the last volume, and now every other season, late in the fall, he bought a straw hat and a box of bleach.

An intimate knowledge of the character and personality of the amoeba isn't as vital as I had thought. It makes no difference how interestingly you talk about the amoeba when the landlord comes around—you can't get his mind off the rent. I am now almost ashamed to admit that there is a diploma with Latin and seals hanging in my parlor, framed in fine weathered oak. The frame's good as new. There's a secondhand dealer on my block. I must drop in and see him—maybe he buys scientific pamphlets, too.

Making Maple Sugar

We children could hardly wait in the Spring until time to make maple sugar.[9] As soon as the weather began to loosen up a bit, we were hanging on father's heels asking him hadn't he better tap the maple trees. Popcorn whitened in a skillet gets awfully dry along toward the end of February.

Then one sunny afternoon after his patience had gone to tatters, he would reach up on top of the cupboard and take down a woolen stocking, with the open end doubled back and tied with a string. Taking out of it the three-eights bit, right and shining as a silver dollar, thanks to its protective covering during the winter, he would try it on his thumbnail and set out to the maple camp.

Selecting a spot on the south side of the trees, as he always said that the sap ran better on that side, he would take the old broom that we kept standing on end on the back porch, and whisk off the dirt and loose bark. Planting the head of the brace in the middle of the stomach he would lean toward the tree and twist with his free hand. The nose of the bit was pointed up so that the sap could run out more easily.

Then he drove in the wooden spout, letting it stick out a few inches, using great care to get it in just right.

"If you didn't get the spile in right," he would say, "you had just as well stick a corncob in a hole."

On the spout we hung a bucket. But the cedar buckets got gummy and made the sap taste all gooed up, 'specially late in the Spring. Tin pails were best, and best when painted.

There'd be a bucketful in a night, sweet till you'd nearly hurt yourself drinking. And it would take off warts if you put it on just as the moon was coming up and never tell a living, breathing soul in the world.

Hitching up old Bess to the flat sled we would go after the buckets to bring them up to the boiling house. The old sled had had its hickory runners off and when the unshod side would grate on a rock, off we would go on our ears, father looking at us out of the tail of his eye and the corners of his mouth working, but never laughing right out so that we could see

---

9 From *Leslie's Weekly*, May 15, 1913

him: work was work and must be gone at earnestly. There was enough sin and foolishness in the world without mixing it with work.

Just before the buddy sap began to run and the quality began to go down he'd start the fire in the boiling house. That wasn't any fun, especially if you had to bring in all the short sticks and limbs you could find and had to watch the fire and skim. Skimming is all right after it begins to get sweet and thicken up, but goodness, how long it takes some sap to begin getting good!

Around the edges of the skimmer it got thick and crusted first, but you didn't dare lick it—when anybody was looking! How would you like to take a bite of maple candy and think that somebody you didn't know from Adam's off ox had had his tongue against it? That's what you would tell Brother Kale and the rest of them when they were out of sight a little, a tiny taste wouldn't hurt anybody—'specially if they never knew anything about it.

When you had to wrap a rag around the handle of the skimmer and it got all stuck up, it was good, too, especially the end that draggled in the syrup. Anyway, there weren't any germs in those days to make you give up everything that had any fun in it.

Syruping off was the most fun and, or course, some older hand had to do it. It's a strange thing that a boy can't ever do anything except the hard work about any kind of a job; he can stir all day, but when time comes to syrup off a more experienced person must do it, but if he works hard maybe next year he can do it.

It did take a lot of boiling to get it down. An average, everyday sort of tree would give up about ten or twelve gallons of sap during a season. Some of them would run above this and some drop below, as you might expect. Our "bush" consisted of 200 trees, and by the time we got all the sap hauled, we thought it couldn't be one under a thousand.

You can count each tree making you about five pounds of candy in a year, and when your father is getting twenty cents a pound, it makes each tree worth a dollar. And when you are wearing copper toes and have your mittens tied to each other with a string running over the back of your neck, a dollar is a vast sum of money. Why, a dollar, all your own and not have to divide it with any of the young 'uns, would buy almost anything in the world that a fellow would really want. You can get a dandy iron-handled IXL for a quarter.

We didn't know what a big thing the maple syrup and maple candy business was. Of course most of it—practically all, for that matter—is made in the East. New York comes first, with Ohio second and Vermont third. Last year the combined maple candy business in the United States amounted to a little more than five million dollars.

From the very day we started boiling the sap, we children were always getting ready to sugar off. That was the most fun of it all—it was the red ear of the husking. When the syrup was still so thin that it took mighty steady nerves to keep from dripping it off the spoon, we would begin testing it to see if it was ready for sugaring off. After stirring and skimming for a few minutes, we would take a spoonful of it and drop it on the snow. If it turned hard then it was ready to sugar off, but if it just flattened out and didn't do anything in particular it would have to be stirred a few months (so it seemed) longer. But if it hardened in the snow and would melt in your mouth and make you wish you had a million sugar trees—then we kept a slow fire under it and sent out the joyous word to everybody in the neighborhood to come over at early candle lighting to the sugaring off.

Lis Culp was always the first one there, coming across the back forty with his dogs. He couldn't go out to the barn without a passel of dogs at his heels, whistling and calling to them till you'd think something was after him. But he never was very much on work; advice his forte. And arguing. You couldn't head him off arguing; if you got in ahead of him and were getting him into a corner, he would swing around and agree with you and end the whole thing by saying, "That's just what I told you in the first place. Good wood-cuttin' weather, ain't it?"

The girls with long aprons on giving the syrup the last stirring, the boys lifting the pans and pouring the syrup in to the molds. All the sugar running over the molds was to be eaten up—but that wasn't very much of a job. The job was keeping any to take down to Oxford to sell. Everybody laughed and cut up and had a good time and jokes flew so thick and fast you couldn't keep up with them to save your life. After being housed up all winter we just couldn't keep from enjoying every minute. Just as everybody was getting quieted, somebody would laugh and off they'd be again. Everybody except two: always over in one corner or out walking by themselves was sure to be one couple, talking in low voice, so sad looking you'd think the world was coming to an end.

How we hated the "sugar sand." It is composed mostly of lime and gets on the bottom of a pan and keeps the pan from boiling. And we'd have to scrape and scrape and scrape to get it off and if you tasted it, it was bitter as iron root and would pucker up your mouth till it made you shiver. That's how bitter it was! If you left it in the pan it made the syrup cloudy and the sugar gritty. Pa used to say everything in the world had some use, otherwise it wouldn't be here. He said that about flies, too. But I know well two things that nobody in the world could find any use for. Flies kill people, so the doctors say. Sugar sand works people to death by making them scrape and scrape. Sometimes there would be so much sugar sand in the syrup that we would have to put in milk or the white of an egg to clarify it.

It does take a lot of boiling to get ready to sugar off and have the crowd over. You boil and boil (I mean the syrup) till you wish to blazes the thing would blow up, or you'd get sick and they'd have to carry you to the house on a blanket and Mary Fordyce would come and look at you (wasn't she pretty and smart as an encyclopedia?) and turn her head to one side and cry. Then you'd sit up and promise to get well for her sake—if you never, never had to boil any more syrup. That was the way they always did in the story books, only it never happened that way to you. When you got sick and thought to goodness you were going to die; Tig Scattergood had cut you out and Mary Fordyce wouldn't look at you any more than she would at a turtle. And instead of carrying you to the house on a blanket, Pa would walk up beside you, make you stick out your tongue, feel your forehead, and give you some old-fashioned painkiller. One dose of that would get your mind off dying and off Mary Fordyce and off everything except your stomach. It would burn a streak right down your gullet clear to the last button on your vest and you'd resolve that the next time Tig said anything to you you'd hold him with one hand (it'd be easy—he couldn't skin a cat and didn't have any more muscle than a grasshopper) and pour a whole bottle down his mouth till he learned to respect a fellow's rights among ladies.

After the sugaring off was done, father would have them all come up to the house and, oh, the things to eat! Where mother kept all those things we never knew. Just as quick as we could, we cleared the things off the dining room floor and then father would get down his fiddle. Then we'd all sing, "We'll all go down to Rowsers," till awfully late, so late that something would get into your eyes and pull over our heads in spite of everything we could do. The last thing we could remember would be the sad couple over in the corner helping each other on with their coats, and Lis Culp setting off across the woods forty whistling and calling to his dogs.

The Joyous County Fair

Do you remember how along about this time of year we used to have the county fair?[10] Of course you do! Don't go putting on airs and letting on you don't know what I mean. You know you were there and about the greenest, gawkiest one on the grounds. I guess you remember the time you climbed clear to the top of the ladder to see those "red bats" and came down looking mighty sheepish. That wasn't very long ago, either, and here you are now sitting around in white pants trying to act as if you had been born at Bar Harbor. My land! How some people do put on airs and try to let on they don't know what a long-neck gourd is.

I bet I could ask you something that would make you squirm in those white pants. Did your ma try to win the prize with the gooseberries or current jelly? Come on now—let's be honest with each other. Didn't your ma wash up her jars and get out her Sunday stationary and write "Current Jelly" with fancy shaded strokes, and paste it on and say, "There, I guess I'll take these down. I don't suppose I'll win anything, but maybe it'll encourage the others to bring something good?" Now didn't she?

I thought so.

And didn't you think they had good fairs in your town, but that if you got on the train and went down to the town where Uncle Doc lived, there they had better ones? And especially if he bought you some white taffy candy with paper around it? Do you remember how the man in a white coat used to pull it with it stretched up there on the hooks, and just about the time you thought it was going to stretch out too far and fall on the ground, he would calmly hang it up again? That was real candy. There was some satisfaction in it. When it got hard and you set your teeth in it you would know you'd got your money's worth. No tin tongs in that. All you could eat for ten cents. Just imagine going into a store now and asking them if they would give you all you could eat for ten cents. They'd throw you out and the court would sustain them!

Gracious! What a crowd! People as far as you could see. No end to them—just people, people everywhere. And what a queer-looking bunch some of them were. Gawky—good land! Some of them looked as if they

---

10 From *Leslie's Weekly*, August 30, 1919

thought that General Nelson A. Miles was conducting the war. The only time anybody ever heard of some of them would be when they would come out of the woods and win first prize with their Chester Whites.

That Balloon Ascension…Saturday afternoon was when the balloon went up, and I'll declare if it didn't look sometimes as if you'd be crushed in the crowd. That's how many people there were. You couldn't move ten feet without bumping into somebody. People would come for miles and miles to see the balloon go up and the parachute jumper risk his fool neck. Do you remember how you wanted to get up on top of Waldron's General Grocery so that you could see them throwing the coal oil on the fire, and your ma wouldn't let you? Your ma wouldn't let you do anything that you wanted to. Now didn't you think that? Didn't you feel pretty mean toward her and wish to get away and have a good time with other fellows? And now…well, it's different now. You'd give a good deal to have her back.

That is the way with things. They slip by so fast—and you never appreciate them until they are gone.

Then there was Machinery Hall only it never had any machinery in it. The only piece of machinery they had in it was a hay loader, and the first time Key Maxwell saw it he said, "I tell you it won't work. I tell you there ain't any kind of machinery that can spit on its hands and fork a load of hay on a wagon. It's just another one of them newfangled contraptions to get your money."

And do you remember the stone-boat? Gracious, that was exciting! I guess it was more like Chateau-Thierry. Griff Alexander would pile stones on the platform till they were heaped up as high as a dinner table, and then the men would line up with their oxen. J. U. Higginbotham would come in with his pair of cattle, but he was the hollering kind. He'd holler and tear and slap his hat till you'd think his house was on fire and the twins asleep upstairs! But he wouldn't get the load ten feet. That was the kind of a man he was. But Charley Leedy was different. He was the quiet kind. He had a tiny little whip you couldn't scare a grasshopper with; he'd just tickle his cattle over the nose with it and talk to them confidentially. Goodness how they would get down and pull! Their toes would dig in and the grass would fly, but never a loud word would Charley say. He'd just say, "Steady old boy. Even her up a little, Mack. Now get down to it!" and wouldn't they pull? Their heads would go down, their tails would stick straight out and their backbones would be as straight as ramrod. Move? Well, I should say that load did! They could have moved Bald Knob if they had it on wheels. Ten feet—twenty feet—thirty feet—forty—that stone-boat would go before they would begin to saw. Then Charley would reach down in his overall and give his cattle a handful of sugar and they'd want to go back and move that load some more. And all the time J. U. Higginbotham would be back there cussing and saying his cattle had laid down on him. Then Charley would take the ten dollars and invite us all up to the cigar counter and tell us to help ourselves. That was the way he would do. If J. U. Higginbotham had won the prize he'd gone off and pitched rings all afternoon and his poor wife at home taking in sewing. It's strange what a lot of difference there is between people—and there ain't any better place for finding it out than at a Fair.

Then when we were smoking our cigars we'd go up to see the Attractions. By golly, that was where a fellow would have a good time. All you needed was half a dollar, and if you didn't have fun it was because there was something wrong with you. You'd better go to the doctor. If you didn't laugh, then you'd just as well quit and tell them whether you wanted *At Rest or Asleep*.

Can't you see them now—that whole line of attractions with their pictures painted on canvas, and a man out in front with a confidential voice? And don't you remember how you were always afraid you were going to be short changed? Of course you do! You wouldn't take your thumb off that dollar till you got your change. No, siree! Those traveling shows were just full of crooks.

There was the picture of the Texas Fat Girl saying she weighed 559 pounds, and a little ruffle of lace around her neck, and arms that looked like the logging industry. And then you'd go in and see her and she'd be there all right, but she wouldn't look as fat as the picture said. Do you remember the time Ted Robinson stood in front of her staring up at her till he just couldn't hold himself any longer and then said, "Was you born this way?"

She just looked at him a minute and then said, "Yes—only smaller."

Bosco the Snake-eater was sure to be there. A fair wouldn't seem natural without him. He'd sit there on his little folding camp stool, looking at his knee caps, not paying much attention while the manager stood out in front with his megaphone and told what a wonderful curiosity Bosco was, and how he was a favorite in Europe, and how queens had seen him perform his marvelous feat, but it didn't seem to interest him to hear himself praised. He'd just yawn and scratch himself and say, "Is there any store in this town carries Syrup of Sprigs?"

When the manager came in and said, "Ladies and Gentleman, we have before us today...," Bosco would stand up and growl and bite a piece out of a snake. When the crowd had gone away he would sit down on his folding chair again and doze off till time for the next snake. It was an easy life and no work to do, but I'd rather stayed at home where I could get fried mush.

But times have changed now.... Things are not the way they used to be. The old county fair is about gone. Why, it's getting so now that a man who comes in and tics his horses so that they can eat out of the back end of the wagon is laughed at! You never see anybody any more out by the side of the road throwing stones to make the dog go back. There isn't anybody any more who has to stop and get the colt out from under the traces because he thinks it is meal time. You never see buggies backed up any more with their tongues over each other and their numbers chalked on that dashboard. It's getting so that you wouldn't know the county fair if it wasn't for the biggest pumpkin. There aren't prize colts at the fair these days, and the man with a pair of matched Clydesdales would attract more attention now than Bela Kun. It's all because of the automobile.

It used to be that a man who came to a fair with an automobile didn't have a friend in the county. They'd talk about him worse than Cosey's Army, and somebody was sure to have a broken leg before night. But now a man who comes to the fair driving a team is looked on as a public nuisance. He's considered as holding up traffic and would vote in favor of free silver. You never hear a horse squeal any more, and you never see two men streaking it off down behind the creamery to stop their teams fighting. There hasn't been a good kicking match at the county fair in six years. The only time you ever see two men streaking it off by themselves is when one of them wants to buy a secondhand Ford. It used to be when you passed anybody you looked to see if they had a colt following—now you look to see if one of the boys is coming on a motorcycle.

It used to be when the parade came down the street with Nick Beffle and Judd Lewis pounding an anvil and Tom Daly playing a flute, everybody had to grab their horses by the bit and swing for dear life, but now Pa sits back in the Ford with his knees crossed, eating an ice cream cone, while Ma looks up from reading how Norma Talmadge was a poor girl before she started in the movies. A few years ago the only Talmadge Ma ever heard of was a Presbyterian.

The chicken show doesn't draw a crowd any more. Pa and Doug Mallach and the rest of them aren't interested in chickens any more. They got some other place to go—they're down at the movie theater looking at Mack Sennett's bathing girls.

It used to be the biggest time was after supper with everybody standing around and visiting and saying how Strickland was growing like a weed and Newt was the picture of his mother, but they don't any more. Instead of that they're all down at the Jewel watching some bride about to be disillusioned.

They don't have balloon ascensions any more. They got flying machines now. Look at that out there behind the Chautauqua grounds—a flying park where you can go up for twenty-five dollars. And by gracious, they got the twenty-five too! You used to work all day for a dollar and have to come in with a lantern to hold your job—and now any old person can pay twenty-five dollars for an airplane ride.

Bosco the Snake-eater and the Texas Fat Girl are having a pretty hard time now. Charlie Chaplin has just about put them out of business. And as for the Siamese Twins—the people would yawn in their faces. If they were triplets and could talk in three languages at once and do a little lightning calculating on the side they might get a tent down behind Machinery Hall, but it wouldn't be a fashionable place to take your best girl. Instead of that, you'd be taking her to watch a pair of feet.

How things change. But there isn't any use in looking back on old times and wishing they would return. There are just as good times ahead. There isn't any use in looking through the wrong end of the telescope. Turn it around and have a good time today! That's our motto.

Seventy-Seven Times Thankful

When I was a boy it wasn't Thanksgiving if we missed church.[11] They don't have singing like that any more—a person could understand every word then. They didn't have just one woman that stood up and did all the work—everybody sang. Even if you weren't a very good singer, it didn't make any difference. The spirit was what counted, and I allow that we had better singing than they have today. When the meeting was over we would all stand around and get acquainted, instead of rushing home as if there were pies in the oven. There's no getting acquainted any more and asking how Tommy's leg is and are Ruth's eyes any better?

My, what a scramble there was to get the preacher! We'd come crowding around him as if he were the king, and his wife would be talking away just as hard as she could, first on one side then on the other. Whoever got the preacher to come home with him Thanksgiving was a mighty proud person. When the preacher would walk off with him, he would hold his head as high as if he had been elected to office. I guess those were great times.

After church our relatives would begin to arrive. The yard would be full of boys and girls—all having a good time, but not making as much noise as they would on any other day. Cousin Phebe was fat, and all of us would come running to help her out of the wagon. But we mustn't ever let on that she was heavy, because she was sensitive! Cousin Phebe wouldn't eat very much because, she would say, she had had a late breakfast. We all knew why it was, but we wouldn't let on for anything. The yard would be full of children, the women folks would be in the kitchen, and we men would be in the sitting room. There would be so many of us that we would have to say "Big John" and "Little John." People don't seem to have many relatives any more.

A person would think that dinner was never coming. They'd make us men sit off in a room by ourselves so that we couldn't tell what they were getting for dinner, so that it would be a surprise when they brought it in. Just a little tiny trickle of odor would creep through, like a wisp of smoke working out of the smokehouse when you are burning green hickory to

---

11 From *Leslie's Weekly*, November 27, 1913. The first four paragraphs of this article as it originally appeared in *Leslie's* have been omitted for concision and clarity.

smoke the meat. Then it would get stronger and stronger till we'd think to gracious that we couldn't stand it.

Then we would go in and sit down at the long table, with the turkey right in the middle, with its breast pointing to the ceiling and a string holding its legs together. Brother Dexter would say grace, because he was the oldest, and we would pitch in, and such jokes and laughter I guess nobody ever heard before. We'd eat and eat till we'd think that we couldn't eat another bite, when they would come around with some white meat. When we'd get that all gone, and were thinking that we couldn't eat another bite for love or money, they would come around with some cranberry pie that Sister Libbie had made. It would hurt her feelings awfully if we didn't eat it, and so we'd tell them "just a small piece"—and they'd pile on a big one. They would always do that on Thanksgiving at our house.

After we were through we would all go back into the sitting room and watch the fire. Sometimes I'd think to goodness that I couldn't keep my eyes open another minute. I'd stretch my legs and pull back the corners of my mouth, but to save me I couldn't keep my eyes from getting heavy.

In the evening everybody would get ready to go home. The ones that lived the farthest away would get ready first. We would hold the blankets near the stove and, while they were good and warm, come running out with them. They would all feel mighty sad that they were leaving and that we were all a year older. How time did slip by! One year we would be teasing one of the nephews about putting cream on his lip and letting the cat lick it off, and it didn't seem more than the next year till he'd be bringing his new bride to Thanksgiving dinner. Say, I guess that was excitement! Of course we would all want to know if this brand-new bride was a good cook or not. She would roll up her sleeves, put on a long apron, and jump into the work to show her new relatives that she was good enough to cook for Ezra.

It would be awfully sad in the evening after everybody left. Mother and I would sit around before the grate, looking at each other and feeling happy, but at the same time kind of sad—I can't explain it—but that was the way we felt—so happy that we couldn't keep the tears back. Then her head would drop over on my shoulder, and I'd stroke her hair, then the first thing anybody knew it was nine o'clock. Then I'd wind the clock and mother would put out the cat, and Thanksgiving would be over.

I guess I'm old-fashioned, for Thanksgiving doesn't seem to me what it used to be. Everybody seems to be afraid of home on Thanksgiving these days. They hate to stay in it. They seem to think that they aren't having a good time unless they are running around somewhere—unless they are out playing billiards or bowling. They must go to a football game and yell and carry on something disgraceful, or go into the country and shoot live things they don't want. People don't seem satisfied unless they do something that takes them away from home. When dinner time comes they go to a restaurant where a man with an apron asks whether they want light or dark. I can't enjoy a turkey unless I know its family history.

When I look at the people sailing around in their cars on Thanksgiving Day and see their hard, set faces, it doesn't seem to me that they are having half the fun that we used to have when we stayed at home and told stories and opened up our hearts to each other. People don't seem to understand why I don't want to go out in a motor car and go ballyhooing around over the country on Thanksgiving. And they don't understand why I think that they could be doing something better than sitting around playing cards—bridge, I believe they call it—on the day during which if we don't give thanks, we never will.

Having things doesn't make people any happier. I don't believe that anybody could be any happier than I was the day I hitched up to our wagon and brought mother, she was Tillie then—back to the little house where I was batching. She went in as my wife, took off her bonnet, looked around and said, "Goodness gracious, this needs cleaning up!" and jumped right in and went to work. And say! such a meal as we had that night—it makes the tears come now to think about it. You can't tell me that these people who go hooting and skyhooping around in an automobile are any happier than we were.

Other people can go to football games and watch a whole pack of men jump on another man who is carrying something, or play bridge, or billiards, or go out shooting birds and animals on Thanksgiving Day, if they want to, but I'm going to stay at home, visit with my relatives and read the Bible on that day. I guess I'm old-fashioned, but sometimes I am glad that I am so.

The Uses of Obesity

It's getting to be the style for authors to write about themselves, and we are are trying to think up something to write about ourselves, but Nature hasn't endowed us with flesh, as it is getting so now that flesh is a valuable literary asset.[12] Irvin S. Cobb has just published a book entitled *One Third Off*, in which he tells of his struggles to reduce, and Don Marquis in the *American Magazine* practically paid his winter's rent on how he dieted.

But curses! We are not fat. If we had to depend on our surplus flesh earning us a living, it would be over the hill to the poorhouse for us inside of thirty days.

The only queer thing about us is our hair. Or to throw all pretense aside—where our hair used to be. We still have a photograph of ourselves taken about the time that people said that there never would be another war and which actually shows us with a cowlick! But now a cow would never recognize the old homestead. She could pass the place by and never realize that it had once been dear to her. But nobody wants to hear about hair that didn't turn out the way it gave promise in its first flush of youth. There isn't even a magazine article about it, let alone a book. Also we suffer slightly from fallen arches, but the fallen arch market is practically dead. But the demand for stout stomachs is keen. Today anyone who has a fat stomach has a literary gold mine. If you work it right you can just about make a living off it. You let it accumulate a while and then begin trying to get rid it and you have, at least, a new Ford. But this hair—you couldn't get a gallon of gas on it no matter how long or how hard you worked!

There are also great opportunities in writing about your children. Ring W. Lardner, with his four boys, just about breaks even on his coal bill, with possibly a little left over for an open fire when company comes; but Nature has never equipped us in this way. Nor have we an "H. the Third" as Heywood Broun of the New York *World*. A couple of months ago the stork brought us a son, but, unfortunately, before recognizing his tremendous earning power, we had him recorded as Junior. Nobody wants to read about a Junior, but "H. III" handled with literary skill, ought to just about pay the meat bill.

12 From *Life*, November 24, 1921

Nor have we an automobile to write about, as has Christopher Morley in the *Evening Post*. When you have a new automobile and a bill comes in, all you have to do is to pound out a few paragraphs and that's settled. All we have is the Long Island Railroad, and if you depended upon paying the gas bill by writing about it, you had just as well telephone the man to come with his pliers and spend the time with your family. If we could just get enough money ahead to get a car, we believe all would be well. But how are we going to get it when we are still a thirty-four and our only son is merely a Junior? Without a car or a stomach, or an "H. III", how are we goin to make any money writing?

The only thing we can think of is our mortgage. We have a perfectly splendid mortgage, one that we have had for a long time, one that acts as if it was going to be with us indefinitely—but what is there to write about in a mortgage? It never gets any thinner and it never breaks down and has to be towed in; and what chance is there to write about it as "M. the First"? None, absolutely none. In fact, we would be better off if we didn't have it at all.

And here is winter coming on—and all we have to write about is where our cowlick used to be and our mortgage. Things look black…just awfully black. That is about the only thing we can make use of that is now fashionable among writers…. You get paid for them just the same as if they were words. And on top of that, they say it is going to be a hard winter…an unusually hard one.

The Six Gold-medal Jokes

Introduction

In a way, the history of this country could be told by its jokes.[13] I suspect the well-known man from Mars could take a volume of our jokes and pretty well tell what we were thinking and doing during certain periods. He would see us waging war with Spain, he would see the short skirt come in—this rocked the country almost as much as the war. He would see the Suffragettes marching, he would see Carry A. Nation whacking away, he would hear about the Full Dinner Pail, he would hear the rattle of a Ford. Motion pictures would appear; Charlie Chaplin would shuffle in.

The jokes [here] have been assembled by going through the magazines, newspapers, and almanacs; some from memory. It's been interesting to uncover some joke of another day, then suddenly remember I'd heard it in my youth. One of my problems has been how much history to put down, and how much humor. For instance, in recounting how this country began to bloom with bloomer jokes, how much should I tell about Amelia Jenks Bloomer herself? Or should I just quote the joke and let history take care of itself? I simply don't know. This little item has given me, I think, more puzzlement than anything else.

A problem has been Mark Twain. How much of him should I use? His best humorous writing had been done by 1890, three years before this begins. Of course, people were still reading him; they still are; I hope they always will. As I was getting this ready, I looked through some of the current magazines and was surprised to see how many "funny" anecdotes there were about Mark Twain. But, on checking back through his life, I found that only about one story in eight was true. In addition, his material is so well-known that I have given him what will seem small space. I expect the Mark Twain fans will be at me, but I can't help it. I did what, at the time, seemed best.

---

13 From *What Grandpa Laughed At* (Duell, Sloan & Pearce, 1949); pp. 5–8; 230–235. "Introduction," originally a separate chapter, is here set as a subheading and run-in with "The Six Gold-medal Jokes." References to "the book" or "the collection" have been omitted from the introduction as it appears here.

The temptation has been to put the big berries on top; that is, set down a number of staunch jokes to "open" the book. But I didn't succumb; I have kept to chronology and have tried to indicate the gradual change in the United States by the jokes, as they come year after year.

I'm surprised at how good some of the jokes are. Their pace is different; more words are used, but it's the same drunken husband trying to creep in at night without waking his spouse. I estimate that more words by a third were used to tell Grandpa a joke than to tell it to grandson.

I personally do not care for stories about talking dogs, or parrots that make comical remarks, or mice that take a swallow of liquor and spit in the face of the cat. Some people must enjoy them, for, in joke collections, they are as thick as cat whiskers. So if you must have your talking dog, or know what the Mama Kangaroo said to the Baby Kangaroo, you'll have to go elsewhere. (*Second thought on part of the author:* There is, after all, one talking dog in this book, but mercifully he speaks only briefly.)

Another personal peculiarity is that I don't care for puns; so you'll find few of them. If you are pun-starved, tune in tonight on almost any alleged radio comedy program and you'll find enough to carry you safely through the crisis.

Another personal comment: my own preference is for jokes with a touch of sadness in them. When I told a friend of mine that I was going to edit this from that point of view, a decided touch of sadness came over him. But I have put that element in, for, to me, if humor were carried just a little further it would be tragedy; in fact, tragedy always hovers in the background. Gene Buck, for many years head of ASCAP and the author of many *Ziegfeld* shows, once told me that he considered Bert Williams the greatest comedian ever seen in America. When I asked him why, he said it was because in all Williams' humor there was an undernote of pathos. And I do believe that; it is the humor that goes deepest. So, if once in a while you find yourself sobbing, you'll know it's that undernote.

It will be seen that in certain years, certain jokes appear, and then are no more. This does not mean they flourished only during this special and particular year and were lopped off on December 31, but that they were most in vogue during that year. As an example, the most popular joke in 1905 was the Dr. Osler joke; this had to do with a speech in which he asserted that human beings had served their purpose in life by the time they reached the age of sixty, and then should be chloroformed. The jokes about it didn't die with 1905; in fact, they flourished for years. Every now and then one of them will still peek its head around the comer, a little frightened.

A problem in this calendar arrangement is where to put the humorists. For instance, Will Rogers joked for thirty years. Where should he go?

It is a bit disconcerting to discover that the jokes pinned on the notables—say, Chauncey Mitchell Depew, William Jennings Bryan, and the much-married Nat Goodwin—are still going the rounds, fastened on the figures of the day. To be specific: the jokes that were told on Eva Tanguay are now told on the bizarre showgirls of today.

I expect readers will say that the jokes are much older than I have indicated. No doubt they are, but my efforts only go back to [the Chicago's World's Fair].

A private pang I have about this is how soon, after it is out, the radio gag writers will have gobbled it; and there's nothing I can do about it. I'll just have to keep away from the radio.

This begins with the Chicago World's Fair and continues up to our entry in the First World War. If this prospers, I plan to get out a second volume, beginning where this leaves off and continuing up to the present. I want to call it *What Grandpa Laughed at the Second Time*. If you never see it, you'll know the old gentleman didn't do so well.

The Six Gold-medal Jokes

Here are the six stories most popular with Grandpa; they appear most frequently in the magazines and newspapers and, today, in the joke collections.[14] They're still alive; they're still going. And they always will be; they are immortal.

In the early days this story was told about as follows. It is a bit stilted and a bit quaint, as all stories were in Grandpa's time, but this very quality added to its value.

NUMBER I. A friend of ours has had an experience, the nature of which

---

14 "The Six Gold-medal Jokes," originally a separate chapter, is run-in and typeset here as a subheading.

is a bit shocking. Recently he was called on to take a trip by pleasure packet, and was delighted in every way. The catering was excellent, the accommodations were even luxurious, but, before he reached his destination, he discovered in his bunk a certain noisome bug. Naturally he was shocked; when he reached his office he wrote forthwith to the president of the company informing him of his unpleasant discovery.

In a short time he received a letter, on most impressive stationery, from the gentleman himself who said, in effect, that he was thoroughly shocked to learn of such conditions on his packets and that he had ordered a thorough investigation and that a severe reproof would be the reward of those who had been negligent. In closing, he thanked the letter writer profusely for having brought the matter to his attention. It was a warm, glowing, appreciative letter.

Our friend was delighted; he had done something worthwhile. But his pleasure was not completely unalloyed, for, on a slip of paper, written in the president's hand and evidently addressed to his secretary, was brief notation which said: "Send this crank the bedbug letter."

The story is still being used, twisted this way or that. The latest version that I have seen is in the New York *World-Telegram*, February 8, 1948, in Frank Farrell's department, and goes this way:

Archie must have missed the diner on his way through the train, because Annette Kaufman found the cockroach mooching around in her Pullman berth. Mrs. Kaufman, touring westward with her concert violinist husband, Louis, posted a complaint at the next stop: An apology from one of the road's executives awaited the Kaufmans at their destination. It deplored the incident and promised immediate fumigation of all cars. As Mrs. Kaufman beamed with personal satisfaction for a good deed accomplished, she noticed another slip of paper in the envelope. It read:

"Send this ___bug letter form Number 3."

Watch for Old Faithful; I'll wager you'll see it inside of six months.

NUMBER 2. This is one of the most famous; you'll soon recognize it:

An inebriated-looking man was sitting in a seat on a train, gazing with his liquor-glazed eyes at large quantities of nothing. But now and then he would manage to stand up and peer at a box overhead in the metal wall rack. After scrutinizing it carefully, he would drop down with a sigh of

229

relief. Finally he got down the box, which was an ordinary paper shoebox, but with holes cut in the sides and top.

A man sitting across the aisle had watched the whole procedure, fascinated. Finally he leaned across and said, "Excuse me, but you seem to have something valuable in that box."

The owner nodded vacantly.

"What is it?" asked the man.

"It's a mongoose."

"A mongoose!" exclaimed the other. "What do you do with it?"

"You see, now and then I have a drink. Sometimes…maybe too much. I see snakes. The mongoose fights them."

By this time the other man was amazed. "I'd like to see your mongoose. I've never seen one."

"Certainly," said the inebriated one, and managed to get the lid off the box. The box was empty.

"Why," exclaimed the man across the aisle, "that mongoose is imaginary."

"So're the snakes," said the drunk, putting the lid back on.

NUMBER 3. A man who had been imbibing far more than was good for him left the boys at the club and started to navigate his way home. He came to a tree that had a circle of iron bars around it, put there by the park department to protect it. When he reached the circle of iron bars, he felt them as a player might do the strings of a harp. Then he started around the tree, but came to a stop and again felt the iron bars, teetering a little as he did so. Again he started on, still going in a circle around the tree; again he stopped and felt the bars. This was too much for the poor man. Putting his face against the bars, he called out in a pathetic, imploring voice, 'Won't somebody please help me? I'm trapped an' can't get out."

NUMBER 4. One night a private citizen was walking along the street, attending to his business, when he saw a man propping up a doorway. Being of a kindly nature, the private citizen said, "Do you live here?"

"Yes."

"Do you want me to help you upstairs?"

"Yes."

The helpful man tried to escort the other up the stairs, but it became apparent that the man was inebriated. So, picking him up, he half-carried, half-dragged him up the stairway to the second floor. "Is this yours?" he asked.

"Yes."

The kindly man saw a door and, when he tried it, the door opened and he put the weak-kneed man inside, and started down the stairs. To his astonishment, when he got out on the street, he saw the dim outlines of another man.

"Do you live here?"

"Yessir."

And now he picked up this man, too, and finally managed to get him to the second floor. "This my floor," said the inebriated man. Assuming that the two roomed together, the kindly man opened the same door and put this man in, and again departed, feeling the glow that comes from doing a good deed.

When he got to the ground floor, he saw a third figure propping up the doorway. "Do you live here?" he asked in a businesslike way.

The other brought his dazed senses together. "Yeah, do," he managed to reply. "But I can't stand to have you carry me up the stairs again and throw me down the elevator shaft."

NUMBER 5. For some time a revenue officer in the Ozarks had been on the trail of a band of moonshiners. Word always seemed to precede him; when he arrived all evidence had disappeared, and so had the alleged moonshiners.

One day, as he was going through the mountains on foot, he came suddenly upon a boy sitting idly on a fallen log. He engaged the boy in conversation, became friendly with him, and said, "Tell me, is there any moonshining going on around here?"

The boy nodded. "There be."

"Oh," said the officer, delighted, "is there a still?"

"There be."

"Where is it, son? I'll give you a five-dollar bill if you'll tell me."

He held up the bill.

The boy's eyes got big. "Hit's up the trail, clean to the summit. They got it thar so's they kin watch."

The officer thanked the boy and got ready to start up the trail. "Please to give me the money," said the boy.

"Oh, that's all right," said the officer. "I'll give it to you when I come back."

The boy shook his head determinedly. "I want 'er now," he said.

"Why can't you wait?" asked the officer.

"Cain't wait," said the boy. "You ain't ever comin' back."

NUMBER 6. When the train stopped at a small station in Scotland, a man got on, lugging a particularly large and heavy suitcase which he proceeded carefully to stow away. Then he sat down and began to stare out the window at the fleeting landscape.

When the conductor came through and asked for the ticket, the man said he hadn't had time to buy a ticket but would now pay, then gave the name of the town where he wished to go. "That," said the conductor, "will be ninety cents."

"I happen to know the fare is only seventy cents," said the passenger. "You are trying to make something for yourself and I'll not pay it."

"I am not overcharging you," declared the conductor indignantly. "You will pay the ninety cents, or get off."

"I'll not pay it and I'll not get off," shouted the man. "And what's more, you can't put me off!" He glared at the conductor defiantly.

The conductor sized up the situation, spied the suitcase, seized it, and flung it through the open window. Such a scream as that passenger let off! "You fool," he shouted, "first you try to overcharge me, then you throw my little boy out the window!"

Part IV
A Corn Country Homecoming

Homer Croy returned ever after to his middlewestern home place, both in mind and in spirit, a fact to which this final section, an epilogue of sorts, readily testifies. When Croy passed away on May 25, 1965, in New York City, his obituary in the *Missouri Historical Review* quoted an interview in which the famous Missouri man of letters once said, "I'd rather be living in Maryville, [Missouri] than any other town in the world, but I have to live in New York to keep something in the icebox. I really never left Maryville. That's my home and always will be. We're just puttin' up' in New York."

Croy's good-humored tribute to his hometown, "Maryville, My Maryville," leads off this section by succinctly and sentimentally detailing the fixtures, fussings, and fetishes of the place that inspired his best-loved work. The final reading, the original Chapter XXVI from *Country Cured*, follows the Missouri man of letters home on one of the countless trips he made back to the farm in late middle life while renting the home place to his longtime tenant, Spide. Carol, who the author mentions in the second paragraph, is Croy's daughter. The rhetorical question with which Croy begins the piece serves as a fitting, resonant conclusion: "In all the world is there a pleasure so completely satisfying as going back to the very land you were born on?"

A year after the publication of *Country Cured* in 1943, Croy had a barn-sized mural painted on his Nodaway County farm depicting the arrival of his parents, Amos and Susan, Corn Country pioneers dating back to 1867.

Maryville, My Maryville

I was unconsciously shocked a few years ago to see my own, my wonderful hometown, referred to in *Editor and Publisher* as a "hog town."[15] I could hardly believe my eyes, but there it was. Why, the best friends I have in the world lived there. I had grown up there and I still live there part of each year.

The town is in Jesse James country. Jesse James wouldn't have sat back, as I did, and let it be called a "hog town." He would have tightened his holster and called on that editor, and this country would have been better off. Jesse wasn't no man to let a fly-up-the-creek editor call the finest town in the United States a hog town. He would have made sausage meat out of him.

But after I cooled down a little, I knew there was truth in it. All night the trucks rumble through the town and all night you can hear the squealing of the doomed hogs on the way to the St. Joseph stockyards.

Hogs—that's where the money comes from—but we have as fine homes and as much culture as any place you can think of without straining your mind.

My wife is from Florida. Before we were married she asked me how big the town was. I told her it was ten thousand. Soon after this she came out here with me, and was shocked to find that it was half as big as I told her. I tell you a man has the right to exaggerate the population of his hometown, just as a fisherman has the right to tell how big the fish was that got away. As long as these are the cardinal principles of America, we'll be a great nation.

The town is Maryville, Missouri, fifty miles north of St. Joseph, Missouri, on U.S. Highway 71, and there's nothing that makes us madder than for people to call it *Marysville*. The town was named for one of our pioneer families, or rather for the wife, Mary. She died when I was a child; everybody loved her and felt a personal loss. Mary Graham is a name that means something to us.

Our town is rich: nobody lives across the tracks. There's not a widow in town who has a printed card in the window which says: *Sewing*. And

15 From *Lincoln-Mercury Times*, July–August 1954

there's not a maiden lady who runs a millinery and lives in the back of the store.

I reckon, everything considered, we're about as typical a town as you could dig up. It's in almost the exact center of the United States. It's in two whoops of where the Pony Express started and where the wagon trains pulled out for the Gold Rush.

Of course the people are engaged in other things besides hogs; cattle, for instance; wherever there are cattle, the thrifty farmer wants hogs. And bluegrass. And just as good as Kentucky ever raised. Some of our people say better. (Our people are never prejudiced.)

Roughly speaking there are three kinds of hogs: black, white and red. A man who raised black hogs would not have a white hog on the place. Men quarrel over the merits of the three kinds and they mean it. Ill feelings flare up. Once one of our men, who went in for the reds, hung a jury because an important witness said that a Chester White was the best all-'round stock hog in the world. The red-hog man said that a man who would swear to a thing like that was not a man to be believed and that his testimony was worthless.

Every Tuesday we have a livestock sale at the pavilion. All kinds of livestock are sold, and always hogs. We've never actually put up a motto, as Ziegfeld did in his letter glorifying his girls, but if we did it would read something like this: *Through These Gates Pass Some of the Most Beautiful Gilts in the World.*

Slapdab in the middle of the town stands the courthouse; on top of the courthouse is the steeple and in this is the town clock. It's the finest town clock you could find in a month's trip by fast dogsled. It has wonderful golden hands and it strikes the hour, day and night, year in and year out. It was striking when I was born and it's been banging away ever since. I used to ride by it on horseback of a morning on the way to high school. I would look up at it and could tell whether I could ease along, or have to ride like Paul Revere. I looked on that town clock, then, as a friend and I still do.

One time it got out of order and the aldermen had to send to Kansas City to get somebody to fix it. It didn't strike for a week. Half the town went crazy. People lost their rhythm of living and were nervous and out of sorts. We almost had street dancing when it again began to send out its lovely tones.

The first thing that strikes a stranger when he comes to our parts is the water tower. There it stands above the town, like a sentinel. It has a beacon light which it holds up to the planes and tells them to get the heck out of here. (I think I am quoting it correctly.) But one time ice formed at the top; a considerable bit of water drained out from under the ice-cap. Suddenly *kerplunk!* the ice came down, squashed open the tank and thousands of tons of water (I think I am getting the figures right) rushed out and flooded all the homes in the neighborhood. That really was a day. The country one-room school where I was going declared a half-holiday so that we scholars could go to town to see the holocaust. (That's what our weekly paper called it.) That was one of the most exciting days I ever lived. The next day we were back in school again, hoping that as soon as the water tower was rebuilt another ice-cap would form.

No manufacturing. We raise instead of make. Once, for a short time, we had a bow-and-arrow factory, but after a while it closed down. Lemonwood bows and reed arrows went out of style. That was our last fling at Big Business.

It's a guinea town. That is, it's not against the law in our town to raise guineas. One hot, sultry day I sat under a tree in the yard of Mrs. Cliff Edwards' farm watching her wash the parts of the separator. I was resting.

Out of a clear sky she said, "It's goin' to rain."

I looked at her pityingly, for that morning on the radio I heard the weather prediction: "Continued dry," it said.

"I guess not very soon," I said politely.

She washed some more blades and put them on the table in the dry sun. "It's goin' to rain tonight," she announced calmly.

I looked up at the cloudless Missouri sky. "How do you know?"

"My guineas told me. When it's goin' to rain, they go to the top of the tallest tree and scream, from time to time, all night. I've never known them to be wrong."

I saw there was no use in talking to such an unreasonable woman and changed the subject. I left feeling sorry for her because she preferred her poor, dumb guineas to the great meteorological department of our great nation. But at about eleven o'clock that night a tremendous rain came; it was making up for all the hot, arid days. It was a regular goose-drowner.

I didn't see Mrs. Cliff Edwards for about a week. "Well, I guess your guineas were right," I said, rather ill at ease.

"They always are," she said, as if the contest between her guineas and the United States Weather Bureau had been a foregone conclusion from the jump.

Our jail isn't as good as it ought to be; we've been getting ready for years to fix it, but we have just never got around to it. It's an old pepper-box type of jail; the whole inside revolves. When the sheriff wants to put somebody in it, he has to call to the prisoners inside; they brace their feet and give a might heave and the cage turns. The sheriff pops the prisoner in, then goes back to his radio. Sometimes the prisoners inside get contrary and won't heave. Then the sheriff is up against it. He's never actually had to sit up all night guarding a would-be prisoner with his hogleg, but he's come close.

Now and then a prisoner escapes, Then there is a tremendous to-do about "modernizing" the jail. But pretty soon the man is picked up and sent back and the thorny problem of the jail is forgotten.

We used to have lots of horsethieves in jail. Nowadays if someone stole a horse and was tried before a fair-minded jury, he would be condemned as an imbecile. If he stole a tractor he wouldn't get less than ten years, and if he stole chickens we'd hang him to the nearest TV aerial. We might even take him inside first and make him listen to a batch of singing commercials. In such situations, we are a hard people and will stop short of nothing.

Six years ago I was on a radio quiz program for the National Broadcasting Company in New York and won as a prize a white pig. The pig was brought to me on the stage, all scrubbed and perfumed, with a string around its neck and the string given to me. The stage was slippery and the pig slid all over the place. This made the chickens laugh and play. When the program was over the producer of the show said he guessed I didn't want the pig. I said I sure did want the pig and that I would ask to have it shipped to my Missouri farm.

I gave the man Lloyd Logan's name and address and wrote Lloyd that he was going to have an eastern visitor.

In about two weeks the radio man called up and asked if the Croy Farm had received the pig. Then I remembered that Lloyd hadn't mentioned this, and so posthaste wrote to Lloyd. Well, it turned out that after the broadcast, the New Jersey farmer had put the pig in a trunk in the back of his car and had started home. On the way the trunk lid fell down and the poor pig had smothered to death.

The radio man said the farmer hand promised to send another pig, and this he did. He must have selected long and carefully, for it arrived safely and it was an exceedingly nice pig, a pure-bred Chester White. It was put in with the other pigs where it grew mightily. And kept on growing.

It was such a splendid pig that it was entered in the 4-H Livestock Show at St. Joseph, Missouri—and became grand champion in its class. The St. Joseph papers told about it and my heart was as light as foam rubber.

Yes, it's a wonderful town. Any time you're driving along U.S. Highway 71, stop in and see us. You can look up and see the clock on the courthouse and if you gaze east down the street, you can see the jail. Don't speed, for we are seriously thinking of repairing the jail and you may find yourself delayed.

The Land You Were Born On

In all the world is there a pleasure so completely satisfying as going back to the very land you were born on, and walking across it and just looking at it?[16] But I must tell you it's not all pleasure, for every joy has a few stickers, on the theory of the rose, no doubt. You labor over a cornerpost and when you have it finished you're proud of it; there it stands, straight and tall and firm. Then you come back, in no time at all, and it looks like the start of a scarecrow. Or a watergap you've taken pride in, has been swept away and there's only a bundle of loose wires and somebody's hen coop.

I seem always to be going home alone, for alas! the old farm doesn't mean much to the other members of my family. My wife has seen it only once. Carol has never seen it. Some day it will be hers, I suppose. I wonder what will happen…

This is a sample of my homecoming. I get off the train and there is Spide standing on the platform where my father used to wait. He heaves my suitcases into his Chrysler—no buggy now—and we start uptown to the Square. I glance up at the gilt hands on the clock and my mind shoots back to the days when I used to drive by in the hack and stare up at them as if they were the Hanging Gardens of Babylon. The clock suddenly bangs out the hour, and there is a throbbing in my throat. Why is it that an old clock can make a baby of you?

Cars are parked around the square. But what I think of is the battle that once raged there. Yes, the battle of the hitch racks…when Pa had said, if they tore down the hitch racks, he'd trade in Wilcox. The farmers had won then, but there had been other and later battles and the merchants had finally triumphed. After a time, Pa was back trading again as if no blood had ever been shed. It just about shakes your faith in war.

We pass the north side of the square where Moses Nusbaum's store was. Today there is no Jewish family in town. But at the State Teachers' College (which has come since those early days) are three Jewish refugee students.

---

16 As in Part II, the title for this chapter, originally numbered simply XXVI in *Country Cured*, has been created from Croy's native phrasing in the first sentence of the chapter.

My eye darts to the courthouse steps and I think of the heartbreaks they've seen—the days during the Depression when farms were sold by the sheriff, and men and wives and children saw them go to the insurance companies. That shakes your faith, too.

We pass the Methodist church where I hid in the areaway. But the years have helped me in at least one particular. I am no longer afraid of my fellow man. I like him.

We pass the Blue Moon cafe. In it are farmers, eating, and I think of the time we used to eat our cheese and crackers in the back of a grocery store. Yes, times change. Also I think of the time in New York when I stole the girl's tip. But these farmers, when they've finished, will plunk down a tip and think nothing of it. Yes, times change.

I pass the house where my father lay like a shadow in the pillows and asked me to pare his fingernails. I think of the featherbed... Spide says, "You didn't catch cold on the train, did you?"

And I say, "I don't think so. I guess I got some of that train smoke."

"That diesel smoke's bad," Spide says.

Here, alone, Phebe[17] lived until eighty-four was upon her. One day she went out to hang her featherbed on the clothesline for an airing; the bench she was standing on tipped and threw her on the ground. Bones were broken, and in St. Francis Hospital she lay waiting for them to mend. But before they could do so, pneumonia came and my second mother was no more.

The water tower jumps up ahead of me, and my mind goes back to the time that Dave and I clumped by it twice a day; and to the time I sold its story to Jesse L. Lasky. Oh boy! I was a businessman that day.

We pass the white schoolhouse and I think of my greatest triumph. When I won the prize in spelling—*Pilgrim's Progress*—certainly the dreariest book ever written. I think of what happened next year when a new teacher came among us and offered a prize for the one who turned in the best showing for nine months of spelling. I won that prize that year, too. The same damned book. It just about soured me on trying to do my best.

Studying was hard work in those days. We moved our lips and whispered the words of the book to ourselves in such an intense effort of

---

17 Croy's father, Amos, remarried after Croy's birth mother died. Phebe is Croy's stepmother.

concentration that when we were finally full tilt, the schoolroom sounded like a hive of bees. One day a girl, much older than I, who was going to the seminary in town, came out to our house to stay over Saturday and Sunday. She brought her books along so she could be ready for her schoolwork Monday morning. After a while she sat down in a chair by the window and got her book ready. To my astonishment, I saw she wasn't moving her lips. She was just sitting there holding the book and looking at it. Now and then she turned a page. I stared and stated at the mysterious ways of higher education.

Our car goes down a swale and I see the exact spot—at least I think it is the exact spot—where I had the only fistfight of my life. Where I actually struck a person. I wonder if Harlen Kennedy remembers it.

I look down the draw and think of the white weasel that I trapped just about *there*—the one the one-horse Farmer told the world about.

The car pulls into the drive lot and the door to the house opens and Nellie Logan (Spide's wife) comes out, and their son Lloyd Logan and his wife Opal, and their children, Robert and Kenneth (Spide and Nellie's grandchildren). They are the ones who run the Croy farm. I am home. My feet are on the very soil.

After chatting a while, Spide and I walk out over the farm, just as Pa and I used to. There's the very place Jim Vert used to come with his dehorning chute and his long thin-bladed, hump-backed saw. I can—so potent is memory—again almost see the blood spurting out on Jim's hands.

There is no longer anybody like Mr. Shannon, the neighborhood man-of-all-jobs. The farms have grown larger; no one would dream, now, of trying to make a living off forty acres. When we need a man to work by the day, we go to town and pick him up there. Usually, he's a pretty poor worker. We miss Mr. Shannon.

And there's where the tree stood with the turtledove nest in its arms. The turtledove I killed with a stone—and saw the dirt on its dead eyes and, later, saw the starving young ones fall out and be no more. When my friends tell gory hunting stories, I have my own ideas running in my head.

And here's the spot where the drummer for the nursery company offered Pa five dollars a day just to drive him around and introduce him to his neighbors. And the spot where Pa refused. It was the first time I ever realized Pa was doomed always to be poor.

As I walk I realize more and more that the farm and I are inseparable; that whatever is deep in me came from its roots.

There is a similar pattern between us. The farm has been up and it has been down; and God knows I have!

The black Aberdeen-Angus are doing fine, and so are the Hampshires. I turn to Spide. "I see you have some Shropshires."

"Lloyd thought he'd try out some."

"Well," I say with the manner of an expert delivering the findings of a lifetime, "don't be too sold on them. They're tricky."

Going home is a time of adventures. And no two times are the adventures ever the same, as no two days in our lives are ever the same. Once I arrived the day before a very exciting time; at least, it's exciting to us. The Women's National Corn Husking Contest which originated in our county and which, until the war, was held every year. The National Corn Husking Contest was originated by Henry A. Wallace when he was Secretary of Agriculture, but we started the women's! It was a gay occasion, with cars from everywhere and newsreel cameras dashing here and there for "shots." At least it was considered a gay occasion by the grinning visitors who piled out of the cars and watched the farm women buckle on their pegs.

Men were posted in the wagons to drive for the women, a starting gun was fired, and slowly—interminably it seemed to me—the wagons inched across the field. Those women knew how to strip ribbons, pick up down-corn, and keep on the throwboard. They were the farm women I had known all my life—tanned, shapeless, amazingly capable, equal to any emergency, overworked and underpaid. At first glance, however, they didn't look like women, for most were in overalls, with men's hats pulled down over their hair. They were there to work and that was exactly what they were doing; regularly, in a sort of rhythm, the ears of corn beat on the throwboards. But the women were feminine after all, no matter what their cover-alls said. For a quarter of them were wearing high-heeled shoes. If my mother had come out to the field in a pair of high-heeled shoes, I'm sure Pa'd 've sent her back to the house. Times change and conditions change. But people don't; for these women were as my mother was—except for the item of the shoes. Sometimes it seems to me, people are the one constant factor in the whole scheme of things.

When the gun went off the second time, the women climbed into the wagons and the wagons started for the scales where the corn would have to be weighed; and the gleanings, too, and the overlooked corn. One woman, before she would allow herself to be driven through the cheering lines, brought out her lipstick. I am glad Pa never saw a Women's National Corn Husking Contest. He had stood up under many things, but a lipstick in a cornfield might have proved too much.

I asked one of the winners what she was going to do with the money. It was going into a college fund, she said. Then glanced proudly at her son she had by the hand.

The contest was held near a farm owned by former President Herbert C. Hoover. I had never been on his farm, so now we drove to it and I walked across it, thrilled to have such a distinguished fellow farmer. When I saw the condition the farm was in, I knew it was just as well he had stuck to politics.

Once, at the behest of his political guides, he had come back to make a speech, just as Parmer Willkie had gone to Elmwood, Indiana, to show what a callus-handed son of the soil he was.

Mr. Hoover's fellow farmers came to see one of their kind.

The crowd became so great that Mr. Hoover adjourned to his front porch and started to talk to his friends. His friends were more friendly than he knew, and crowded on the porch. Suddenly there was a noise, and a shock, too, and Hoover and his friends and the porch went down. There was a scramble but, after a few moments, Mr. Hoover was able to right himself and went on with the alarming condition of the country.

The porch is still there, in about the fix the speech left it in.

When I got back to New York, I went to the Dutch Treat Club, and there was my neighbor. I went to him, after he had finished lunch but was still sitting at the table, and said: "Mr. Hoover, I'm going to say something to you that no one else in this club has ever said."

He glanced at me, evidently wondering what to make of this approach.

I said, "I walked across your farm in Missouri a few days ago." Now he did look with interest. "Well, how is it?"

I told him just what I had seen. That it was in poor condition; the outbuildings were falling to pieces, the house needed painting, the fences were down, the gullies were washing and the soil itself was overcorned. Even, I said, one side of his cave had fallen in.

He asked questions and I told him just how the farm impressed me. Then he wanted to know if I would be interested in buying it. I told him that I did not think I would.

After I left, he went on smoking; but more thoughtfully, it seemed to me. Maybe it had dawned on him that he hadn't been cut out to be a farmer.

All visits are not so glamorous; there are plenty of hard, practical problems to solve. And so Spide and I and Lloyd stand on the south side of the barn and try to work them out. How much land should go in wheat? How much in corn? How much in rye? This is complicated by the fact that the government must always be reckoned with. We will be paid so much for raising this; and so much for *not* raising that. It takes a bit of figuring.

As we walk across the farm, I see a cornpicker at work. It is not on our land, but in a few days one will be snatching off the ears on our land. I think back to the days when my father shucked corn and my mother came out and helped him, and that night poured tallow in the cracks in his hands. And I think back to the days when I husked, too—surely the hardest work in the world. The land doesn't yield as it did then. Fertilizer is going on it—something my father never dreamed of. And there are a million bugs and insects busy at the corn and at the land, pests he never heard of. The vast fertility of the prairie soil has been depleted. But it's still black loam, still the finest cornland in the world.

We have dinner. Nellie sits in the chair nearest the kitchen, where my mother used to hop up. Spide only bows his head, for the Logans are Catholics. I think of my father sitting in Spide's chair, and a choky feeling pushes into my collar. A little disappointment about dinner, for the cooking isn't as good, and the food isn't as good, as I remember it. After all, there's nothing to season food like a couple of plow handles.

After dinner, house problems. Every room must be inspected. A new ceiling will have to go into this one. But Nellie's son-in-law, who lives in Omaha, is a plasterer. "When his vacation comes we'll invite him to see us," says Nellie. So that's taken care of.

Why, this is the very room where my father used to fall asleep over his livestock paper. The very one where I used to read the farm papers.

What does the farm boy of today read? Well, he reads the farm weeklies and semimonthlies (*Wallaces' Farmer* is still going strong) and he listens to the National Radio Hour and to the market prices as they come in over the Midwest stations. The mail-order monthlies are all gone; but there has come to take their place a plague of cheap movie magazines and radio guides and comic supplement magazines detailing the adventures of Superman and his kind. And the hired man, today, instead of having pictures of racehorses pinned on his wall, has Poses of Beautiful Art Models. Sometimes I wish the mail-order magazines hadn't gone their way.

We look at the bathroom. The nondecaying wallpaper has about decayed. So that goes down on the list. It is a single duty bathroom; merely a bathroom and nothing else.

I am asked by my curious city friends what a woman on a farm does when she wants to be alone. The answer is simple. She does as the women have done for three-quarters of a century. Goes to an arrangement in the back yard, or in the edge of the orchard, designed for that very purpose. Naturally in winter time there are certain problems to solve. But she solves them and never once thinks of herself as underprivileged.

That Croy bathroom means something to me, for it was the first in all the neighborhood. People came as if to a shrine. I turn to Nellie and say: "How many bathrooms are there in this neighborhood?"

She and Spide count it up. On the ten farms nearest ours there are two bathrooms. They still go out back. And that's today in the black loam section.

We go upstairs to the northwest bedroom and my heart goes flutter. This is the room where I had my panel of "Six Famous American Authors." There's where the old Barlock used to repose; on the wall was a picture of Victor Hugo and right under it I read *Les Misérables*.

"Homer, the roof leaks," says Nellie.

This is the room where I packed my telescope with the mousehole. How long ago that was! Yet how recent. I remember my mother said: "Homer, I wish you didn't have to go off to the city with a hole in your telescope."

My mind races away to St. Joseph where I saw my second streetcar, and I think of something that happened, later, when I came to have as a friend the man who invented the electric streetcar, Frank J. Sprague, and he told me this streetcar line was the second in the United States.

We go into "Renzo Davis" room. Two sacks of shelled corn are on the floor. "We don't dare leave our hybrid at the barn," says Spide. "Mice."

"This room should be papered," says Nellie.

From room to room we go, and from place to place, then outside. The kitchen foundation is getting weak in the knees; we'll have to have the cement man out.

We go into the basement under the parlor, and I think of the time my father got the acetylene gas craze and had a machine installed in this cellar room. The machine was supposed to dump pockets of carbide into the water and make gas for our lights. One night the machine didn't work and Pa told me to take the lantern and go down and see what was the matter. I came into this room, opened the machine and peered into its depth, aided by the lantern. Suddenly there was an explosion and I was knocked as flat as a doily.

In the back yard, behind the "new" house, is the house where I was born. If there are any chickens in it, I'll wring their necks. Thank God, there aren't. In the floor is the augurhole where I used to see the water drain off and wonder where it went; and under the clock shelf is the very nail where our *Hostetter's Almanac* hung. And a little to the left is the wall where Pa kept the International Harvester calendar, with circles around the dates when the cows would freshen.

Then to the henhouse. The roof leaks. I don't know why it is, but henhouse roofs always leak. Put *that* down, too.

We have supper and that evening the neighbors come in, the boys and girls I've grown up with; and with them their children. And, here and there, a grandchild. It just doesn't seem possible. But there *they* are, staring popeyed as if I was Rip Van Winkle. We talk about the weather and crops, just as we used to; and how the schoolteacher is panning out. Then about what the government says we'll have to do next. *That's* all new. And puzzling. But on the good side. Our farmers like what the government is doing.

We have a sort of procedure to go through. After we've talked about local things, it is my place to tell them about New York. Not one in the room has ever been in New York, except one boy who saw it when he was a soldier. And none of them ever hope to see New York. They want to know what kind of house I live in, and when I tell them I don't live in a house at all but in an apartment, with no front yard and not a sprig of grass, they shake their heads. I'd better've stayed on the farm. When I tell them that six feet from my front door is the front door of a man I have seen only twice, they put it down as some of my imaginings. After all, he wrote *West of the Water Tower* and only half of that was true.

When I tell them that certain people in Connecticut live on five acres yet call themselves farmers, it makes them smile. But when I tell them that all the work these city "farmers" do is to dress up in fancy clothes on Saturday morning and walk around with a pair of vineclippers in their hands, it makes 'em laugh right out. They say they would like to see a city farmer in his fancy clothes try to ring a hog. Well, so would I. Probably the hog'd have a good time, too.

Once, when I told them that the mayor of New York had ordered a cow put in the zoo so that New Yorkers could see one, they said I was going too far.

They know about the tall buildings, for they've seen them in the movies; but the subway is different. When I tell them that the train I go to Washington Heights on, runs three miles under the ground without stopping, they glance at each other again. Well, let him talk. His father and mother tried hard enough.

After my "lies" are over, the conversation again swings back to neighborhood matters. Mysteriously Nellie and Opal get up and tiptoe out and there is a clinking in the kitchen. Refreshment time; pretty soon we are eating ice cream and homemade cake. Not ice cream made on the back porch, in a salt-water freezer, but fetched out from town. And not as good, either.

The children are getting restless. It's half-past nine. Why, we haven't been up that late since Grandpa died.

After a while they've gone and the house seems lonely and empty—just as it did when I was a boy. A train whistles in the distance and an exquisite agony lays hold of me.

And now, as I lie in my old room, I think: Some day I'll be no more, and when that day comes I'd like to have my ashes sprinkled on the farm.

The next day we go in to trade, but now it takes only a few minutes to clip off the six miles. What wouldn't I have given if old Dave had had six cylinders? It's a farming town, the guidebooks say, then add: "Industry— none." They're a little off, for there's the lightning rod factory. A dozen people employed there, counting, of course, the office workers.

You're nobody if you're not proud of your hometown. We have some "names" that we're proud of—men who were born in the county and who have distinguished themselves. There's George Robb Ellison, judge of the Missouri Supreme Court. Remember I mentioned a boy who went to Harvard and came back with a feather-edge haircut? Well, that was George. And there's Merrill E. Otis, Federal Judge, Kansas City. (He's the one who sentenced Pendergast.) Dale Carnegie, the writer and lecturer. Ed H. Moore was born in our county and lived there all his early days; then went to Oklahoma and beat Josh Lee and became United States Senator. (Should never have left Missouri.) Forrest C. Donnell became Governor of Missouri. Yep, one of our boys. Have you heard of Dawson City, British Columbia, near Alaska? Named for one of our boys.

On one of these trips, I was told that Newt Kennedy was sick and wanted to see me. His hands were on the outside of the covers—those great hands that had tamed so many wild mules. But now the joints were knobby and the flesh wasted away between them; and his eyes that had twinkled so many times, were sunken and hollow.

I sat down beside him, deeply affected. After a while the paid woman who was waiting on him left the room, and he and I were alone together. The years slipped away; we were back on adjoining farms. I spoke of the captured weasel, but he had forgotten it.

But he hadn't forgotten breaking the mules. He laughed—then had to cough—this giant, this strongest man in the neighborhood, this man who got so much fun out of living, this boyhood hero.

His voice grew weak, for I stayed too long, living over the old days. Finally the paid woman came in. But Newt still had a message. "We had lots of fun, didn't we?" he whispered, for his voice was about gone.

"We did," I said.

It was the last time I ever saw him. But I will remember him all my life—Newt Kennedy, the man who taught me to have fun.

On these trips I stay a week, sometimes two. It sounds sentimental, I suppose, but the farm does something to me; brings me closer to the realities. Closer to the heart of America; to what the plain, simple people are thinking and doing. The Corn Belt people. My people.

The day comes when I must leave. I go down to the depot, alone usually, and look at the platform of the old, familiar station. Then the train comes in and I get on.

About the Author
by Cameron Shipp

The distinguished novelist tossed his loudly checked coat on a chair, loosened his bright red tie with the sunflowers on it—the tie was twenty or thirty decibels louder than the coat, about the key of a four-alarm fire—thrust his long legs under a kitchen table and wrote a letter.[1]

He toiled briefly, his ancient typewriter rattling with a machine-gun staccato, then reached in a crowded filing cabinet and fumbled for an envelope. Examining several, he found one to his satisfaction. In the upper left-hand corner was a return address: "Office of the Collector of Internal Revenue, Washington, D.C."

The novelist grinned, stuck it in the machine and typed under it: "Department of Fines."

Then he addressed it like this:
      Known to the Police as:

      Mahatma Bill Williams
      715 Kenneth Road
      Glendale, California
The letter, on the stationery of a Spartanburg, SC, undertaker, said:

      Taking Cow to Bull Day

      Bill: Are you interested in making a lot of money? Answer me frankly.
      —Croy, Night Manager, Eliza Peabody Home for
      Wayward Girls
In bold, block letters, he signed it simply, "H. C."

Persons of superior intelligence may fail to be inspired to belly-laughs by this kind of japery, but it is a fact that professional writing men are bowled over by it. In the bourbon and beer-stained bistros of Broadway, on the pretty sidewalks of Paris and in the studios of Hollywood there are always scores of

---

1 Cameron Shipp's article originally ran in *True*, 1948, and appeared as the final chapter in Croy's *What Grandpa Laughed At* (Duell, Sloan & Pearce, 1948); 238–55.

admiring literary gents who frequently poke through the unpaid bills in their pockets in search of the latest dispatch from Homer Croy.

The great Croy has so many astonishing, lovable and downright scandalous distinctions that setting them down all in one paragraph would be distracting. But as millions of readers know, Croy is the tall, towering cornstalk of Missouri letters, the author of *Corn Country, Country Cured, They Had to See Paris*, and *West of the Water Tower*, among a spate of exceptionally fine books, all best-sellers, and also of innumerable motion pictures, short stories, radio sketches and magazine articles.

Croy is the author, too, of more fondly remembered pranks and quaint sayings than have been put on public view since the demise of vaudeville.

Once upon a time he was living in Paris, in a small *pension*, where the mustached old virago of a landlady kept a small pet turtle in a large basin in the front parlor.

Croy scoured the pet shops and fishmarkets of the Left Bank for several weeks, purchasing turtles with the passionate precision of a millionaire matching pearls for a frontline cutey-pie. Then he started.

He replaced the landlady's turtle with one a few millimeters larger. No one noticed. Several days later, he swiped his turtle and replaced it with one still larger. Incredible! The turtle was growing!

And, brothers, it grew. In a month, by gradual stages, that four-bit-sized reptile had developed—apparently—into a pot-walloping critter the size of a soup-plate. The virago was struck all of a heap with excitement. Newspaper photographers crowded the *pension* to depict the phenomenon, and neighborhood scientists examined it with awe.

Having gone about as far as he could for size, Homer let the turtle stop growing and rested for a week. Astonishment subsided—until a fiendish idea invaded the Croy imagination. Why waste all those matched turtles crawling around his bathroom? In the dead of night, Croy sneaked into the parlor and reduced the big turtle by one swap. And he kept on reducing it until he had whittled it down to size again at the end of three more weeks.

They say that landlady never was quite the same again. She became a mild and amiable woman, victim of a sort of chronic astonishment. They also say that Homer Croy had to move. This stunt was subsequently debited to various Paris newspapermen; some kind of tribute to Croy the Pioneer.

And it was in Paris that Homer incited a riot. One evening he attended an old-fashioned French festival known as the Fete of the King, at which Homer won the prize, an ornate and imposing papier-mâché crown.

When the party broke up at a late and hilarious hour, Homer donned his glittering headgear and paraded down the Place de l'Opera, leading a shrieking crowd of revelers. As they emerged into the I section, excitable Frenchmen and their *jeunes filles* automatically joined the procession, shouting "*Vive le Roi!*"

Gendarmes trotted from all directions and quelled the riot just before troops were called out. The French thought it was a Royalist demonstration.

"I thought it was too," says Homer. "*Vive le Croi, Oh boy!*"

Most chroniclers of intellectual folkways are under the impression that goldfish-eating originated at Harvard University, but that is not so. Here are the facts. Homer Croy started it. What the young Harvard men didn't know was this: when the great Croy walked into a living room, stuck his hand into the goldfish bowl, pulled out a bright yellow sliver and started munching, he was actually chewing carrot sticks.

After a gargantuan meal of hog jowls, this tasteful notion came upon Homer one evening in the red-plush parlor of a Missouri crossroads home, where Courtney Riley Cooper was a guest. Homer munched so realistically that Cooper had to be rushed to a Kansas City hospital to prevent his gagging to death. Mr. Cooper spread word of this feat quickly and widely, growing paler around the gills every time he told it, and the repercussions were as you know—a new thing at Harvard and a procession of vaudeville skits. Croy moved on to other enterprises.

One evening he invited Cal Tinney, the Oklahoma wit, to be his guest at the Rockefeller Center Ice Show. It was summer. Topcoats were not being worn. Homer and Cal had agreed to meet in the lobby.

When he arrived, Tinney was knocked bug-eyed by the splendor of Croy's raiment. His suit was a horse blanket of wonderful and fabulous checks and his tie was a screaming yellow. But what struck Tinney was the fact that a piece of paper was attached to Croy's right pants leg, about knee level. People were grinning.

A considerate man, Tinney started to call attention to the piece of paper, but Croy divined his intention, put his fingers to his lips and shushed him. Tinney soon found out why.

Strangers invariably noticed the piece of paper, which resembled a price tag. They would start to pass, then halt, return and say in hushed voices:

"Pardon me, sir, but the price tag is still stuck to your pants leg. See?"

Homer would bow gratefully. And he would say: "Yes, yes *I know*."

Some startled informants backed quickly away, muttering to themselves. Others insisted on telling Croy again, figuring perhaps he hadn't understood. To these, Homer said:

"Yes, thank you very much, sir. I know it's on there. You see, the suit is not paid for, and when I go to the store to make a payment, the man checks it off on that little piece of paper."

Croy had a stream of strangers backing away from him in confusion and embarrassment for thirty minutes before the show started. It turned out, Tinney discovered by searching questions, that Croy had two pairs of pantaloons to the particular suit, one for formal wear, the other for fun on the street.

"It's amazing," Homer says, "how people dote on telling you things like that. One time I was pursued two blocks by a man who was trying to inform me that something was stuck to my britches leg. They always do it with discretion; they sidle over and whisper. It just goes to show how kindhearted people are when it doesn't cost them money."

These and other artful pranks which we shall examine, especially more of the fabulous correspondence, are merely the outward and rambunctious signs of an inwardly serene spirit.

In order to pin the great Croy down like a bug and examine him carefully, it is necessary to consider one hard biological fact. We might as well do that right now.

If there is anything certain about the natural history of that noble but usually undernourished animal, the American writing man, it is the fact that the species breeds best around 40 degrees north latitude, 95 degrees west longitude—provided it escapes from this climate shortly after puberty and settles around 59 west longitude and 42nd Street, Manhattan. The best writing animals come from the central U. S. A., but wild impulses and unquenchable thirsts soon drive them east, where they crowd into the bistros and nuzzle up as close as they can get to publishers.

Homer was born on a farm near Maryville, Missouri, which is about as close to the middle of the United States as you can get. He was born the year the Brooklyn Bridge was built, which is as close as he will come to telling his age. He came into the world with an intense ambition to get away from agriculture, loathing farm chores like a Bedouin hates baths, and being smitten from infancy with the notion that the world panted to read the things he could put on paper.

He had an auspicious start as a literary man at the University of Missouri, where he was the world's first student of journalism and where he failed to get a degree because he flunked senior English.

He found employment on the St. Joseph *Gazette*. Eugene Field had worked on that sheet, and so had Walter Hines Page.

Homer's chief memory of his experience there is one of the tenderest comments on youth ever penned. With restraint and nostalgia he tells of his boyish experience in a house of ill fame.

Like all farm lads, Homer had listened with wagging ears to the forthright, strictly anatomical comments on women by the sages of his day, the farm hands. But his experience was nil. As a matter of fact, it wasn't direct experience the boy craved so much as satisfaction of curiosity. Homer, of course, attacked the problem with flamboyant imagination. He equipped himself with a drawing pad and a few pieces of charcoal and applied timidly at the door of one of St. Joe's chief bagnios.

"I'm an artist," he said. "I want one of the girls to pose for me."

The madam gazed steadily at him. "I never heard of anything like that before," she muttered.

Homer's paper collar began to shrink. "I'm willing to pay," he whispered.

"The price here is two dollars. But I guess in your case I can make it a dollar."

Finally, a tittering girl trudged upstairs with our hero. She entered a room and faltered: "What do you want me to do?" Homer was close to collapse. "I want you to to…if you don't mind, p-p-please take off some of your c-c-clothes."

She took some off. "Is that all right?" "Yes," squeaked Homer. "Just hold it."

Homer, who even today can barely draw a straight line, sketched rapidly, not daring to look directly at the girl. She finally came over and looked at his wiggly lines.

"Is that supposed to be me? Lissen, feller, come over here and we'll just talk."

On the way out, Homer shook hands with the madam and thanked her. "Was everything all right?" the lady inquired.

"It certainly was," said Homer. "I—I think I ought to give you another dollar." He popped it into her astonished hand and shot out the door.

I think this is one of the sweetest chapters in American literature.

Another Croy classic is his chapter on "Lost Manhood" and the patent medicine ads, a note on adolescence likely to inspire any man to sentimental recollection. Homer tried to get this into *Country Cured*, but the publishers blushed and threw it out. When he wrote *Wonderful Neighbor*, a sequel, he put it back in. The editors apparently didn't notice it this time.

Croy's latest book, *Corn Country*, a magnificent piece of reporting, is in his best tale-spinning mood.

Croy got on to New York as fast as he could and worked for a spell under the late great Theodore Dreiser, then editor of three Butterick publications. Both Dreiser and Croy were awkward when the tall, angular-jointed youth applied for a job. Dreiser asked a question:

"You're from Missouri? Then where is Washington, Missouri?"

"It's in Franklin County, sir, not far from St. Louis. That's where they make the corn-cob pipes."

"You're hired," said Dreiser. "I've put that question to a hundred men and not one knew the answer. Washington is where my wife comes from."

Remember that if you want an editorial job in New York.

Homer began to write, produced a vast quantity of humorous pieces and then did *West of the Water Tower*, a pretty unusual book for those times. It was a problem book, the story of what happened to a boy who did wrong by a girl. It was the reverse twist and the utter Missouri honesty of the writing that fetched both the critics and the readers usually it's lo, the poor girl and to hell with the distressed boy. But because Homer was so well known as a professional funnyman by now, his publishers insisted upon bringing the book out anonymously. It became a bestseller.

Finally, as happens to all best-selling authors, Hollywood beckoned. Jesse L. Lasky sent for Homer. Mr. Lasky quickly informed Homer that he hadn't read the book but liked the idea about the boy. Homer told him the story, hitting the high spots.

"We might just possibly buy it," Lasky said, offhandedly. "I will make you just one offer—seven thousand, five hundred dollars."

Homer could hardly believe it. That was a whole heap of money. He couldn't speak. While he couldn't speak; Mr. Lasky regarded him keenly. "All right then, eight thousand dollars," he said.

"That's not very much money," Homer muttered, repeating a phrase he had learned at Harper and Brothers, "for a valuable literary property. You must remember, it's a bestseller."

Croy looks back on this horse-trading as the supreme moment of his life. He sat there and wriggled, ready to accept any firm offer, fumbling for a graceful way to retreat, until Lasky upped his bid to $25,000—the highest price ever paid up to that time for an American novel.

A little later, he went to Hollywood to write pictures for Will Rogers. Homer was supposed to do a sequel to his other bestseller, *They Had to See Paris*, the story of one Pike Peters.

"Well, Homer," said Will Rogers, "the Fox people tell me you have a great story for me. Where's the script?"

Homer struggled through his pockets and finally produced a piece of paper about the size of a dollar bill.

"Here it is," he said.

Rogers read it at one glance, grinned and said, "That's good. Okay. Let's go ahead and make a movie out of it." And they did. It was Will Rogers' first talking picture and the forerunner of several more, all by Croy. Here is Homer's script, in full:

"Pike Peters loses his money in the Depression and adjusts himself to the situation."

Now you know how to make money in Hollywood.

Like Homer, you may not know how to keep it. Homer bustled into real estate in Forest Hills, Long Island, and lost everything. During this period, the gas and electric light people cut him off and the grocers refused to speak to him. A novel he had thought was pretty wonderful while he worked on it for a year turned out to be a dud.

I knew him well during this period, saw him daily, in fact. But not one of us realized, until some ten years later, that Homer was having trouble. And all the time, going hungry often as not, he pecked out little pieces for obscure magazines, big pieces for important magazines, toiling like a village seamstress to make ends meet. The difficulty was, one end was in New York, the other in Missouri.

Homer still had the farm, the farm he escaped from. He wouldn't work on it for $900 a day, but he holds such a strong sentimental attachment for that piece of Missouri dirt that a twenty-mule team couldn't take it away from him. The barn needed painting. The south forty needed fertilizer. The roof leaked. Homer paid and paid, and finally, due to a stroke of luck and an industrial movie production, paid off the mortgage.

But the farm has handsomely repaid Homer. He has written about it constantly. It is probably the best-known farm in America today, having inspired more novels, stories, anecdotes and tall tales than any comparable patch of ground in American literature except Louis Bromfield's. Gents, there's a lesson in it.

If you yearn to become a successful writer, get yourself a Missouri farm to escape from. The reason Homer writes so well and so industriously is that he is afraid he will have to go back and work that farm. And I think the reason he kept the farm all these years is so he would have something to be afraid to go back to.

This celebrated enterprise is now in the black, due to Homer's thrift and an honest tenant, and fetches Croy about $2,000 a year, along with chitlins, hams, beans, bacon and butter. It was a godsend during the war. Homer was much courted by hungry editors.

In honor of his pioneer father and mother, Croy hired a fine mural artist a few years ago and had a covered wagon painted across the side of his bam. It is a beautiful thing and the glory of Maryville.

Today, Croy is easily one of the three or four best-known and most popular literary men in New York City. The favors he does for friends— gently insulting them meanwhile—are uncountable. No one has ever seen him angry. He has licked New York by being honestly what he is—a gentleman from Missouri. And he has kept his friends largely by employing that fabulous letter-writing technique of his. Actually, Croy has not only bound his friends to him with hoops of wit and thoughtfulness, but has revolutionized the art of correspondence. And has added the element of mystery to it. The mystery: how does Homer get hold of his staggering collection of letterheads and envelopes? He has been showering wisdom and foolishness on me, for instance, for the past twenty years, has never yet used his own stationery, has never yet matched envelope to letterhead and has never failed to deceive me, at least momentarily.

The envelopes are always exotic. Once I thought I had a letter from His Majesty King Ibn Saud of Arabia. The note inside was on the stationery of a girls' camp in Maine. I have in my Croy collection letterheads from a hostelry in Alaska which specializes in reindeer steak; from Lowell Thomas, the Mount Rushmore Memorial Commission, from Beatrice Fairfax, the White River Boosters League, the Xenia Hotel and Ambassador Joseph E. Davies.

These letters, all on unmatching stationery sometimes more startling than the envelope, are never dated. Nothing as obvious as "Monday, Oct. 20," for Homer. The Croy dateline technique:

Taking Girl to Haymow Day
Soft-Corn Sorting Day
Calf Weaning Time
Poison Ivy Time
Saturday, Just Before Taking Bath
The Sabbath, Just Before Toddling Off to Sunday School

Nor does he fumble around with idiotic parting lines. In all literature, there is probably nothing more insincere or inept than the average sign-off. "Yours." The hell you say. I doubt it. "Faithfully." Also doubtful, and smug. "Yours till Niagara Falls." Well, at least, the feller was trying on that one.

Here are some Croy sign-offs:

Croy, the Rugged Individualist of Toad Hollow
Croy, the Sir with the Fringe on Top
Croy, Writer and Roué
Croy, the Honest Hog Caller
Croy, Pin-Up Man of the Harems
Croy, the Man Who Hates Sin and Form 1040

Croy, the Man Who Wants to Live to 90 and be shot by
a jealous husband
Croy, a Fine Man in a Fine Body (No Laughter, Please)
Croy, a Good Force in a Naughty World
Croy, General Custer's Last Surviving Scout
Big-Hearted, Tousle-Headed Croy
Croy, Terror of All Evildoers.

As you can readily tell from these samples, opening a letter from The
Croy is like finding a rosebud on the breakfast tray.

If you get the idea that Homer is slightly sex-mad, how wrong you
are! He just knows that the world turns on its sexes, and you can take it
from there. The chief charm of those short letters is neither Homer's exotic
datelines and sign-offs, nor yet his quaint sayings. These are his trademarks,
good for bellylaughs, grins, and quoting at bars or in men's rooms. How
many letters do you get from people who want to do something for you?
How many of those charming, warming, offhand-gesture letters with a
smile and a wink in them, as encouraging as a hail and salute across the
heads of a crowd of strangers? How many do you write?

Ninety-nine percent of the people who send letters to me do so
because (a) they want me to do something for them, or (b) they want to
sell me something. My own record is probably average. It runs this gamut
from A. to B.

Homer never wants anything, never describes his health, even when
asked, never mentions his troubles. Croy correspondence is devoted
exclusively to your amusement or to your interests.

One of Homer's letters suggested, in two lines, a book he thought I
ought to write. It was followed by an introduction to a publisher. (We did
business, too.) Then, on Artificial Insemination Day:

Cam: How you getting along with the book? Anything
I can do? There will be no charge. I have a new tome
out this spring. It has a good characterization and fine
spelling. I may be in Mexico City this winter. Bring
your ulcers.
—Croy, Sex's Atomic Bomb.
Another, written on Apple Sorting Day:

260

Cam: Here is something to make a man pause and think about the nobility of the human race. A man writes and asks me to do a foreword for a book—seemingly without remuneration—and it comes on a one-cent postcard. Please explain human nature to me.

—Goldilocks.

On Exchanging Presents Day, this came on a postcard, addressed to Master Cameron Shipp:

An editor called up today and said she wanted some material about you for a blurb. I shook her to her foundations. I simply told her the truth. She said she was going to leave tonight for Pottstown, Pennsylvania. To recover, I guess.

—Croy, the Honest Hog Caller.

Another, dated Prophylactic Day:

Cam: I will collect you Sunday morning and take you out to Forest Hills, the original site of the Funny Hat Club. I'll call at your hotel, in the lobby, and telephone up so as not to come in and disturb anyone who may be with you and you know what I mean.

—K'roy Was Here.

A man named Dale Carnegie once wrote a book called *How to Win Friends and Influence People*, and this book had a right smart sale, two and a half million, a world's record at the time for a nonfiction book. Anyone in the congregation recall to whom that book was dedicated? It was to Homer Croy, who, Mr. Carnegie observed, didn't need to read it.

"I think one of the deep feelings of anyone coming to New York is to want the home folks to think he is doing well," Homer told me in one of the few moments when I had him pinned down to serious talk. (He calls it "Fraternization," or "Intellectual Conversation.") "I was lonesome when I first came, and I developed as many correspondents as I could. I didn't say outright I was prosperous, but on the other hand, I didn't say I *wasn't* either. Then I hit on something very nice."

The something very nice was a friend who was a clerk at the Hotel Astor, and who let Homer get his mail there. Homer used their fine, crested stationery and got quite a reputation with the homefolks.

Then he thefted letter paper and envelopes from other hotels and—as you would suspect—got them mixed up. He put the wrong stationery in his envelopes, and so mystified the citizens of Maryville that they suspected Homer of leasing suites at all the fashionable hostelries. This was fun. He also purloined stationery from the Eden Musee, wrote on it, and stuffed it into Fiss, Doerr & Carroll Horse Auction envelopes. The homefolks were delighted. Homer has been at it ever since, and what delighted the corn-raising kinfolks of Missouri has also delighted the intellectuals of the Dutch Treat and the Players Clubs.

Today, the operation is far-flung. Volunteer thieves operate on a global basis, pinching stationery in every country. Homer travels a good deal himself, in the interest of his literary, lecturing and radio chores, and is the most accomplished writing-paper purloiner of all time. What started as the device of a country boy to impress the corner drugstore crowd back home has turned into a trademark and—never discount country boys—a profitable one.

Homer knows perfectly well that when editors cast their discouraged eyes on the morning mail, they are more than likely to open his letters or manuscripts first.

Far be it from me to suggest that any beginner, or any professional either, try this, but the manuscripts are as thoroughly tricked up as the letters. One I saw in an editorial office recently was tagged on the first page: "Approximately 5,000 words by Homer Croy, that Good Man. Every word a song at sunset."

On the cover page was pasted a picture, cut from a magazine. It showed a number of nude and callipygian ladies in a Roman bath, and with them was the inevitable naked Cupid with pink, smick-smack buttocks. The typewritten legend said: "Homer Croy's First Bath. The Baby Cried."

Homer once put down on paper the things he believed in. Here they are:

> "*I believe* that most people do the best they can, considering their limitations and their prejudices and the toll their mental limitations have levied upon them."

"*I believe* that kindness is just about the finest thing in the world. And, it seems to me that kindness has its roots in understanding."

"*I believe* that most people would rather be kind than cruel, but that their animal inheritance is just below the surface and is the cause of much of the intolerable ferocity that human beings so often exhibit toward each other."

"*I believe* there is no secret of happiness and that complete happiness is an impossible goal. But that one can get a great deal of satisfaction as one goes along by not expecting too much and by squeezing dry all the little pleasures."

"*I believe* in the innate dignity of human beings and I hold this to be one of their finest qualities."

"*I believe* no one is free from worry, and that the person who is happiest and who accomplishes most is the one who spends his time and vitality doing instead of chafing."

"*I believe* that most people hunger for approval as the roots of a flower do for water."

"*I believe* that praise is just about the most powerful stimulus in all the world. And, unfortunately, about the least employed."

"*I believe* that every person is part devil and part pretty fine, and that we must accept these phases as they come."

He also set down the things he liked.

The whistle of a train at night.

Getting into a bed with fresh clean sheets.

Sitting in front of a fireplace.

Fish jumping in a lake at sunset.

Sitting down to dinner with friends.

A child toddling toward me.

Meeting a dear friend I have not seen for some time.

The welcome from a dog.

The smell of coffee cooking early of a morning.

A walk all by myself at dusk along a country road.

Who's Who in America lists Croy as "best known as a humorist." But men who have been close to him for years and have been both the beneficiaries and the victims of his japes would be inclined to edit that. For my part, I'd say, "best known as a human being."

Acknowledgements

Chapters VIII, IX, XVI, XXVI from *Country Cured* by Homer Croy ©1943 by Homer Croy. Copyright renewed 1971 by Mrs. Homer Croy. Reprinted by permission of HarperCollins Publishers.

"The Beautiful Chip," "Newt Writes the One-horse Farmer," "Our Hat-tipping Problem," "I Lose my Manhood" from *Wonderful Neighbor* by Homer Croy ©1945 by Homer Croy. Copyright renewed 1971 by Mrs. Homer Croy. Reprinted by permission of HarperCollins Publishers.

"Introduction" from *Jesse James Was My Neighbor* by Homer Croy, ©1949 by Homer Croy. Used by permission of Dutton, a division of Penguin Group (USA) Inc.

Chapters from *Corn Country* by Homer Croy ©1947 by Homer Croy. Used by permission of Dutton, a division of Penguin Group (USA) Inc.

"Introduction," "The Six Gold-Medal Jokes," from *What Grampa Laughed At* by Homer Croy, ©1948 by Homer Croy. Used by permission of Dutton, a division of Penguin Group (USA) Inc.

Editor's Note: Most of Croy's work is available via interlibrary loan. Two excellent sources for background information are the Western Historical Manuscript Collection, Columbia, and "Homer Croy, Maryville Writer" by Charles O'Dell in the *Bulletin of Northwest Missouri State University*, Volume XXXIII, August 1972.

About the Editor

A seventh-generation Iowan and the author or editor of more than a dozen books on place and outdoor life, Zachary Michael Jack hails from his family's Civil War-era Heritage Farm. Jack has lived in states across the Corn Belt, including Missouri, Illinois, and Iowa, and has published widely on the Midwest's most iconic twentieth-century writers, most recently in his books *Iowa, the Definitive Collection* (2009), *Liberty Hyde Bailey: Essential Agrarian and Environmental Writing* (2008) and *Uncle Henry Wallace: Letters to Farm Families* (2008). A scholar of Border State history, culture, and literature, he served as an assistant professor of English at Tusculum College in east Tennessee, and has been a featured reader at the Ozarks Studies Forum, a contributor to *Elder Mountain: The Journal of Ozark Studies*, and a guest editor for the journal *Southern Rural Sociology*. A former Iowa public librarian and newspaper section editor, Jack now serves as an associate professor of English at North Central College in Naperville, Illinois, where he specializes in creative nonfiction, literary journalism, and place-based environmental writing.

 Ice Cube Books began publishing in 1993 to focus on how to live with the natural world and to better understand how people can best live together in the communities they share and inhabit. Since this time, we've been recognized by a number of well-known writers, including Gary Snyder, Gene Logsdon, Wes Jackson, Patricia Hampl, Greg Brown, Jim Harrison, Annie Dillard, Ken Burns, Kathleen Norris, Janisse Ray, Alison Deming, Richard Rhodes, Michael Pollan, and Barry Lopez. We've published a number of well-known authors as well, including Mary Swander, Jim Heynen, Mary Pipher, Bill Holm, Connie Mutel, John T. Price, Carol Bly, Marvin Bell, Debra Marquart, Ted Kooser, Stephanie Mills, Bill McKibben, and Paul Gruchow. As well, we have won several publishing awards over the last seventeen years. Check out our books at our web site, with booksellers, or at museum shops, then discover why we strive to "hear the other side."

Ice Cube Press (est. 1993)
205 N Front Street
North Liberty, Iowa 52317-9302
steve@icecubepress.com
www.icecubepress.com

singing with the corn,
snapping to the beans
hugs, kisses and cheers to
Fenna Marie & Laura Lee